FOOD, SHELTER AND TRANSPORT IN SOUTHEAST ASIA AND THE PACIFIC

CHALLENGING THE 'UNCONVENTIONAL WISDOM' OF DEVELOPMENT STUDIES IN THE THIRD WORLD

FOOD, SHELTER AND TRANSPORT IN SOUTHEAST ASIA AND THE PACIFIC

P. J. RIMMER
D. W. DRAKAKIS·SMITH
T. G. McGEE
(eds)

RESEARCH SCHOOL OF PACIFIC STUDIES
Department of Human Geography
Publication HG/12 (1978)

THE AUSTRALIAN NATIONAL UNIVERSITY CANBERRA

First published in Australia 1978
Set up and printed at
The Australian National University

© The Australian National University 1978

HD
9016
.A789
F66

National Library of Australia
Cataloguing-in-Publication entry

Rimmer, Peter James; Drakakis-Smith, David
William; McGee, Terence Gary, eds.
  Food, Shelter and Transport in Southeast
  Asia and the Pacific: Challenging the
  'Unconventional Wisdom' of Development
  Studies in the Third World.

  Bibliography.
  ISBN 0 7081 0670 6.

  1.

P R E F A C E

This monograph comprises papers presented at a Seminar on 'Food, Shelter and Transport in the Third World: Policy Implications of Informal Sector Studies' held at The Australian National University on 29 and 30 July 1977, together with a foreword, sectional overviews and afterword.

The contributors to this volume were invited to reconsider their original papers in the light of discussion at the Seminar. Most contributors took the opportunity to do so and prompted a change in title to accord more closely with the nature, content and general thrust of the discussion. Indeed, the final product owes much to the thoughtful comments made by all participants in both formal and informal discussions held during the two day Seminar.

Finally, we acknowledge our debt of gratitude to Wang Gung-wu, K.J. Ratnam and Martin Rudner for chairing the three sessions; to Hans Gunther and Theo Baumann who were responsible for the cartography; to Keith Mitchell for producing the cover, to Barbara Banks and Christine McMurray for assistance with referencing; and to Pauline Falconer for typing the manuscript.

P.J.R.
D.W.D-S.
T.G.M.
Canberra

TABLE OF CONTENTS

viii

Table of Contents (continued)

LIST OF TABLES

List of Tables (continued)

LIST OF FIGURES

List of Figures (continued)

LIST OF PLATES

FOREWORD

CHALLENGING THE 'UNCONVENTIONAL WISDOM' OF
DEVELOPMENT STUDIES IN THE THIRD WORLD

PETER J. RIMMER, D.W. DRAKAKIS-SMITH
and T.G. McGEE

For much of the period since 1945 during which Third World countries
have been emerging from colonialism into political independence the
'conventional wisdom' about development has had three main threads.
First, the Third World countries are engaged in a developmental
experience which is very similar to that of the developed Western
countries such as England and the United States.   Second, once the
problems of political custody and stability have been solved the
best policy for increasing economic growth is one which involves
the development of the most productive sectors of the economy.
Third, growth as measured by the increase in Gross National Product
is the major goal and ultimately its increase will enable Third
World countries to share in the same standards of living and
'affluence' as the developed countries.

        Studies of development in the Third World like many other
aspects of academic research have been characterised by fashions.
In the 1960s this 'wisdom' was challenged for a variety of
reasons.   A new 'unconventional wisdom' which stresses questions
of 'quality of life' and the persistence of 'unequal income distribution' in Third World countries has emerged.   The persistence and
growth of low-income populations in Third World countries has
challenged the 'conventional' answer to development and placed
greater emphasis upon the need for developmental inputs to be
directed towards the low-income, low-productivity activities of
Third World countries which are subsumed under the rubric of the
informal sector.   Such thinking has become quite influential and
embodied in the policies of such institutions as the International
Labour Office and the World Bank.   More recently the 'unconventional
wisdom' aimed at encouraging the informal sector has, in turn, begun
to be challenged.   This is reflected by the contributions to this
monograph on Food, Shelter and Transport in Southeast Asia and the
Pacific based on a Seminar held at the Australian National University on 29-30 July 1977.

        This challenge to 'unconventional wisdom' was not the original
intention of the Seminar.   Its initial objective was to draw
together a diffused body of researchers in Australia to discuss the
policy implications of their work on various aspects of the informal
sector.   Papers given at the Seminar were deliberately chosen to
provide a set of desirable and distinctive features; they had to be
original and, for the most part, based on detailed fieldwork; they
had to be wide-ranging and notably different from most considerations of economic dualism by combining the more usual studies of
food distribution systems with housing and transport so as to lead

towards a more complete analysis of the urban economy; they had to
be multidisciplinary and combine different levels and types of
approach (survey research methods, participant observation and
attempts at broad conceptualisation); and they had to focus on
Southeast Asia and the Pacific, thereby providing a valuable anti-
dote to generalisations based on African and Latin American
experience (J.C. Jackson, pers. comm.).

What emerged from the discussion of the papers was a direct
challenge to 'unconventional wisdom'.   The nature of this reaction
which can be distilled either strongly or, at times, hesitantly
from the chapters of this monograph can broadly be seen as taking
three main directions.   First, there is criticism of the over-
simplification of the 'informal sector'.   Inductive studies indicate that it is an overgeneralisation which distorts the much more
complex economic structures of Third World economies.   Second, the
dualistic division into 'formal-informal' sectors pays insufficient
attention to the linkages between the two sectors which are crucial
in explaining the functioning of the economies of these societies.
Third, great doubt has been placed on the policy prescriptions
flowing from the 'informal sector' models.   This is mutually felt
by the radicals who argue that informal sector encouragement simply
leads to persistence of poverty and to the advantage of the formal
sector, and by those supporters of conventional wisdom who favour
a return to the policies of the 1950s.

A general overview to the monograph is given in Chapter 1 and
the remaining chapters are grouped under three headings — Food,
Shelter and Transport.   An overview to each section relates the
individual chapters to common trends and an afterword provides an
immediate reaction to the general thrust of the Seminar.

CHAPTER 1

AN INVITATION TO THE 'BALL': DRESS FORMAL OR INFORMAL?

T.G. McGEE[*]

1. INTRODUCTION

The current flurry of concern in development studies about the 'informal sector' can be rather nicely captured by the metaphor of the 'ball'. Previously, participants were expected to dress formally, now it has become fashionable to allow informal dress. But the main features of the ball have not radically changed. The band is still the same and the dances still occur in the same order. Much the same people are invited. What is more, there are a lot of people at the ball who are distinctly uncomfortable in 'informal' dress. They would like the ball to go back to formal dress. Who knows next year they may succeed.

The metaphor of the 'ball' may be too simple, but it certainly captures a rather cynical view of what is happening in development studies at present. Most of the debate on development policies is occurring at 'balls' in the developed world to which only an atypical representation of the underdeveloped world is invited. The majority of 'poor' in the Third World who are the subjects of this debate are excluded despite the fact that they are correctly dressed. It is doubtful if our deliberations will greatly improve their lot.

Having set the scene let me welcome you to the 'ball' and stress that dress is 'informal'. The following discussion is devoted to three main questions which are felt to be central to any discussion of the informal sector.

(a) What is the origin of the concept of the informal sector?

(b) Is the informal sector capable of operational definition as opposed to theoretical definition?

(c) Are policy prescriptions which advocate 'developing' the informal sector viable 'developmental strategies'?

---

* Dr T.G. McGee is Senior Fellow, Department of Human Geography, Research School of Pacific Studies, The Australian National University, Canberra.

2.   ORIGIN OF THE INFORMAL SECTOR CONCEPT

Strictly speaking the 'informal sector concept' appears to have
arisen in the work of Hart (1971, 1973) circulated in cyclostyled
form at a conference on 'Urban Unemployment in Africa' held at the
Institute of Development Studies, University of Sussex in 1971.
The concept was taken up and developed in the International Labour
Office (1972), Kenya Mission report.   Since that date the concept
of the informal sector has become a major analytical tool in
'developmental' theory.

It should not be imagined that 'informal sector' conceptualisation just happened.   The trends in development thinking in
the 1960s which provided the intellectual framework for the emergence of the informal sector have been discussed (see McGee, 1976).
However, it is worthwhile briefly reviewing these trends.

Up until the middle of the 1960s there was surprisingly little
attention paid to the problems of the poor in the Third World
cities.   True, while there was no lack of recognition that the
occupational structures of the Third World cities were characterised
by what was regarded, in the light of the developed countries'
historical experience, as an excessive concentration of the city
populations in the tertiary sector (see Lambert, 1965), there was
little evaluation of the features of this population apart from
rather broad assertions of its low productivity, 'marginality',
revolutionary potential and general poverty (see, for instance,
Gutkind, 1968; Frank, 1969).   One might suggest at least three
reasons for this lack of research attention.

First, for many economists, it seems that their models of
development tended to concentrate upon the economic growth features
of the modern sector at the expense of the activities of the
population engaged in the informal sector.   This attitude was
partly the consequence of assuming that the only way for poor
countries to 'develop' was to repeat the historical experience of
the developed countries (see, for instance, Rostow, 1960).   Thus
only the economic activities of the modern sector could be conceived
as growth-promoting, while the activities of the 'informal sector',
in which the proto-proletariat was concentrated, were a blockage to
growth.   Only the dualistic models of writers such as Fei and
Ranis (1964) recognised the significance of the interaction of the
two sectors of the economy as an important factor in the growth
process.   Thus the 'informal sector' was construed by economists
of all shades of ideological position as an inhibiting sector.   To
the Marxists and neo-Marxists its existence was a symptom of the
poverty-creating capacity of international capitalism.   To the
'similar path writers' who favoured rapid growth within the capitalist structure, its existence was a blockage.   Neither polar
position, it seems to me, was willing to explore the question of
whether the 'informal sector' contributed to economic growth.

A second reason is that the modern-traditional dichotomy,
which has been a central conceptual model for the analysis of social
and economic change, has encouraged a one-sided emphasis on the
process of development as a penetration of traditional systems by

the 'elements' of 'modernisation' which are thought to be equated with developments. The major limitation of this approach, apart from its acceptance of a linear theory of social and economic change, has been its portrayal of traditional society as a static, homogeneous culture with a consistent body of norms and values which are opposed and antithetical to modernisation (see Bernstein, 1971, for a major review; also McGee, 1974c). As Gusfield (1967, p. 355) has suggested, there is ample evidence that traditional cultures may supply skills and values 'which are capable of being utilized in pursuit of new goals and with new processes'. Milton Singer (1971) also has perceptive comments to make on this same theme. The activities of the informal sector population, despite the fact that they often involve highly ingenious adaptations and utilisation of traditional technology or practices, have been ignored because they have been portrayed as traditional, and thus of little interest to the process of social and economic development.

Finally, one may point to the fact that the systems of statistical enumeration of occupations have been most inadequate for recording the activities of the informal sector. Most existing systems of enumeration tend to record information pertinent to the economic and service activity of the wage-earning population of the modern or formal sector. As Hauser (1971, p. 1) has pointed out, the 'efforts of nations to differentiate in the population that part which consists of "workers" is...a recent phenomenon' occurring in the United States only after 1870. This technique concentrated at first upon the identification of 'gainful workers' engaged in a profession, occupation, or trade, but later changed to the 'labour force approach' wherein people were asked to report their actual activity for a period of time as well as time spent 'seeking work'. This technique was generally transferred to the various countries of the Third World. Its limitations for the underdeveloped countries are obvious since it is largely based upon an assumption of employment or work in which the majority of the labour force are 'employees', and does not account for those forms of 'work' which are performed in household enterprises in both agricultural and non-agricultural situations. Thus Hauser (1971, 1972), Myrdal (1968, p. 994ff) and others, such as Maunder (1960), Mouly (1972) and Davies (1973), have argued strenuously for a new system of occupational/labour force data collection in the Third World.

These statistical data collection systems have been further rendered inefficient by the fact that they often collect data only from enterprises which have some form of legal recognition. For instance, Halpenny (1972) points out that in Uganda the Official Survey of Industrial Production is limited to establishments with 'an *average* of ten or more employees in industrial production throughout the year', which excludes a large number of smaller units of production. There are similar problems with surveys of commercial establishments which exclude retailing by hawkers because they are not licensed, as indicated in the research on hawkers in Hong Kong (see McGee, 1974a). Therefore, the activities of the proto-proletariat have never been enumerated satisfactorily, further contributing to the ignorance of their role and contribution to the economy.

In the late 1960s, however, there appeared to be a growing realisation of the importance of the size and activities of the

informal sector.   Again, while it is not always easy to identify
the causes of this growing realisation, one may suggest at least
several themes.   First, there has been, in some quarters, a growing disillusionment with development as being conceived solely as
'economic growth'.   In particular, here one may point to the
important contribution of writers such as Seers (1969) and Goulet
(1971) who have raised questions concerning the quality of life
which development may bring about.   Some of this disillusionment
has certainly stemmed from the highly popularised ecological crisis
of the 'developed world'.   Now it would appear further complicated
by an 'energy crisis' which has caused many people to ask whether
the countries of the Third World can reach the same levels of
energy consumption as the developed world.   Thus, there has been a
growing interest in the features of the labour-intensive systems of
the peasantry and proto-proletariat which do not rely on the high
energy consumption of 'fossil fuels'.

    A second and perhaps more important factor in the change of
attitude has been the growing focus on what has been labelled the
'employment problem' of the less-developed countries.   From the
middle of the 1960s a rapidly proliferating series of papers emerging from individual writers and from such international organisations as the International Labour Office, United Nations, regional
organisations, etc. (see Morse, 1970; Lewis, 1967; Grant, 1971) has
drawn attention to the fact that an increasing proportion of the
labour force of the rapidly growing cities of the Third World is
not being absorbed into what has been labelled 'full productive
employment' (see Friedmann and Sullivan, 1972, p. 1).   In addition
to high rates of unemployment among the urban populations, often
young and relatively well educated, there is '...a reserve army of
low-productivity workers in rural and urban areas, among whom the
waste of human potential is massive' (Turnham and Jaeger, 1971,
p. 10).   What is more, this pattern does not appear to vary
greatly between the countries of the Third World which have
experienced rapid economic growth and those which have had slower
rates of development.   For instance, in Brazil, despite comparatively high rates of economic growth in the sixties, unemployment
and underemployment have increased during the 1950s and 1960s (see
Diegues, 1966).   And, in Indonesia, with comparatively low rates
of economic growth, unemployment has also increased (see Keddie,
1973).   A series of studies has focused upon this problem in the
three continents of the Third World, and the statistics they
present, even subject to the problems of the applicability of data,
all tell the same story — a picture of a rapidly increasing labour
force within both rural and urban areas, increasing rates of
unemployment, and absorption into low-productivity informal activities in urban areas which will accelerate in the decades of the
1970s and 1980s in most of the Third World countries (see, for
instance, Oshima, 1970-1 for Asia; Hofmeister, 1971 and Jones, 1968
for Latin America; Charles Frank Jr., 1971 for Africa; also Turnham
and Jaeger, 1971 for a broad overview).   Thus, in 1970 the International Labour Office estimated that over 300,000,000 new jobs
would be needed outside agriculture in the decade of the 1970s in
the underdeveloped world.   The reasons for this situation are well
known.   A combination of population explosion, urban growth and
limited employment opportunities generated by capital-intensive
industrialisation have all combined to create the problem.   For
instance, in Latin America, the Economic Commission for Latin
America (ECLA) estimates record that while industrial production
has increased its share of the Gross Domestic Product from 11 per

cent in 1925 to 23 per cent in 1967, the proportion of the total
labour force employed in industry has remained stable at 14 per
cent.   At the same time employment in agriculture and mining has
declined from 60 per cent of the labour force in 1925 to 43 per
cent in 1969.   As a consequence, the construction and service
sectors have absorbed the redistribution of the labour force,
increasing from 26 per cent in 1925 to 43 per cent in 1969, of
which approximately 50 per cent are in the categories of 'other
services' and 'unspecified activities', in which many of the proto-
proletariat are located (Frank, 1972, citing ECLA publications).
Similar patterns have been observed in Africa and Asia but they
have not accelerated to the point of Latin America as yet.   But as
Weeks has perceptively commented, the failure to create employment
structures which can successfully absorb labour in high-productivity
activity is also a symptom 'of a development strategy seeking to
reproduce a Western consumer goods economy' (Weeks, 1971, p. 69) in
the less-developed countries which rely on Western derived capital-
intensive techniques*.   Whatever the reasons, the end-product is
that the 'employment crisis' has resulted in a growing concern with
the development of employment strategies for the countries of the
less-developed world which has increasingly had to accept the fact
that certain activities of the informal sector are likely to play
an increasingly important role in the cities of the Third World,
and therefore there is a need to focus research upon them.

Finally, one may suggest that a very important reason why the
informal sector's activities have come to be recognised has been
the radical revision of concepts concerning the process of class
formation in the less-developed countries.   Hardly surprisingly
this has emanated primarily from a group of writers, principally in
Latin America and Africa, who represent a stream of broad neo-
Marxist thought, perhaps most forcefully expressed in the writings
of Fanon (1963) and analysed structurally in the writings of Frank
(1969), Worsley (1972), Beckford (1972) and Amin (1974).   In
particular the writings of Worsley have focused upon the significance of the emergence of the semi-proletariat (proto-proletariat)
in urban centres as a major element in the class structure of urban
area.   Active revolutionaries such as Mao and Cabral had also
drawn attention to this group as presenting a 'difficult' revolutionary potential.   While there has been much debate over the role
of this group, the importance of the analysis has been to break
down the rigid Marxist categories of bourgeoisie, proletariat, and
lumpenproletariat by stressing the emergence of this new class —
victims of 'urbanization without industrialization' (Worsley, 1972,
p. 209) — as well as questioning the repeated emergence of a large
middle class which was associated with the urban revolution in
Western countries.

Basic to all these factors which have led to a growing awareness of the role of the informal sector are two sets of polarised
assumptions, which rest upon an assessment of the demographic underpinnings of the current urbanisation process in the Third World.

---

* In this respect the author broadly agrees with the school of
thought which sees this 'unemployment problem' as arising from the
'development of underdevelopment' and the dependency of peripheral
economies upon the metropolis within the international capitalist
system.

At one pole is a group of writers who see the process of occupational formation occurring in the Third World cities as basically
involutionary; that is to say, a combination of very high rates of
natural increase in both countryside and city and a large volume of
actual and potential rural-urban migration involved in the urban
transformation poses grave demographic constraints on the possibility of labour absorption in high-productive, capital-intensive
sectors, thus forcing people into low-productive activities which
proliferate and involute.   To my knowledge no one except the most
optimistic of revolutionaries has attempted to put a time limit on
the capacity of the labour systems to involute — primarily because
the economic and social operations of the involutionary process
have been insufficiently investigated.   The second group of assumptions may be described as evolutionary; that is to say, while they
accept certain of the demographic underpinnings which have earlier
been enumerated, they are more optimistic about the progress of
occupational formation as one in which there will be sectoral lags
in the rates of labour absorption in certain sectors (for instance,
industry), which will cause a growth in the 'informal sector'.
This process will be temporary and eventually occupational mobility
and economic growth will correct these sectoral imbalances in a
manner which will produce not dissimilar occupational structures to
those of the developed capitalist world (see Kilby, 1971; Garlick,
1971).

       In fact the gross figures of predicted urban and labour force
increase in the less-developed countries strongly support the first
of these positions.   United Nations' estimates, while admittedly
crude, suggest that the total world urban population living in
centres of 20,000 or more may grow by 1,326,000,000 to 2,336,000,000
between AD 1970 and 2000, some 972,000,000 of whom will be absorbed
in urban centres of the less-developed world.   This increase of
population in urban centres of the less-developed world will only
shift the overall level of urbanisation from 19 to 31 per cent,
although some regions such as Latin America will have well in
excess of 50 per cent of their population in urban places.   Thus,
it is possible to argue that the problem of urban absorption will
still remain a very large problem even by AD 2000.   (These
estimates are based on Davis, 1969, 1972; and UNDESA, 1969.)   Of
course, it may well be that in some countries this problem of
labour absorption in urban areas will be successfully tackled, as
appears to be the case at present in Hong Kong and Singapore, but
for the majority of countries, particularly those with large, dense
populations such as India or Indonesia, the problem is a grave one
for the future, unless successful strategies of labour absorption
can be developed (see McGee, 1971 and 1977a).

       3.   THE DELINEATION OF THE INFORMAL SECTOR

Broadly one may suggest that there are three dimensions by which
one can seek to delineate the urban informal sector.   First,
structurally it is possible to identify the informal sector participants as carrying out their activities primarily within the one
sector of a dualistic model of the economic structure of a Third
World city.   The transfer of the comparatively well-established
dualistic model of the less-developed countries' economy, which
distinguished between the capitalist towns and subsistence

countryside (Lewis, 1958), was primarily the work of Geertz, who in
his work on a Javanese town, published in the early 1960s, drew
attention to the dual economic structure of the town divided between
a *firm-centred* economic sector '...where trade and industry occur
through a set of impersonally-defined social institutions which
organize a variety of specialized occupations with respect to some
particular productive or distributive end' and a second sector
labelled the *bazaar-economy*, based on '...the independent activities
of a set of highly competitive traders who relate to one another
mainly by means of an incredible volume of *ad hoc* acts of exchange'
(Geertz, 1963, p. 28).   Lately, this model has been greatly broad-
ened by the work of Milton Santos (1971, 1972 and 1976) who has
stressed the relationships between these two sectors in the form of
two interacting and interlocking circuits of economic activity
summarised in Table 1.1. The types of economic activities found in
the upper circuit are banking, export trade, modern large industry,
modern services, wholesaling, and some forms of transport (airlines,
etc.).   The lower sector consists of non-capital-intensive
industry, services and trades, etc.   There are of course, intermediate types of activity but these do not invalidate the model.
Independently, apparently, economists associated with the International Labour Office (1972) have also suggested a model of the
dualistic structures of the economies of the less-developed
countries which, while it is applied to the total economy, can be
equally fitted into the urban economy as well.   Thus, the International Labour Office (1972, p. 6) distinguishes between an
'informal sector' of the economy characterised by:

(a) ease of entry;
(b) reliance on indigenous resources;
(c) family ownership of enterprises;
(d) small-scale of operation;
(e) labour-intensive and adapted technology;
(f) skills acquired outside the formal school system; and
(g) unregulated and competitive markets;

and a 'formal sector' of the economy of which the principal features
are:

(a) difficult entry;
(b) frequent reliance on overseas resources;
(c) corporate ownership;
(d) large-scale of operation;
(e) capital-intensive and often imported technology;
(f) formally acquired skills often expatriate; and
(g) protected markets (through tariffs, quotas and trade licenses).

While this division is broad, and is surprisingly little developed
as an analytical framework in the International Labour Office's (ILO)
(1972) publication, from the point of view of our previous arguments
concerning the informal sector, the proto-proletariat are clearly
identified as participants in the 'informal sector' or lower circuit
of the Third World cities' economies.

A second approach to defining the proto-proletariat is an
institutional approach which classifies the proto-proletariat on
the basis of the mode of production in which they are engaged.

TABLE 1.1:   THE TWO CIRCUIT URBAN ECONOMY CHARACTERISTICS

Characteristics	Upper circuit	Lower circuit
Technology	Capital-intensive	Labour-intensive
Organisation	Bureaucratic	Generally family-organised
Capital	Abundant	Scarce
Hours of work	Regular	Irregular
Regular wages	Normal	Not required
Inventories	Large quantities and/or quality	Small quantities, poor quality
Prices	Generally fixed	Generally negotiable between buyer and seller
Credit	Banks and other institutions	Personal non-institutional
Relations with clientele	Impersonal and/or through documents	Direct, personal
Fixed costs	Important	Negligible
Publicity	Necessary	None
Re-use of goods	None, wasted	Frequent
Overhead capital	Indispensable	Not indispensable
Government aid	Important	None or almost none
Direct dependence on foreign countries	Great, outward-oriented activity	Small or none

Source: Adapted from Santos (1976).

This is an approach which I have favoured following Chayanov (1966) and Franklin (1965, 1969) which distinguished between three main systems of production — capitalist, socialist and peasant — in which:

> ...the fundamental differentiator is the labour commitment of the enterprise.   In the peasant economy the individual entrepreneur is committed to the utilisation of his total labour supply - that of his family, who may and do often find alternative or additional sources of employment. This accounts for the diversities of historical peasant societies, but if these sources are not available the *chef d'enterprise* must employ his kin...

> In the capitalist and socialist systems of production labour becomes a commodity to be hired and dismissed by the enterprise according to the changes in the scale of organisation, degree of mechanisation, the level of market demand for products.   It is for this reason especially, not so much because of the introduction of mechanisation and the factory system, that the capitalist system of production has been disruptive of traditional societies. It introduces to society a hitherto unheard of scale for the evaluation of the human individual.   (Franklin, 1965, pp. 148-9.)

The advantage of such a distinction between systems of production is that while it recognises the fact that the majority of
peasant enterprises may be family farms, it does not exclude the
fact that peasant enterprises, such as family-organised industry or
retailing, may exist in cities.   This is what Franklin means when
he says:

> ...The scheme ignores the agricultural-industrial division.
> At this level of generalisation the division has little
> importance.   Agriculture is carried out under all three
> systems of production and so is manufacturing.   Admittedly,
> in peasant-folk-traditional societies, agricultural
> activities predominate without excluding the appearance
> of a capitalistic system of production - but it is the
> systems, not the societies which are our concern.   (Franklin,
> 1965, p. 148.)

Following this definition most of the proto-proletariat of the
Third World cities fit clearly into a peasant system of production.
There are, however, problems with this definition in the city
situation, because members of a household may often be operating in
both modes of production.   For instance, among the hawkers in Hong
Kong it was common to find that members of a hawker's household
might be engaged in factory work, but were still working in the
hawker establishment in their spare time (McGee, 1973).   There are
also semantic difficulties because many social scientists are unwilling to accept the possibility that peasants may live in cities
(see the exchange between Isaac, 1974 and McGee, 1974b).   Another
variation of this model has been devised by Friedmann and Sullivan
(1972) combining a labour force and institutional model of Third
World cities that present a tri-sectoral model of the urban economy
divided between individual operators, which includes the 'open
unemployed' and occupations such as street vendors, casual
labourers, etc., the family-enterprise sector which includes household enterprises, and the corporate production sector which includes
employees of government, large firms, etc.   While I think this
model presents very useful possibilities for analytical insights, it
also is not without its problems of fitting populations into the
various categories.

The third approach is that suggested by Hart (1973).   Hart's
work in Ghana has shown that there is a wide range in the size and
scale of activities within the informal sector which a delineation
on the basis of the Franklin (1965) or the Friedmann and Sullivan
(1972) model could not encompass.   Therefore, he has developed
classifications based on the income opportunities available to
people in the city.   The accompanying list in Table 1.2 is not
exclusive but it is not hard to see how income figures collected
within this framework might lead to a more precise definition of
the participants in the informal sector.   For instance, working at
a household level, it may be possible to determine in situations
where households earn incomes from two sectors which sector is the
larger contributor.   Another aspect of this framework which offers
fruitful possibilities is that some idea of the contribution of the
informal sector to total income generated in a city might be produced, in addition to figures on the flows of income between the
two sectors.

TABLE 1.2:   INCOME OPPORTUNITIES IN A THIRD WORLD CITY

Formal income opportunities

(a)   Public sector wages

(b)   Private firms (wages, dividends, etc.)

(c)   Transfer payments — pensions, unemployment benefits.

Informal income opportunities: legitimate

(a)   Primary and secondary activities — farming, market garden-
      ing, building contractors and associated activities, self-
      employed artisans, shoemakers, tailors, household manufac-
      turers of beer and spirits.

(b)   Tertiary enterprises with relatively large capital inputs
      — housing, transport, utilities, commodity speculation,
      rentier activities.

(c)   Small-scale distribution — market operatives, petty
      traders, street hawkers, caterers in food and drink, bar
      attendants, carriers, commission agents, and dealers.

(d)   Other services — musicians, launderers, shoeshiners,
      barbers, night-soil removers, photographers, vehicle
      repair and other maintenance workers; brokerage and
      middlemanship (the *maigida* system in markets, law courts,
      etc.); ritual services, magic and medicine.

(e)   Private transfer payments — gifts and similar flows of
      money and goods between persons; borrowing; begging.

Informal income opportunities: illegitimate

(a)   Services — hustlers and spivs in general; receivers of
      stolen goods; usury, and pawnbroking (at illegal interest
      rates); drug-pushing, prostitution, poncing ('pilot boy'),
      smuggling, bribery, political corruption Tammany Hall-
      style, protection rackets.

(b)   Transfers — petty theft (e.g. pickpockets), larceny (e.g.
      burglary and armed robbery), speculation and embezzle-
      ment, confidence tricksters (e.g. money doublers),
      gambling.

Source: After Hart, 1973, p. 69.

It should not be imagined that these attempts to delineate the informal sector have gone without criticism. At least three major criticisms can be offered of the model. First, it is possible to criticise the dualistic concept of the economy which is implicit in the formal-informal division. Second, there are great difficulties in applying the concept to the real world. Third, there are severe problems with developing the policy implications of the concept. Each of these criticisms is considered in turn.

4.   CRITICISMS OF THE DUALISTIC CONCEPT

The criticism of the dualistic concept of the informal-formal sector has at least two elements. First, the model may be criticised because it fails to approximate reality*. Second, the model has very low explanatory power because it does not pay sufficient attention to relationships between the sectors. Turning to the first criticism, it is fairly obvious that many of the features used in the ILO catalogue of features of the informal sector occur in a very modified mix in many countries. Ease of entry into so-called informal sector occupations has been shown to be very restricted. For instance, studies by Gerry (1974), Harriss (1977), Lomnitz (1977), Lynch (1977) and McGee and Yeung (1977), have all shown that entry into occupations such as small industry and street vending is highly selective and involves the use of kin and the payment of fees to people already involved in these occupations. Also, there is the feature of *reliance on indigenous resources*. While it is true that substantial amounts of the fresh and processed food sold by street vendors are locally produced, many other activities in the 'informal sector' are reliant upon imported goods. Thus Gerry (1974) shows that many small industries in Dakar are reliant upon imported materials. One could continue this critical catalogue of all the so-called features of the 'informal sector' *ad infinitum*. The fact is that virtually every feature of the model of the informal sector can be shown to be characterised by substantial exceptions (see also Bremen, 1976).

A more powerful criticism may be offered of the explanatory power of the model. The model of informal-formal sector activity in the city is essentially descriptive. It tells us very little about the likely future of these sectors even in the very short term. However, an emphasis on the model's elements ignores the fact that these are part of the much larger economy of the city, the national and indeed an international economic system. When the informal-formal sector model is used for explanatory rather than descriptive purposes the dualism is often seen as a consequence of internal processes such as rapid population growth, etc. rather than a result of the position of Third World countries in an international capitalist system.

---

* A failure to approximate reality does not mean that the model is useless. As many writers have indicated the use of polar models is designed to help in understanding reality not necessarily in reproducing it.

The emergence of the broad body of dependency theory, largely
emanating from research by Latin American writers in the sixties,
provided an explanatory body of theory which offered the opportunity to correct this inward-looking model building.   Dependency
theory emphasised that the structure of Third World societies and
their cities was primarily a result of the manner in which they had
been integrated into an international capitalist system from the
sixteenth century (see Wallerstein, 1974a and 1974b for a discussion
of this process of expansion).   The continuing pattern of integration, which is responsible for a particular socio-economic formation
— peripheral capitalism, is very different from the capitalist
mode of production in the developed capitalist countries.   While
there have been significant variations in the form of this capitalist integration during the expansion of the capitalist system, a
misunderstanding of which has been the major reason for the
vigorous debates among dependency theorists (admirably summarised
in essays in Oxall *et al.*, 1975, and Chilcote and Edelstein, 1974),
the importance of this body of theory to the mode of production of
Third World cities is that it offers an explanation for the persistence of these low-income, low-productivity activities and populations in the Third World cities in terms of an international system.

The economic structure of the Third World cities and countries
can be described in a Marxist sense as a distinct mode of production
— peripheral capitalism.   This involves a capitalist sector deeply
integrated into the international capitalist economy and a variety
of petty capitalist forms of production in which the articulation
of the relationships between these two sectors is primarily a
response to the pace of expansion of the dominant capitalist sector.

The features of this peripheral capitalism are as follows:

(a)   a combination of capitalist and petty capitalist forms of
       production under the hegemony of the first form; and

(b)   a combination of these two forms in which one is grafted
       onto another and which is characterised by a capitalist
       expansion which occurs in a series of leaps rather than
       entirely domestic evolution (see Obregon, 1974, for fuller
       explanation).

This is seen for instance in the importation of capital-intensive
technology from the developed capitalist core which does not generate sufficient labour opportunities but still leads to increasing
productivity in the capitalist sector.   This pattern has important
consequences for the ability of the petty capitalist sector to
accumulate capital internally and carry out domestic expansion (see
Bienefeld, 1975; Bradby, 1975, pp. 53-73).

Bettelheim summarises this argument succinctly when he says
'...that it is the *world domination by the capitalist mode of
production*, resulting from economic, political and ideological
relations the effects of which are called colonization and imperialism, that has favored the maintenance (or in some cases the development) in the dominated countries of production relations and also
of political and ideological relations which have "blocked" the
development of the productive forces' (Bettelheim, 1972, p. 291).

This can be further explained by recourse to the mechanism of
'conservation - dissolution' which means 'that within a capitalist
social formation the non-capitalist forms of production, before
they disappear, are "restructured" (partly dissolved) and thus
subordinated to the predominant capitalist relationships (and so
conserved)' (Bettelheim, 1972, p. 297).   Le Brun and Gerry make
the point that '...generally speaking it is the dissolution aspect
which dominates the conservation aspect in developed countries of
the capitalist mode of production.   Petty production is therefore
residual and tends to disappear.   In Europe this dissolution
mechanism operated during the period of transition which, due to
the Industrial Revolution, led to the establishment of a self
sufficient capitalist mode of production.   In the countries of the
periphery it seems it is the conservation aspect which dominates
...' (Le Brun and Gerry, 1973, p. 9).   Bettelheim (1972, p. 298)
says 'This is the aspect that is interpreted, in ideological terms,
by the metaphor of the "dualistic character" of these social formations - a metaphor that *conceals* the specific type of domination by
the capitalist mode of production that is characteristic of these
formations'.

    If indeed the tendency to conservation is dominant in the
peripheral social formations it is important to ask why the dominant
mode of capitalist production is not acting to dissolve the non-
capitalist modes.   At least three reasons seem apparent.   First,
the activities of the petty production sector seem essentially
unprofitable for the capitalist mode of production in the periphery
because, as Le Brun and Gerry point out (1973, p. 10) the mode is
essentially oriented '...towards the production of exports for
metropolitan consumption and/or transformation for re-export, and
the production of consumption goods for the more favoured strata of
the population'.   Second, as Meillasoux (1972 and 1973) argues,
the persistence of this large petty distributive and production
sector, in which underemployment and low income are universal,
enables the persistence of a cheap surplus labour force which is an
important factor keeping the wage levels down and providing adequate
labour when it is needed.   This petty production sector can also
be utilised by the capitalist sector for putting-out operations
when it is necessary to cut costs in the capitalist sector, as
occurs in Hong Kong.   Finally, the existence of a large petty
production and distribution sector characterised by predominantly
family employment is important from the point of view of the
bureaucracies of the Third World states because they cut down the
need for social welfare investment.   This means more capital can
be invested in areas which often directly benefit the capitalist
sector.   (Castells, 1977, labels the public sector the *administration* sector and argues persuasively that its principal role is to
act in liaison with the large capitalist interests against the
poor.)   More debatably, the persistence of these populations may
cut down the possibility of political unrest.

    Looked at from this perspective there is only one mode of
production (peripheral capitalism) in Third World countries within
which the articulation of relationship between dominant capitalist
modes and petty capitalist modes will vary markedly from country to
country.   As, for instance, in the contrast between the 'export
platform' economies such as Singapore and Hong Kong based on
increasing industrialisation compared to 'neo-colonial' economies reliant on primary exports such as Bangladesh or Senegal.

(See, Frobel, Heinrichs and Kreye, 1976, and McGee, 1977b.)   The
relationships will also vary markedly between different economic
activities as I indicated in the study of hawkers in Hong Kong
(McGee, 1974a).

5. PROBLEMS OF APPLYING THE FORMAL-INFORMAL CONCEPT

Turning next to the problem of applying the model of the formal-
informal sector to the reality of the Third World city, Mosley
(1977) has suggested that there are at least four 'working' definitions that are applied to attempt to distinguish the formal from
the informal sector.   These are:

(a)   the *accounting definition*: those activities falling outside
       the net of official and company register statistics;

(b)   the definition according to the *size of firm*: self-employment
       or employment in an establishment not subject to, for example,
       minimum wage legislation, unionisation, restrictions on the
       use of child labour;

(c)   the definition according to the pattern of *industrial* rela-
       tions practised in the firm: informality here could denote
       involvement in an establishment not subject to, for example,
       minimum wage legislation, unionisation, restrictions on the
       use of child labour;

(d)   definition according to the *relationship of the producing
       unit vis-a-vis the state*.

     All these definitions have at least one common characteristic.
The informal sector is a residual category which is outside the
legal or statistical boundaries acceptable to the *formal* requirements laid down by the national state or city.   The problem is
that in reality the application of these regulations makes it very
difficult to define where the formal sector finishes and the
informal sector begins.   Thus in some activities such as beer-
making in African cities there is a clear distinction between formal
manufacturing units and the myriad of informal illegal beer-making
shops.   In others such as retailing the distinction is much
clearer; for instance, in some Southeast Asian cities there is a
continuum of retailing which does not permit allocation to either
formal or informal sectors.   In Hong Kong, for instance, there are
vending units which utilise employed labour in excess of five
persons but are illegal (see McGee, 1974).   Should these units
be placed in formal or informal sectors?   The fact is that it is
almost impossible to allocate economic activities in Third World
cities to these either/or categories.

     In addition to this *descriptive categories mix* another diffi-
culty emerges.   This is the problem of *scale of activity*.   How
does one cut off the formal from the informal sector in one particular activity?   For instance, when does formal sector construction
activity begin in cases where sub-contracting occurs?   It is well
established that the construction industry in many Third World
countries utilises systems of sub-contracting which fit most of the
earlier definitions of informal sector (see Germidus, 1974; see also

Chapter 6).   Does this make a particular construction unit formal or informal?

The solution to these problems of attempting to fix economic activities into watertight categories has been discussed notably by Breman (1976) and Gerry (1977).   (Friedmann and Sullivan, 1972, were also aware of the problem.)   Breman (1976, p. 1905) introduces the concept of the 'fragmented labour market' in which '...the structure of the market is not dualistic but has a far more complex ranking'.   The features of this market recognise that in the conditions of labour surplus which prevail in the majority of Third World cities individuals take every opportunity to ensure some form of employment.   In support of this assertion Breman indicates labour is very fluid, moving about between and within various sub-labour markets.   The existence of a large body of casual labour which works partly for large-scale enterprise (e.g. building labourers) and partly in petty construction is an example of this phenomenon.

Gerry (1977) has added another dimension to this labour market perspective which is closely aligned with the mode of production analysis that was presented earlier.   This is presented in Table 1.3.

While this classification still suffers from some of the same problems of the formal-informal classifications, it is much more realistic in recognising the various parts of the labour force in Third World cities, especially when it is related to a theory that attempts to show the advantages to the dominant capitalist mode of production accruing from the present situation in Third World countries.

The Breman and Gerry conceptual frames at least challenge the view that the formal-informal sector has either a conceptual or operational utility.   The model is too simplistic, and masks the real economic relationships which operate in Third World cities. This brings me to the last section of the chapter which concerns the question of the viability of development policies aimed to encourage the 'informal sector'.

6.   'DEVELOPING' THE INFORMAL SECTOR:
A VIABLE DEVELOPMENT STRATEGY?

There is a certain ambivalence in discussing this question because the author has written at least two reports which suggest that policy measures should be developed to aid the informal sector — in this case street vendors (see McGee, 1974a and McGee and Yeung, 1977).   Yet, the author now has real doubts about the prescription. In other words, to reintroduce the metaphor of the title of the paper, the author now finds himself wearing both formal and informal clothes, and it is getting increasingly uncomfortable.   What is more, the author is not so keen on dancing and wonders whether he should be at the ball at all.   Let me explain what these personal meanderings mean.

TABLE 1.3:   RELATIONSHIPS IN THE LABOUR MARKETS
OF CAPITALIST AND PERIPHERAL CAPITALIST SOCIETIES

Fraction of labour force	Mode of reproduction of labour-power	Functional status *vis-a-vis* capitalist mode of production	Capital - labour relationship
A. Workers in capitalist industry (i.e. 'formal sector')	Repetitious sale of labour-power in the capitalist production process	Labour directly functional in capitalist production and accumulation	Real subjection of labour by capital
B. Casual workers in capitalist industry (i.e. industrial reserve army)	Intermittent sale of labour-power plus some petty commodity production and/or services	Alternating membership of capitalist labour force as well as of functional relative surplus population, according to cycles of capitalist accumulation	Real (but intermittent) subjection of labour by capital alternating with formal subjection of labour by capital
C. Workers exercising skills within a coexisting mode of production (marginal pole of the economy?) subordinated to the capitalist mode of production (i.e. the 'informal' sector)	Petty commodity production (including some apprentice exploitation)	Simultaneously functional in both direct and indirect senses	Typically formal subjection of labour to capital on a relatively permanent basis
D. Unsuccessful sellers of labour-power, the 'unemployed', urban 'lumpenproletariat', Marx's 'dangerous class'	Combined elements of A,B and C, but also possibly begging, extortion, political 'employment', family parasitism, 'illegal transfers'	Occasionally functional (politics rather than economics) but more typically disfunctional (disruptive, costly) or possibly nonfunctional (?)	Minimal relations with organised capital

Source: After Gerry, 1977, p. 12.

When the International Labour Office (1972) report on Kenya
started this concern with the informal sector the author joined
those who saw its prescriptions for 'development' of the informal
sector as a positive development strategy.   At the lowest practical level the success of such policies might lead governments to
stop attacking the activities and housing of the poor.   If the
poor could be allowed to work and live without this harassment,
perhaps they could accumulate capital and contribute to their
development.   At least the rapidly growing populations of the
Third World cities might be absorbed into some form of viable
employment.   All this seemed very reasonable at the time and
assuaged the author's liberal conscience.

But in view of the present state of the 'art' there now seems
to be three positions that may be taken with respect to policies
which may be developed to encourage the 'informal sector'.   The
first position is that because there is insufficient evidence it is
impossible to argue that policies which favour the informal sector
will have *only* negative or *only* positive developmental results.
Therefore, the least that can be done is to continue with policies
designed to support the informal sector on the assumption that they
will at least have some short-term benefits to the low income
populations of Third World countries.

A second possible position is that because policies which
favour 'informal sector' development encourage the persistence of
low income, low-productivity activities, there should be an increased input into the higher productivity sectors.   This, hope-
fully, will lead to increased economic growth and an eventual
spread of income throughout the population of Third World countries.
In effect this would mean reassertion of the conventional developmental wisdom.

Finally, there is a more radical position which sees these
attempts to preserve the existing economic structures as essentially
designed to benefit international capitalism and the dominant mode
of capitalism in these peripheral capitalist societies.   True
there are matters of degree here.   The original International
Labour Office (1972) report on Kenya suggested a redistribution of
investment in such a manner as to change the existing set of relationships between the dominant capitalist mode and petty capitalist
mode.   Leys (1973 and 1976) has shown how the political economy of
Kenya in practice made this redistribution of income impossible.
Mosley (1977) has also argued that even if there was a redistribution of income to the 'informal sector' it would have only meant
increasing flows of capital to the 'formal sector' because income
increases within the informal sector would lead to more purchases
of formal sector goods.

This leads to the conclusion that policies which favour the
informal sector ultimately shore-up existing class relationships in
the majority of Third World peripheral capitalist societies.   Such
policies advocate a continuation of poverty of the majority of
Third World urban populations.   The implication is that rather
than tinkering with such policies of 'general aid' aimed at retool-
ing economies there should be policies that advocate radical changes
in existing class relationships and income distribution in the
Third World countries.

Ultimately, each individual concerned with the plight of the low income populations of Third World countries will have to make his own choice as to which position is more correct.

REFERENCES

Amin, S. (1974),   *Accumulation on a World Scale: A Critique of the Theory of Underdevelopment*, (2 vols), New York.

Beckford, G.L. (1972),   *Persistent Poverty: Underdevelopment in Plantation Economies of the Third World*, New York.

Bettelheim, C. (1972),   'Appendix I: Theoretical Comments' in A. Emmanuel, *Unequal Exchange: A Study of Imperialism and Trade*, New York, pp. 271-322.

Bernstein, H. (1971),   'Modernization Theory and the Sociological Study of Development', *Journal of Development Studies*, 7(2), pp. 141-60.

Bienefeld, M.A. (1975),   'The Informal Sector and Peripheral Capitalism: The Case of Tanzania', *Bulletin, Institute of Development Studies*, 6(3), pp. 53-73.

Bradby, B. (1975),   'The Destruction of the Natural Economy', *Economy and Society*, 4(2), pp. 127-61.

Breman, Jan (1976),   'A Dualistic Labour System? A Critique of the Informal Sector Concept', *Economic and Political Weekly*, xi(48): 1870-1875;   xi(49):1905-1908;   xi(50): 1939-1944.

Castells, M. (1977),   *The Urban Question: A Marxist Approach*, London.

Chayanov, A.V. (1966),   *The Theory of Peasant Economy*, Homewood, Illinois.

Chilcote, R.H. and   *Latin America: The Struggle with Edelstein, J.C. (eds)   Dependency*, New York.
(1974),

Davies, D.G. (1973),   An   essay on employment concepts: the
                                    definition of labor forces in terms of
                                    socialization,   paper presented to an *ad
                                    hoc* seminar on Short-term Employment
                                    Creation Prospects in Southeast Asia,
                                    Southeast Asia Development Advisory
                                    Group, Washington.

Davis, K. (1969),   *World Urbanization 1950-1970: Volume 1
                                    Basic Data for Cities, Countries and
                                    Regions*, Population Monograph Series 4,
                                    University of California, Berkeley.

Davis, K. (1972),   *World Urbanization 1950-1970: Volume 2
                                    Analysis of Trends, Relationships and
                                    Development*, Population Monograph
                                    Series 9, University of California,
                                    Berkeley.

Diégues, M. (1966),   'Urban Employment in Brazil', *Inter-
                                    national Labour Review*, 93(6),
                                    pp. 643-57.

Fanon, F. (1963),   *The Damned*, (trans. C. Farrington),
                                    Paris.

Fei, J.C.H. and G. Ranis   *Development of the Labor-Surplus
  (1964),   Economy: Theory and Policy*, Homewood,
                                    Illinois.

Frank, A.G. (1969),   *Latin America: Underdevelopment or
                                    Revolution*, New York.

Frank, A.G. (1972),   *Lumpenbourgeoisie: Lumpendevelopment;
                                    Dependence Class and Politics in Latin
                                    America*, New York.

Frank, C.R. Jr (1971),   'The Problem of Urban Employment in
                                    Africa' in Ridker, R.G. and Lubell, H.
                                    (eds), *Employment and Unemployment
                                    Problems of the Near East and South
                                    Asia*, Delhi, pp.   783-818.

Franklin, S.H. (1965),   'Systems of Production: Systems of
                                    Appropriation', *Pacific Viewpoint*, 6(2),
                                    pp. 145-66.

Franklin, S.H. (1969),   *The European Peasantry: The Final
                                    Phase*, London.

Friedmann, J. and
  Sullivan, F. (1972),

The absorption of labour in the urban
economy: the case of developing
countries, School of Architecture and
Urban Planning, University of Califor-
nia, Los Angeles.

Frobel, F., Heinrichs, J.
  and Kreye, O. (1976),

'Tendency Towards a New International
Division of Labour', *Economic and
Political Weekly*, xi(57), pp. 159-70.

Garlick, P.C. (1971),

*African Traders and Economic Develop-
ment in Ghana*, Oxford.

Geertz, C. (1963),

*Peddlers and Princes: Social Change and
Economic Modernization in Two Indonesian Towns*, Chicago.

Germidus, D.A. (1974),

'Labour Conditions and Industrial Relations in the Building Industry in
Mexico', *Development Centre, Organization for Economic Co-operation Employment Series* No. 11, Paris.

Gerry, C. (1974),

*Petty Producers and the Urban Economy:
A Case Study of Dakar*, World Employment
Programme, Research Working Paper No. 8,
International Labour Office, Geneva.

Gerry, C. (1977),

Shantytown production and shantytown
producers: some reflections on macro-
and micro-linkages, paper prepared for
Burg Wartenstein Symposium No. 73 on
Shantytowns in Developing Nations,
Wenner-Gren Foundation, New York.

Goulet, D. (1971),

*The Cruel Choice: A New Concept in the
Theory of Development*, New York.

Grant, J. (1971),

'Marginal Man', *Foreign Affairs*, 50(1),
pp. 112-24.

Gutkind, P.C.W. (1968),

'The Poor in Urban Africa' in Schmandt,
H.J. and Bloomberg, W. (eds), *Power,
Poverty and Urban Policy*, Beverley
Hills, pp. 355-96.

Gusfield, J.R. (1967),

'Tradition and Modernity: Misplaced
Polarities in the Study of Social Change',
The American Journal of Sociology, 72(4),
pp. 351-62.

Halpenny, P. (1972),   Getting rich by being "unemployed":
                            some political implications of "infor-
                            mal" economic activities in urban areas
                            not usually represented in official
                            indices, paper prepared for Universi-
                            ties Social Sciences Conference,
                            Nairobi.

Harriss, B. (1977),   Quasi-formal employment structures and
                            "behaviour" in the unorganized urban
                            economy, and the reverse: some evidence
                            from South India, paper prepared for
                            Institute of British Geographers Sympo-
                            sium on The Urban Informal Sector in
                            the Third World, School of Oriental and
                            African Studies, University of London,
                            London.

Hart, K. (1971),   Informal income opportunities and
                            urban employment in Ghana, paper pre-
                            pared for conference on Urban Employ-
                            ment in Africa at the Institute of
                            Development Studies, University of
                            Sussex.

Hart, K. (1973),   'Informal Income Opportunities and
                            Urban Employment in Ghana', *The Journal
                            of Modern African Studies*, 11(1),
                            pp. 61-89.

Hauser, P.M. (1971),   A new approach to the measurement of
                            the work force in developing areas,
                            unpublished paper [limited circulation].

Hauser, P.M. (1972),   Population change and developments in
                            manpower, labour force, employment and
                            income, paper prepared for UNECAFE
                            seminar on Population Aspects of Social
                            Development, Bangkok.

Hofmeister, R.H. (1971),   'Growth with Unemployment in Latin
                            America: Some Implications for Asia',
                            in Ridker, R.G. and Lubell, H. (eds),
                            *Employment and Unemployment Problems of
                            the Near East and South Asia*, Delhi,
                            pp. 819-48.

International Labour   *Employment, Incomes and Equality: A
  Office (1972),   Strategy for Increasing Productive
                            Employment in Kenya*, Geneva.

Isaac, B.L. (1974),   'Peasants in Cities: Ingenious Paradox
                            or Conceptual Muddle', *Human Organiza-
                            tion*, 33(3), pp. 251-57.

Jones, G.W. (1968),   'Underutilisation of Manpower and Demo-
                             graphic Trends in Latin America',
                             International Labour Review, 98(5),
                             pp. 451-69.

Keddie, J. (1973),   'The Mass Unemployment Explosion', *Far
                             Eastern Economic Review*, 82(52),
                             pp. 41-3.

Kilby, P. (1971),   *Entrepreneurship and Economic Develop-
                             ment*, New York.

Lambert, D. (1965),   'L'Urbanisation Accélerée de l'Amérique
                             Latine et la Formation d'un Secteur
                             Tertiaire Refuge', *Civilisations*, 15(2),
                             pp. 158-70.

Le Brun, O. and   A theoretical prelude to class analysis
  Gerry, C. (1973),   of petty producers in Senegal,
                             unpublished paper.

Lewis, W.A. (1958),   'Economic Development with Unlimited
                             Supplies of Labour', *Manchester School
                             of Economics and Social Studies*, 22,
                             pp. 139-91.

Lewis, W.A. (1967),   'Unemployment in Developing Countries',
                             The World Today, 23(1), pp. 13-22.

Leys, C. (1973),   Interpreting African underdevelopment:
                             reflections on the ILO report on employ-
                             ment, incomes and equality in Kenya,
                             paper prepared for Institute of Common-
                             wealth Studies, University of London,
                             London [limited circulation].

Leys, C. (1976),   *Underdevelopment in Kenya: The Political
                             Economy of Colonialism*, London.

Lomnitz, L. (1977),   Mechanisms of articulation between
                             shanty town settlers and the urban
                             system, paper prepared for Burg Warten-
                             stein Symposium No. 73 on Shantytowns in
                             Developing Nations, Wenner-Gren Founda-
                             tion, New York.

Lynch, O.M. (1977),   Potters, plotters, plodders in a
                             Bombay slum: Marx and meaning or mean-
                             ing vs. Marx, paper prepared for Burg
                             Wartenstein Symposium No. 73 on Shanty-
                             towns in Developing Nations, Wenner-Gren
                             Foundation, New York.

McGee, T.G. (1971),   *The Urbanization Process in the Third
                             World: Explorations in Search of a Theory*,
                             London.

McGee, T.G. (1973),   'Peasants in Cities: a Paradox, a
                             Paradox, a Most Ingenious Paradox',
                             Human Organization, 32(2), pp. 135-42.

McGee, T.G. (1974a),   *Hawkers in Hong Kong: A Study of Policy
                             and Planning in the Third World City*,
                             Centre of Asian Studies, University of
                             Hong Kong, Hong Kong.

McGee, T.G. (1974b),   'Peasants in Cities: Ingenious Paradox
                             or Conceptual Muddle, a Reply', *Human
                             Organization*, 33(3), pp. 258-60.

McGee, T.G. (1974c),   'In Praise of Tradition: Towards a
                             Geography of Anti-development',
                             Antipode, 6(3), pp. 30-47.

McGee, T.G. (1976),   'The Persistence of the Proto-proletariat:
                             Occupational Structures and Planning of
                             the Future of Third World Cities',
                             Progress in Geography, 9, pp. 1-38.

McGee, T.G. (1977a),   'Rural-Urban Mobility in South and
                             Southeast Asia: Different Formulations
                             ...Different Answers?' in J. Abu-Lughod
                             and R. Hay Jr, *Third World Urbanization*,
                             Chicago, pp. 257-70.

McGee, T.G. (1977b),   Conservation and dissolution in the
                             Third World city: the "shanty-town" as
                             an element of conservation, paper
                             prepared for Burg Wartenstein Symposium
                             No. 73 on Shantytowns in Developing
                             Nations, Wenner-Gren Foundation, New
                             York.

McGee, T.G. and   *Hawkers in Southeast Asian Cities:*
  Yeung, Y.M. (1977),   *Planning for the Bazaar Economy*, Ottawa
                             [in press].

Maunder, W.F. (1960),   *Employment in an Underdeveloped Area:
                             A Sample Survey of Kingston, Jamaica*,
                             New Haven.

Meillasoux, C. (1972),   'From Reproduction to Production: A
                             Marxist Approach to Economic Anthro-
                             pology', *Economy and Society*, 1(1),
                             pp. 93-105.

Meillasoux, C. (1973),   'Développement ou Exploitation',
                             L'Homme et la Societé, 33/34(1),
                             pp. 55-61.

Morse, D.A. (1970),   'Unemployment in Developing Countries',
                               Political Science Quarterly, 85(1),
                               pp. 1-13.

Mosley, P. (1977),   Implicit models and policy recommenda-
                               tions: reflections on the employment
                               policy in Kenya, paper prepared for
                               Institute of British Geographers
                               Symposium on The Urban Informal Sector
                               in the Third World, School of Oriental
                               and African Studies, University of
                               London, London.

Mouly, J. (1972),   'Some Remarks on the Concepts of
                               Employment, Underemployment and Unem-
                               ployment', *International Labour Review*,
                               105(2), pp. 55-60.

Myrdal, G. (1968),   *Asian Drama: An Inquiry into the
                               Poverty of Nations*, (3 vols), Harmonds-
                               worth.

Obregon, A.Q. (1974),   'The Marginal Pole of the Economy and
                               the Marginalised Labour Force', *Economy
                               and Society*, 3(4), pp. 393-428.

Oshima, H. (1970-1),   'Labour Force Explosion: The Labour
                               Intensive Sector in Asian Growth',
                               *Economic Development and Cultural
                               Change*, 19(2), pp. 161-83.

Oxall, I., T. Barnett and   *Beyond the Sociology of Development:
D. Booth (eds) (1975),   Economy and Society in Latin America
                               and Africa*, London.

Rostow, W.W. (1960),   *The Stages of Economic Growth: A Non-
                               communist Manifesto*, Cambridge.

Santos, M. (1971),   *Les Villes du Tiers Monde*, Paris.

Santos, M. (1972),   Economic development and urbanization
                               in underdeveloped countries: the two
                               flow systems of the urban economy and
                               their spatial implications, unpublished
                               paper, University of Toronto, Toronto.

Santos, M. (1976),   *L'Éspace Partagé*, Paris.

Seers, D. (1969),   'The Meaning of Development', *Inter-
                               national Development Review*, 11(1),
                               pp. 2-6.

Singer, M. (1971),   'Beyond Tradition and Modernity in
                              Madras', *Comparative Studies in Society
                              and History*, 13(2), pp. 160-95.

Turnham, D. and Jaeger, I.   *The Employment Problem in Less Developed
  (1971),   Countries*, Paris.

United Nations Department   'Growth of World's Urban and Rural
  of Economic and Social   Population 1920-2000', *Population
  Affairs (1969),   Studies*, 44, United Nations, New York.

Wallerstein, I. (1974a),   *The Modern World System: Capitalist
                             Agriculture and the Origins of the
                             European World Economy in the Sixteenth
                             Century*, New York.

Wallerstein, I. (1974b),   'The Rise and Future Demise of the
                             World Capitalist System: Concepts for
                             Comparative Analysis', *Comparative
                             Studies in Society and History*, 16(4),
                             pp. 387-416.

Weeks, J. (1971),   'Does Employment Matter?', *Manpower and
                             Unemployment Research in Africa*, 4(1),
                             pp. 67-70.

Worsley, P. (1972),   'Franz Fanon and the Lumpenproletariat'
                             in Miliband, R. and Saville, J. (eds),
                             The Socialist Register 1972, London,
                             pp. 193-230.

PART I

FOOD: OVERVIEW

T.G. McGEE[*]

The supply of food to the rapidly growing urban areas of Southeast Asia and the Pacific is a crucial element of both the international and national marketing networks. Yet, hardly surprisingly, major attention is more often focused upon the periodic famine crises which are the result of various forms of natural disaster, or on incipient Malthusian situations in which population growth appears to be exceeding the rate of food production (see George, 1976 for an excellent review of this aspect).

It is a fact, however, that an important portion of urban food supply is provided by locally-produced goods in which the distribution networks from producer to seller are dominated by people who are part of the 'informal sector'. While it has been customary to regard such networks characterised by a myriad of traders and wholesalers as inefficient, the fact is that these marketing networks perform a remarkably effective function in providing urban dwellers with regular supplies of foodstuffs. There is no doubt, however, that these distribution systems exhibit marked complexity and variation from country to country.

As James Jackson points out in Chapter 2, attempts to build theoretical models which can be used to try and understand this complexity are fraught with great dangers. However, the work of anthropologists such as Geertz (1963) and, particularly Mintz (1959), are not without their value. Thus, Mintz (1959, p. 20) suggests that a distribution system must be seen as a 'mechanism to facilitate the exchange of goods and services while the market places are the *loci* where concrete exchange takes place'. In the case of the following studies the general market-place is the urban area; the specific market-place is the public market. There are, of course many other types of urban market-place selling foodstuffs which range from supermarket through store to street-seller. There are also very diverse patterns of exchange of goods and services which range from simple flows in which producers sell their own goods to complicated networks in which large numbers of intermediaries are involved in the purchase and reselling of goods before they finally reach consumers. Such networks play a major role in linking urban areas to the countryside. They provide employment and income for large numbers of people in the labour surplus situations of many Third World countries.

---

* Dr T.G. McGee is Senior Fellow, Department of Human Geography, Research School of Pacific Studies, The Australian National University, Canberra.

Historically two broad models of the structure of these marketing networks have dominated research in Southeast Asia and the Pacific.   The first of these developed by Geertz is summarised by Jackson in Chapter 2.   The second model which is outlined in Brookfield's contribution to *Pacific Market-places* (1969) has been the basis of views about indigenous Pacific marketing which explains its rather slower development and lack of sophistication.

On the basis of empirical data collected in the early seventies, Jackson, and Bathgate in Chapter 3, challenge these earlier models, suggesting that the marketing networks are far more complex and that different patterns are beginning to emerge.   Thus, Jackson shows that the hierarchical model of marketing networks in which foodstuffs flow through a series of chains in which goods are sold and resold at many points before reaching the consumer, depends greatly upon the type of produce.   In some commodities, such as fish, there is increasing concentration among wholesalers while in others, such as vegetables, more traditional patterns prevail. Bathgate shows that there can be sharp variations between different villages in developing the production of goods for markets which are a reflection of cultural and other factors that certainly need more investigation.

The fact that marketing systems are becoming more specialised is hardly surprising.   The improvement in transportation and increased capital investment in food storage have begun to affect the structure and organisation of foodstuff marketing.   As Forman and Riegelhaupt (1970) have shown in Brazil the traditional patterns of relatively short-distance marketing have changed radically in the last fifteen years leading to increased regional specialisation which is well brought out in the Jackson study.   While this process is still only incipient throughout the Pacific, it is becoming increasingly true of the market systems which supply Suva the capital and largest city of Fiji (see Baxter, 1976).

Such developments in the marketing systems have important consequences for policy formation.   Both Jackson and Bathgate warn of the dangers of government interference without adequate understanding of the structure of these marketing systems and the changes that they are undergoing.   This has great relevance to policies which encourage the persistence of 'informal' marketing systems which may end up 'fossilising' at times when they are involved in processes of change which are leading to more 'workable' marketing systems.

REFERENCES

Baxter, M. (1976),   Specialised transport of produce to
                                  Suva, Nausori and Navua markets: a
                                  tentative analysis of a survey
                                  conducted in June 1976, Centre for
                                  Applied Studies in Development,
                                  University of the South Pacific, Suva.

Brookfield, H.C. (ed.),   *Pacific Market-places: A Collection of*
    (1969),   *Essays*, Canberra.

Forman, S. and   'Market Place and Marketing System:
    Riegelhaupt, J.F. (1970),   Toward a Theory of Peasant Economic
                                  Integration', *Comparative Studies in
                                  Society and History*, 20(2), pp. 188-
                                  212.

Geertz, C. (1963),   *Peddlers and Princes: Social Change
                                  and Economic Modernization in Two
                                  Indonesian Towns*, Chicago.

George, S. (1976),   *How the Other Half Dies: The Real
                                  Reasons for World Hunger*, Harmonds-
                                  worth.

Mintz, W. (1959),   'Internal Market Systems as Mechanisms
                                  of Social Articulation', *Proceedings of
                                  the Annual Spring Meeting of the
                                  American Ethnological Society*, Seattle,
                                  pp. 20-30.

CHAPTER 2

TRADER HIERARCHIES IN THIRD WORLD DISTRIBUTING SYSTEMS:

THE CASE OF FRESH FOOD SUPPLIES IN KUALA LUMPUR

JAMES C. JACKSON[*]

1. INTRODUCTION

The adoption of a dualistic or two-sector model has long been a feature of analyses of Third World economies and has been incorporated into planning proposals by national and international authorities (Lewis, 1958; Fei and Ranis, 1964; International Labour Office, 1972; *Second Malaysia Plan 1971-1975*).   The application of this notion specifically to the Asian urban context is commonly attributed to Geertz (1963); it has been much used in studies of urban Southeast Asia and it now often figures prominently in the general literature on Third World cities (McGee, 1967, 1973; Santos, 1971; Yeung, 1973).   Despite frequent use, and the undoubted insights it has brought by directing attention to elements of urban life previously largely ignored, the concept is little more refined, and no more readily applicable in practice, than it was a decade ago and it has been attacked as vague, crude, arbitrary, and oversimplified (Sethuraman, 1976; Bromley, 1977; Harriss, 1977). Although McGee (1976, p. 13), in particular, contends that the existence of syncretic intermediate types of activity does 'not invalidate the model', one frequent criticism has been that many enterprises do combine characteristics from each sector.   Like similar 'ideal-type' constructs it has suffered from a general reluctance to investigate fully this lack of conformity.   It has also suffered from a tendency to accept it as a general law derived from an accumulated body of appropriate research rather than as a framework into which much research has been fitted.   Dichotomisations of this kind, Hauser (1965, p. 514) has warned, 'perhaps represent all too hasty efforts to synthesize and integrate what little knowledge has been acquired in empirical research'.

Since the application of the concept to urban Southeast Asia derives much of its inspiration from the work of Geertz (1963), the supposition underlying this chapter is that we may gain in the search for a workable analytical framework by re-examining his generalisations.   To do so, raises three critical points.   First, his field enquiries were conducted in a small market town in east-central Java which resembled 'any of a hundred other small Javanese towns' and, at the time, had a population of 24,000; two-fifths of its employed labour force were storekeepers, traders, or peddlers,

---

* Professor J.C. Jackson is Professor of Modern Asian Studies, School of Modern Asian Studies, Griffith University, Nathan, Brisbane, Queensland.

one-third were unskilled workers, and only 7 per cent were civil
servants, teachers, and clerks (Geertz, 1963, pp. 8,20).   To what
extent, therefore, are his generalisations culturally and context-
ually specific?   Can we expect to transfer unmodified conclusions
derived from research on a small, functionally simple settlement in
the lower ranks of the urban hierarchy to large, particularly
primate, and far more complex cities serving as focal points in
national trade systems?   Second, although in his analysis of the
town's economy Geertz does identify the *bazaar* and *firm-centred*
sectors, he does not present this as a simple dualism.   Rather,
Geertz (1963, pp. 53,59) recognises a gradation or continuum — a
term he uses several times — from the one to the other.   Specific
cases of stores and factories are cited ranging from those which
had 'only partially escaped from the bazaar economy' to those 'firmly
established along lines familiar to Westerners' and indicating that
the principal distinction between these is not size but mode of
business organisation (Geertz, 1963, pp. 51-66).   Whether or not
this notion of a continuum negates the two-sector approach, making
it desirable to devise a more complex model, possibly along lines
similar to those adopted by Friedmann and Sullivan (1974), it
certainly emphasises the need to view the kinds of enterprise
commonly associated with each sector as highly variable in terms of
size, scale of operations, and organisation and to consider the
extent to which they are ordered hierarchically.   Finally, much of
the subsequent research on what Geertz called the *bazaar economy*
has dealt largely with identifying the characteristics of the participants (see McGee, 1975).   Geertz himself, however, was concerned
mainly with the nature of the bazaar economy as an operating system.
Partly to illustrate the relevance of the first two of these points,
coupled with the conviction that any official intervention must
take full account of the system and its ramifications, this paper
sets Geertz' generalisations about the bazaar trading system of
Modjokuto, his pseudonymous Javanese town, against the findings of
a detailed investigation of the marketing of fresh foods in Kuala
Lumpur (Jackson, 1976)* — Malaysia's fast-growing and increasingly
primate multi-ethnic capital (Pryor, 1973, pp. 57-8).

2.   GEERTZ AND THE *BAZAAR* TRADING SYSTEM

Based on observations in Modjokuto, Geertz shows that the total
flow of commerce in a bazaar trading system is typically 'fragmented into a very great number of unrelated person-to-person
transactions'; it rests on 'the independent activities of a set of
highly competitive commodity traders who relate to one another
mainly by means of an incredible volume of *ad hoc* acts of exchange'
(Geertz, 1963, pp. 28-9).   To comprehend such a system, he
suggests, we should examine it in three dimensions: 'as a patterned
flow of economic goods and services'; as a set of mechanisms serving
to sustain and regulate that flow; and as a socio-cultural system
embracing those mechanisms.

* Fieldwork for this project, which was financed by a grant from
the British Social Science Research Council, was conducted in Kuala
Lumpur in July, August and September 1975.

Geertz (1963, pp. 30-1) identifies three major characteristics
of the flow of goods and services. First, the goods involved in
the system are 'unbulky, easily portable, easily storable foodstuffs, textiles, small hardware and the like, whose inventories
can be increased or decreased gradually and by degrees; goods which
permit marginal alterations in the scale of trading operations
rather than demand discontinuous "jumps"'. Here, in keeping with
many observers, he apparently sees the bazaar system as largely
restricted to those areas in which difficulty of achieving economies
of scale through mass production or trade in standardised or indi-
visible items makes large-scale forms of organisation unprofitable.
Second, the flow is characterised by a very high turnover of goods
and by the fact that the volume involved in any single sale is
extremely small. 'Goods flow through the market channels at a
dizzying rate', he claims, 'not as broad torrents but as hundreds
of little trickles, funnelled through an enormous number of transactions'. Moreover, this movement is not direct; it entails
passage of the goods, and particularly less perishable commodities,
through the hands of a multitude of intermediaries so that the
proportion of retail sales (i.e. sales to consumers) to wholesale
sales (i.e. sales to traders who sell to others) is 'rather small'.
Geertz likens this marketing chain to 'a long line of men passing
bricks from hand to hand over some greatly extended distance to
build, slowly and brick by brick, a large wall'. This leads him
to see its highly labour-intensive nature as a third outstanding
feature.

Geertz (1963, pp. 32-42) then identifies three regulatory
mechanisms as of central importance to the functioning of the
system. First, is its use of variable rather than fixed prices
and its reliance on bargaining as a means of establishing price in
each transaction. This, he maintains, 'tends to focus all the
trader's attention on the individual two-person transaction: the
aim is always to get as much as possible out of the deal immediately
at hand'. The trader, therefore, is looking perpetually for a
speculative profit, 'not attempting to build up a stable clientele
or a steadily growing business'. Rather, he sees his activities
'as a set of essentially unrelated exchanges with a very wide
variety of trading partners and customers, which taken together
form no over-all pattern and build toward no cumulative end'. This
seemingly creates a situation in which 'the primary competitive
stress is not between seller and seller, as it is for the most part
in a firm economy, but between buyer and seller', a difference
which affects the general style of commercial life. Whereas the
firm-type vendor seeks to attract customers, the bazaar trader is
more concerned with clinching each individual deal; 'the idea is
not so much to create or stimulate a market for whatever you have
to sell; rather it is to be present when a chance to sell appears,
and most especially, to be capable of making the most of it'.

Second, 'the primary integrative factor' in the system is the
complex, ramified network of credit linking larger and smaller
vendors which leads to 'a hierarchic ranking of traders' in terms
of their credit relationships and secures their particular positions
in the flow of trade since it is not simply a means of making
capital available but a method of establishing and stabilising
'more or less persisting commercial relationships'. Third, the
trading system is typified by a fractionalisation of risks, and,
therefore, of profits. The larger traders 'do not accumulate

liquid reserves in order to hire labour, land, capital equipment
for more highly systematized productive purposes but to enable
themselves to cut in on a large number of profitable deals'.
Wherever possible, they seek to augment the proportion of total
trade flowing through their hands and will thus engage in a wide
variety of deals as opportunities arise, frequently in conjunction
with other traders, thereby spreading both risks and profits. They
remain, however, highly individualistic operators and they do not
co-operate with other traders to form larger more permanent
alliances for this purpose.

        Perhaps not surprisingly, some of Geertz' (1963, pp. 42-7)
observations on the socio-cultural system in which these mechanisms
were embedded in Modjokuto are more obviously culturally and con-
textually specific.   Thus, he explains how and why the bazaar
economy appears traditionally to have occupied an 'interstitial'
position in Javanese society while the absence of guilds and
similar commercial associations is equally a local peculiarity.
The other two major social and cultural characteristics he dis-
cusses, however, are of wider significance: the existence in
bazaar trading of a highly developed division of labour and the
sharp separation of 'specifically economic from diffusely non-
economic social ties'.

        The major structural pattern, he maintains, derives from the
division of labour, or 'occupational system', which varies along
two axes: according to the type of goods sold and according to
each trader's place in the distributive network.   As a result, the
role of traders which, for the majority, is defined along both axes,
'seems to be almost hyperspecialized' and reveals a relatively high
degree of stability.   'In what is otherwise a very fluid system,
the tendency for most individuals to persist in one sort of trading
rather than shifting easily among various sorts is of course
evidence of the full-time, technically demanding, non-amateur
nature of the trader role as an occupation'.

        Finally, business relationships between traders and between
vendors and customers are 'highly specific' and 'carefully insulated'
from general social or particularistic ties resulting in a markedly
'impersonal, calculating, rationalistic approach to economic
activity'.   Non-economic ties are used to enforce obligations or
to gain assistance, but members of the same family will operate
independently in the market and 'regard one another within that
context with nearly as cold an eye as they would any other trader'.
The standing of the participants in the system is measured largely
therefore by their achievements as reflected in the scale of their
activities and their wealth and'rapid mobility, both upward and
downward, is common'.

        In Geertz' view then the bazaar trading system possesses a
series of distinctive characteristics.   To what extent are these
manifest in the marketing system for fresh foods in Kuala Lumpur?
Does investigation of the trading networks through which these
commodities reach the consumers of the Malaysian capital reveal
aspects requiring greater emphasis or further enquiry before more
refined analytical approaches to the study of the total urban
economy can be developed?   The remainder of this chapter is devoted
specifically to these questions.

3. FRESH FOOD MARKETS IN KUALA LUMPUR

Like its counterparts elsewhere in the Third World, Kuala Lumpur is
essentially a low income city in which probably between 45 and 50
per cent of total household expenditure goes on food (Jabatan Perang-
kaan, 1975, p. 4)*.   Approximately two-thirds of the city's residents, however, fall into the lowest income groups for whom food
absorbs at least three-fifths of total expenditure (Wilbur Smith and
Associates, 1974, pp. 7-5, 9-4 and Table 9-2; Department of Statistics, 1960, p. 5, Table 1).   Unlike the situation in the West, this
is the outstanding feature of urban demand and the most significant
elements in the city's retail structure for the mass of its inhabitants are the various food outlets.   Rice is the main food purchased by all ethnic and income groups.   For virtually all other
foods there is a distinct avoidance of the frozen, chilled, packaged, or processed types now common in the West and an entrenched
preference for freshness.   The principal supplements to rice in
local diets are wet fish and a vast range of vegetables — these
items are virtually in daily demand.   Other fresh foods, consumed
in smaller quantities or less often, include fruit, poultry, eggs
and meat.   The multitude of small independent provision stores in
the city rarely stock these items, dealing instead in rice, sugar,
bottled, canned and preserved foods, beverages and cooking oils.
Consequently, there is a virtual absence of shops specialising in
the sale of vegetables, fish or fruit.   Supermarkets, which have
appeared in Kuala Lumpur since the early 1960s, carry mainly canned,
bottled, frozen and processed foods; they do stock some fresh foods,
but these are generally of the more expensive, exclusive or exotic
types.

   The major sources of fresh food supply for the entire city
population, therefore, are petty mobile vendors and market traders
and the greater part of this passes through its network of public
markets.   Each of these markets represents an officially provided
fixed site for the daily use of licensed traders who are grouped
according to the goods sold.   Physically, the markets take two
forms.   Most are either open-sided permanent buildings or temporary
structures with a corrugated iron roof supported by pillars set
within a wire perimeter fence.   Each such building contains rows of
concrete or wooden benches, or stalls, provided by the authorities
and usually arranged with a central corridor; within the compound,
but outside the building, empty selling spaces, or pitches, are
provided at lower rentals on which licensees may erect their own,
often temporary, structures.   In contrast, are the *open* markets
where the authorities have merely provided an appropriately sur-
faced site but no building; this site is divided into selling
spaces (pitches) on which licensees can erect their own structure
at their own expense.   Unlike other parts of the Third World, and
importantly in sharp contrast to Modjokuto, these markets contain
very few vendors of cooked foods, textiles, or craft products and
each market does not specialise in a particular commodity.   Their
function is to supply fresh foods to the city's inhabitants and
each forms the kernel of a larger retail cluster usually with shops,
street traders, and hawkers in adjacent roads and lanes.

---

* The location of cities in Malaysia is given in Figure 4.1

As instanced by the Jalan Drury 'market' in the heart of Kuala
Lumpur's Chinatown (Jackson, 1975) there are other small groupings
of fresh food vendors operating in public space to which the term
'market' might be applied.   However, the survey was restricted to
those markets in the Federal Territory currently under, or scheduled
for early transfer to, the Health Department of City Hall, the
authority responsible for public markets*.   In terms of function
and size the eighteen markets covered in the study fall into four
categories.   Unlike Singapore, where specific markets specialise
in the wholesaling of particular commodities, Kuala Lumpur possesses
only one Wholesale Market (Pasar Borong).   Located 2.6 kilometres
north of the city centre, this comprises a large fenced compound
containing several permanent single-storey buildings.   These
buildings house a total of 370 stalls, none of which is vacant,
which are rented out to wholesalers; 47 per cent of the licensees
dealt in vegetables, 33 per cent in fish and almost 16 per cent in
fruit.   A large open site within the compound is occupied each
morning by temporary pitch operators who usually erect collapsible,
often makeshift, tables on the spaces provided; at least four-
fifths of these are vegetable sellers.   Pasar Borong, therefore,
is the focus of the city's wholesale trade in vegetables, fish and
fruit — other foods are of little or no significance.

For convenience, the remaining markets have been labelled
public since they draw substantial numbers of domestic consumers
buying for household needs.   Of the total of 2370 recorded
licensees dealing in uncooked foods** in these markets 34 per cent
specialised in fresh vegetables, 9 per cent in fish and roasted
pork, 7 per cent in fruit, 2 per cent in beef, 2 per cent in mutton,
and 14 per cent in other produce, mostly groceries.   Functionally,
however, these markets are of three types and they have differing
relationships with the city's population.   Eleven can be classed
as *small neighbourhood markets*.   These are all located in

---

*   As a result of negotiations between the Federal and Selangor
State Governments, on 1 February 1974 the City of Kuala Lumpur was
enlarged to form the Federal Territory, an area directly under the
Prime Minister's Department and totally separate from all State
jurisdiction.   Administration of the Federal Territory is now entrusted to Kuala Lumpur's City Hall which, at the time of the survey, was still in process of taking over responsibility for various
facets of this much larger unit.   Despite the current administrative transition, which complicated the acquisition of official data,
in the circumstances it seemed desirable for the study to cover all
markets in the Federal Territory under, or due to come under, the
jurisdiction of the City Hall Health Department.

** For the purposes of this study all 'uncooked foods', which are
purchased for incorporation in domestically-prepared meals, were
regarded as 'fresh foods' to permit inclusion of vendors of *towfu*
(bean curd) and dried and preserved vegetables and fish (mostly
handled by what are termed here 'grocery' traders); these are distinguished from 'cooked foods' which can be consumed with no further
preparation.   Incredibly, the criteria for identifying informal
sector enterprises suggested by Sethuraman (1976, p. 81) appear
specifically to exclude trade in fresh foods.

predominantly low income areas, they concentrate particularly on
the supply of vegetables, fish, and pork, the items in greatest
daily demand, and they are patronised almost entirely by customers
living in the immediate vicinity.   Three other markets also perform an essentially neighbourhood function supplying basic foods to
poor customers who come daily but, in addition, have larger catchments and draw a more diversified clientele.   This includes residents of nearby high income areas who come less often and buy a
wider range of foods so that, for instance, fruits, especially
imported varieties, which are an expensive luxury to the poor, are
more readily available in them.

      The city's three largest public markets — and more particu-
larly Pasar Besar (Central Market) and Raja Bot Market — are
altogether different.   To some degree each performs a wholesaling
function — especially for foods not handled in Pasar Borong such
as poultry and eggs — supplying retailers from other markets and
hawkers.   In addition, they serve three different types of domestic
consumer.   A significantly large proportion of customers interviewed in these markets came from high income residential areas,
often some distance away, usually for a weekly or bi-weekly visit
to purchase a wide variety of foods.   They are also patronised by
residents of the catchments of many small neighbourhood markets
who use their local markets most frequently for normal daily requirements.   However, they visit these large markets less often to
acquire items consumed infrequently or foods for which the aggre-
gate level of demand is so low that provision needs to be cen ral-
ised, such as fruit, beef or mutton, and to take advantage of the
greater range of variety, quality and price.   Since some of the
most dense residential areas in Kuala Lumpur lie close to the city
centre these markets also perform an important neighbourhood
function for the predominantly poor inhabitants in the vicinity who
use them to satisfy their daily needs.

4.   SYSTEMS OF FRESH FOOD SUPPLY

No official records are kept of the flow of foods through these
markets.   The questionnaires administered to traders were, therefore, designed to identify the chains through which they acquire
their supplies and to permit assessment of their varying roles in
the fresh food distributing system.   Since virtually all market
vendors specialise in a particular commodity, and sometimes in a
limited range of varieties, the supply chains for each food category were treated separately.   To simplify analysis and to highlight differences between these supply chains, the results for the
major foods are presented separately in diagrammatic form for the
Wholesale Market, the three largest public markets, and the smaller
markets.   These diagrams merely represent lines of commodity movement between supply points and traders and between traders and
consumers.   Since it was impossible to acquire reliable data on
the quantities or values of produce involved in these movements,
the diagrams afford no measure of volume.   Additionally, they por-
tray each system in simple spatial terms taking no account of
differences in temporal patterns of stock replenishment.   In other
words, every reported linkage has been plotted regardless of
frequency of use.   Given these drawbacks, however, it is clear that
each food item sold in the markets is characterised by its own
supply system.

These systems differ for three principal reasons.   First, in
view of the strong local preference for freshness and the associated
consumer habit of buying small amounts with great frequency, they
are greatly conditioned by the degree of perishability and potential
for storage of the commodities concerned; this directly affects
desired speed of turnover and, therefore, frequency of acquisition.
Traders dealing in the most perishable foods and those for which
prolonged storage reduces acceptability, such as fish, vegetables
and pork, tend to acquire the bulk of their stock anew each day.
Vendors of these foods characteristically seek to buy just sufficient stock each day to clear before trading finishes, although few
are fully successful.   In order to achieve this objective, the
usual practice in these trades is for prices to be reduced as
closing time draws near.   Daily acquisition is also common in the
mutton, poultry and coconut trades but, because these are more
readily held over without impairing quality, many of these traders
do replenish stock less frequently.   Daily acquisition is less
common for the least perishable foods such as eggs, imported fruit
and groceries.   Significantly, the practice of reducing prices to
clear the day's stock is rarely adopted by those selling poultry,
mutton, and eggs which, for differing reasons, are easily carried
over.   Vendors of each commodity, therefore, not only acquire
their supplies at different frequencies but the proportion of total
normal stock accounted for by each purchase varies greatly.   At
the one extreme are vendors of foods, such as vegetables and fish,
who aim at complete daily turnover to ensure the highest level of
freshness; grocery dealers, in contrast, stock the least perishable
items and generally make replacements as necessary to maintain a
steady inventory.   The turnover and the flow of goods in each
trade thus differ greatly.

The nature of these supply systems also reflects the extent
of variation within each category, the tendency of vendors in some
trades to specialise in a specific range of varieties, and the
degree to which supplies are imported, derived from sources close
to Kuala Lumpur, or drawn from more distant parts of the country.
Fish wholesalers, for instance, are intent on channelling daily
to the city the amounts and range of varieties they expect will be
required by retailers in the light of the current state of the
market.   The complexity of the vegetable supply system is largely
a product of the many different types of vegetables demanded by the
capital's residents.

Finally, remarkably little food reaches Kuala Lumpur's market
retailers direct from producing areas; a mere 3 per cent of respondents in the public markets sold their own produce and less than 18
per cent received any supplies either from producers or from assemblers or agents in the areas of production.   These were mostly
wholesalers-cum-retailers in the largest markets.   The vast
majority of retailers obtain their stocks from supply points within
the city or in its immediate vicinity so that distributing systems
are greatly affected by the character and localisation of the
wholesaling function for each commodity.   They are also influenced
by the extent to which retailers make a personal selection of their
acquisitions.   Few vendors of meat, poultry, eggs or coconuts
attend wholesaling points to choose their requirements.   Normally,
traders in these commodities, which are least open to variation and
easiest to grade, place orders with a fixed supplier for regular
delivery.   In contrast, almost all vegetable and fish retailers go

early every morning to select their stock for the day's trading, as
also do many fruit sellers; in these cases, they either use their
own transport to return to their stalls or pitches with their purchases or they hire transport for the purpose.   In the absence of
grading, these commodities vary greatly in quality, size and price,
as well as in the particular varieties available daily, so that
personal selection affords distinct advantages.

         In view of these differences, the supply systems for the major
foods sold in Kuala Lumpur's markets were divided into four categories.   The city's sole Wholesale Market is the prime focus for
the distribution of fish, vegetables and fruit, although smaller
amounts of the last two foods are also handled by dealers in the
largest public markets.   By law, virtually all fresh meat must
pass through the government abattoir at Syah Alam twenty-two kilometres south-west of the city centre.   Wholesaling of poultry,
which is absent from Pasar Borong, is conducted by large-scale
vendors in Pasar Besar and Raja Bot market who combine this with
retailing.   Finally, stocks of groceries are acquired through
dealers in the city who operate from premises outside the market
network.

(i)   Supply systems focusing on Pasar Borong

Fish. Nearly all the fresh fish sold in Kuala Lumpur's markets is
of marine origin and virtually all that consumed in the city is
funnelled through the Wholesale Market.   This situation is readily
explained.   The rich, warm-water grounds off Malaysia's long
coastline contain over one thousand species of fish of which more
than one hundred are commonly sold in the markets.   Adequate and
regular provision of the range of types, sizes, and prices demanded
by Kuala Lumpur's multi-ethnic population mean that wholesalers
must draw supplies from several sources depending on availability.
Malaysian consumers will accept iced but not frozen fish, which
they maintain has poorer flavour, and since wet fish deteriorates
rapidly in the local climate, the supply system is designed to
afford the speediest handling possible.   Moreover, since customers
buy fish frequently and in small amounts for immediate consumption
and also seek different varieties according to taste, dietary
patterns and price, retailers limit their daily purchases strictly
to the amounts and range of varieties they expect to sell during
the day in the light of stocks reaching the Wholesale Market.
Typically, they achieve this by buying tiny lots of different
varieties from several wholesalers.   It is, therefore, in the
nature of the fresh fish trade, serving as it does local peculiari-
ties of demand, that supplies to the city should concentrate at a
single point.

         Fish wholesalers in Pasar Borong rely principally on three
source areas (Fig. 2.1A).   Almost two-thirds of the respondents
obtained some stock from the neighbouring state of Perak, chiefly
from Pangkor, Krian, Teluk Anson, and Hutan Melintang — all places
200 to 350 kilometres from the city.   Slightly over half reported
receiving fish from places on the Selangor Coast, which are the
capital's nearest points of supply, and well over half sold imported
fish mainly of higher grades from south Thailand.   Very little fish
reaches the city from southern parts of the peninsula, but almost
two-fifths of those interviewed did report receiving stock from the

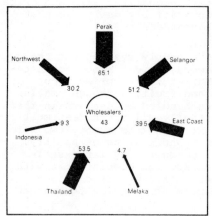

A. Pasar Borong Wholesalers : Supply of Fish

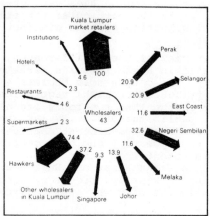

B. Pasar Borong Wholesalers : Distribution of Fish

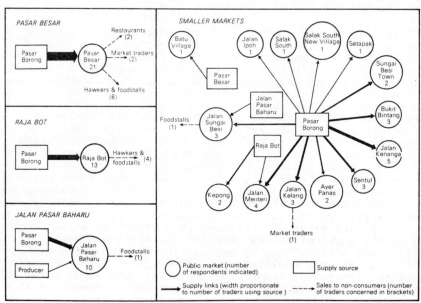

C. Public Markets: Supply and Distribution of Fish

Fig. 2.1:   The marketing chain for fish.

east coast, almost entirely via Kuantan and Kuala Terengganu.
Another 30 per cent drew fish from Alor Setar, Kuala Muda, and
Penang in the north-west.

Almost all these wholesalers acquired their stocks from regular suppliers on a consignment basis (see Low, 1967; Elliston, 1967
and Yap, n.d. for additional studies of the fish marketing system).
At each landing point there are assemblers or agents, some with
their own fishing gear, who receive the catch and have it sorted
according to species and packed in boxes in layers of crushed ice.
In return for a commission from producers, the assembler decides
where to send the fish on the basis of telephone negotiations with
wholesalers over the estimated 'expected' price at which consignments will be accepted and sold.   He may, as a result, distribute
it to several buyers, often in different towns.   Whether the
assembler contacts the wholesaler, or *vice versa*, depends largely
on the state of the market since when there is a shortage the onus
is on wholesalers to obtain suitable supplies and when there is a
glut assemblers must find outlets.   The relationship between the
two is not fixed, however, partly because of variations in the
quantities and types of fish caught, and arrangements are made anew
each day through a process of negotiation.   But most wholesalers
and assemblers do have distinct preferences which are established
through experience and often partially cemented by credit relationships.   Moreover, they deal mostly with regular contacts since
both seek to move as much fish as possible with the greatest speed.
The standing of wholesalers, and their success in acquiring a
regular supply of many varieties whatever the circumstances, rests
on their reputation as reliable and fair dealers who offer competitive prices which they will honour, accept the fish consigned to
them, and settle accounts quickly.   In a field where risks are
high, it is in their interests to maintain good relations with their
suppliers to ensure regular receipt of appropriately varied stocks.
In order to make their decisions about daily supplies, wholesalers
require the fullest up-to-date information on market conditions and
they keep in frequent touch by telephone with landing points and
other markets to gauge the amounts, types, and prices of fish
currently available.

When agreement has been reached on consignments, the assembler
arranges immediate road transport to Kuala Lumpur.   Fish was
delivered to almost 84 per cent of respondents in the survey in
hired lorries which make regular daily runs on arrangements made by
suppliers; the rest came in lorries owned by assemblers or agents.
When these reach Pasar Borong, wholesalers collect their consignments and re-sort the fish according to type, size and freshness
ready for the day's sales.   In the past, wholesalers operated on
fixed commission, but they are now essentially buyers, rather than
simple commission agents, who pay the consignor an agreed net price.
The wholesaler receives different prices for each type of fish he
sells according to size, freshness, time of sale and the particular
customer.   In order to avoid preparing complex and detailed
accounts (which would require the precise recording of each individual sale) and to effect early settlement, the wholesaler returns
an average price based on the day's sales which must be as near as
possible to that originally quoted in negotiation with the assembler.
Initially, the wholesaler pays for the transport, but he makes
deductions for this and other costs, together with an allowance for
his profit margin, before remitting the net proceeds to the assembler
who in turn distributes them, less his commission, to the producers.

Assemblers and consignment agents are located in all the
major landing centres. Their function is not to hold fish, but to
arrange for its immediate direct distribution to points of consumption. The remarkable freshness of the fish sold in Pasar Borong
is testimony to the efficiency and speed with which this onward
transfer is effected. Indeed, once loads have been assembled in
producing areas, fish rarely take more than ten to twelve hours,
usually half this time, to reach Kuala Lumpur wholesalers. Surprisingly, perhaps, in view of the distance involved, this short time-
lag applies equally to supplies from Thailand.

The amount of fish imported from north of the border has
risen substantially since the late 1960s. Stocks are acquired in
Songkhla, a provincial seat and major fishing centre in southern
Thailand, through Chinese agents who send lorries loaded with boxes
of iced fish to Bukit Mertajam in Province Wellesley. These usually
leave Songkhla in mid-afternoon and begin to arrive in Bukit Mertajam, after a 235-kilometre journey, about 8.30 p.m. Bukit Mertajam
despite also receiving and forwarding fish from north-western parts
of Peninsular Malaysia, is termed by locals as the *headquarters* of
the trade in Thai fish. There the Chinese dealers, of whom there
are about thirty according to one informant, have premises cluster-
ing around an open square where this fish is sorted, re-packed, and
loaded onto other lorries which leave for Kuala Lumpur and other
towns later in the evening. The lorries from Songkhla return to
Thailand next morning with the empty boxes. After travelling the
385 kilometres from Bukit Mertajam to Kuala Lumpur, the fish usually
reach Pasar Borong between 3 a.m. and 4 a.m. It has thus taken
little more than twelve hours to move from southern Thailand to the
Kuala Lumpur wholesalers with the entire journey, and associated
transfer, timed to ensure arrival at the most opportune time.
Nothing could illustrate more forcefully the long distances
travelled by wet fish consumed in the capital, the speed with which
this is achieved, or the general rush to hit the Wholesale Market
when prices are at their peak at the start of trading.

Each day fish wholesalers experience a short period of intense
activity during which stocks arrive, are sorted, and are sold to
guarantee speedy transmission of this highly perishable commodity.
When stocks arrive they are sorted quickly and, by agreement among
members of their association, selling begins punctually at 4.30 a.m.
For the next hour or so the market is flooded with purchasers
selecting suitable amounts and types for the day's retailing elsewhere in the city. This phase of hectic trading then subsides
rapidly and by 8.30 a.m. most fish wholesalers have finished direct
sales for the day and the building devoted to the trade is largely
deserted. Much business remains to be done, however, mostly by
telephone, in order to dispose of any surplus by re-consignment
elsewhere and to arrange for the next day's supplies.

Most sales are made by these wholesalers to the city's
retailers through individual bargaining with prices falling as
trading proceeds and wholesalers attempt to clear their stocks.
Indeed, three-quarters of the wholesalers interviewed supplied
hawkers, all made some sales to market retailers, and nearly a
third only sold to this category of trader (Fig. 2.1B). Virtually
all the city's fish retailers go personally every morning between
4 a.m. and 5 p.m. to the Wholesale Market to select their

requirements from the day's newly-arrived stock (Fig. 2.1C). These
are then transported to their pitches and stalls by lorry or truck,
typically under contract, or less often by motorcycle, car or trishaw.   In addition, over one-third of the wholesalers sold to
other wholesalers in Kuala Lumpur, typically lesser dealers in
Pasar Borong; smaller numbers supplied restaurants and institutions
within the city.   Surplus fish were either stored in loose ice or
in the market's freezers or, more frequently, were re-consigned to
dealers elsewhere. Almost three-fifths of the respondents indicated
regular distribution to places outside Kuala Lumpur and, although
this included towns in most parts of the peninsula, the main destinations were in Selangor, Negeri Sembilan and Perak.   The supply
chain for fish is thus both simple and compact.

Local and imported fruit. The marketing chain for fruit is less
heavily focused on a single point and since many fruits, particularly imported types, keep fresh longer than fish, speed of transfer
to retailers is less important.   Most traders specialise to some
degree in imported or local varieties.   Imports are chiefly of
oranges, apples and pears which come mainly from China, Australia
and the U.S.A.   These fruits, which are easily stored, are
channelled almost entirely through the Wholesale Market.   Well
over four-fifths of the wholesalers interviewed received their
supplies through agents in Singapore who arrange transport to Kuala
Lumpur by lorry; small amounts also pass through Port Kelang and
Penang and some imported oranges come by road from Thailand through
an agent in Hat Yai (Fig. 2.2A).

Local fruits, most of which cannot be kept for long, are of
two main types: those which are markedly seasonal, such as durian
and rambutan, and those which are available throughout the year,
for example, banana, papaya and pineapple — the latter group being
most common in the markets.   Most fruits are grown throughout the
peninsula, typically by small-scale producers on village house lots
or in tiny orchards, although selected localities are renowned for
specific varieties.   Moreover, only 4000 hectares are under fruit
in Selangor and the largest areas of cultivation lie in Johore,
Perak and Pahang so that Kuala Lumpur necessarily draws substantial
amounts from distant sources.

Almost all of this fruit enters the city's market network
through three points (Fig. 2.2C). Of greatest importance is Pasar
Borong which was the source of supply for over 46 per cent of all
fruit vendors interviewed in the public markets.   However, both
Pasar Besar and, to a lesser extent, Raja Bot market also serve as
secondary distributing points; these markets contain several larger-
scale traders who combine wholesaling and retailing and who receive
their stocks, mainly bananas, papayas and pineapples, directly from
producing areas.   At the time of the survey, the fruit wholesalers
in Kuala Lumpur relied heavily on three major supply areas.   The
most important of these was Johor, from which over two-thirds of
all fruit wholesalers in Pasar Borong received some of their stocks.
The main fruits mentioned in this respect were pineapple, water-
melon and papaya, and the most frequently reported point of supply
was the town of Muar in north-western Johor, 190 kilometres from
the capital.   Second, nearly two-fifths of the Pasar Borong wholesalers and several of those in the other two markets received some
supplies from east coast States — primarily bananas from Pahang,

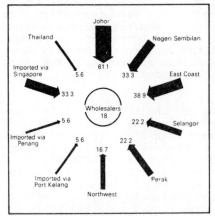

A. Pasar Borong Wholesalers: Supply of Fruit

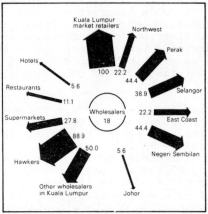

B. Pasar Borong Wholesalers: Distribution of Fruit

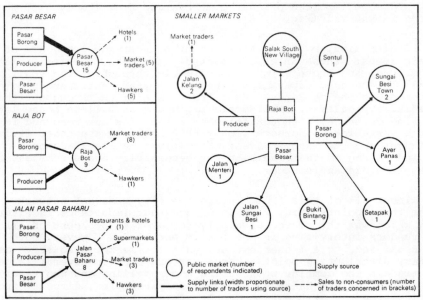

C. Public Markets: Supply and Distribution of Fruit

Fig. 2.2:   The marketing chain for fruit.

the largest supply area for this fruit.   Third, a somewhat smaller
proportion of fruit wholesalers acquired stock from sources within
Selangor or from the neighbouring west coast States of Negeri
Sembilan and Perak.

All wholesalers reported receiving stocks of local fruit from
assemblers or agents in producing areas and almost all claimed to
deal with regular suppliers.   In all cases, these local fruits
were conveyed to the city by lorry, typically in hired transport
arranged by the supplier with the cost, according to most inform-
ants, 'included in the bill'.   The supply system for local fruit,
therefore, bears a strong resemblance to that of fish and vegetables
relying, as it does, on assemblers in producing areas to bulk the
output of many small-scale producers and to despatch this to the
city's wholesalers in response to negotiated orders they have
placed.   In the case of fruit, assemblers appear to acquire their
stocks by one of two systems.   In most instances, particularly
where year-round fruit are concerned, collectors or buying agents
acquire supplies from individual growers on behalf of a Chinese
assembler in a local town.   These are taken to appointed villages
or fixed roadside points, collected by lorry, and despatched to
Kuala Lumpur to fulfil the orders received.   With more seasonal
fruit, however, assemblers often arrange to buy the produce of
particular growers in advance of the harvest on the *pajak* system
which exists, with variations, in all fruit-growing areas and can
apply equally to the produce of an entire orchard or of a particular tree renowned for quality (Lai, n.d.).   When the fruit is
developing but not ripe the local assembler and the grower assess
the potential yield and reach a mutually agreed price for its
advance sale, the money being paid immediately.   When the fruit
has ripened, it is collected and sent to the wholesalers.

Retailers in several of the city's markets draw their supplies
of fruit from dealers in Pasar Besar or, to a much lesser extent,
from those in Raja Bot market, but the Wholesale Market is clearly
the major point for the intra-urban distribution of this commodity
to Kuala Lumpur's public markets.   All wholesalers interviewed
there sell to market traders, almost nine-tenths supply hawkers,
and more than a quarter claimed regular sales to supermarkets (Fig.
2.2B).   Significantly, however, over four-fifths of these wholesalers also send fruit to dealers elsewhere in the country.   At
the time of the survey, the main destinations for these   reconsign-
ments were Negeri Sembilan, Perak and the smaller towns of Selangor,
but over one-fifth also reported sending fruit to places in east
coast States and to those in the north-west.   Apart from its role
in supplying the demands of Federal Territory consumers, therefore,
Pasar Borong holds an important place in national patterns of fruit
distribution.

Vegetables.   Although the Wholesale Market is also the hub of
Kuala Lumpur's fresh vegetable supply system, and daily purchasing
by retailers is equally typical in this trade, the patterns of movement both to the city and internally to retailing points are more
complex.   The principal reason for this lies in the wide variety
of vegetables on sale for these differ markedly in their keeping
quality, in the extent to which production is localised, and in the
share of imports in total supplies.   Malaysia is largely self-
sufficient in virtually all the vegetables in greatest demand.   As

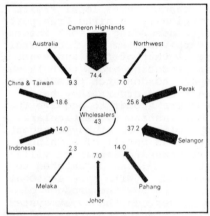

A. Pasar Borong Wholesalers: Supply of Vegetables

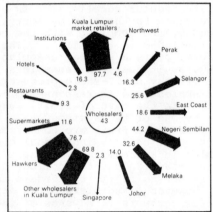

B. Pasar Borong: Distribution of Vegetables

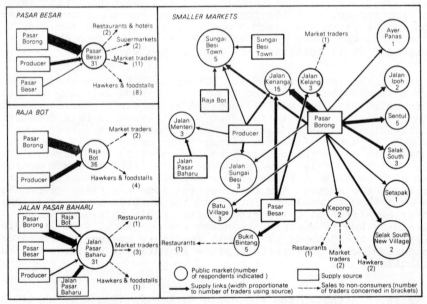

C. Public Markets: Supply and Distribution of Vegetables

Fig. 2.3:   The marketing chain for vegetables.

with fish, however, local consumers place a premium on freshness, particularly of fruit and green leafy vegetables and legumes; most of these cannot be kept for long, even under cold storage, without deterioration so that rapid transmission from producer to public market is imperative. The supply chains by which the three major categories of vegetables — highland, imported and lowland produce — reach the city's consumers thus tend to be quite different.

The most important highland temperate vegetables are English and Chinese varieties of cabbage which are consumed in large quantities by the city's population. Production of these is restricted to the Cameron Highlands, 220 kilometres north of Kuala Lumpur, and currently the capital receives over half this area's total output. Much smaller amounts of other temperate vegetables, such as lettuce and peas, are also received from the Highlands. These are grown by Chinese market gardeners on tiny intensive farms using rotations allowing several crops on the same plot each year; in consequence, cabbage is harvested throughout the year with peak yields in April and August-September and reduced output between November and February (see Agarwal, 1966; Chye and Loh, n.d. and Federal Agricultural Marketing Authority, 1974 for information on production and marketing of Cameron Highland cabbage). Before the city's Wholesale Market opened in 1964 wholesalers handling this produce operated from Pasar Besar and some have remained there combining this wholesaling with retail sales. Today, however, this trade in highland vegetables focuses heavily on Pesar Borong where the majority of wholesalers carry some Cameron Highland produce (Fig. 2.3A). Over three-quarters of those interviewed received stocks direct from the Highlands and it is through these first-level wholesalers that the city's supplies are channelled.

A few producers sell their vegetables to dealers in the Highlands who forward them to Kuala Lumpur, but most despatch their produce direct to wholesalers in Pasar Borong on a regular consignment basis; indeed, 91 per cent of the wholesalers interviewed were supplied regularly by the same producers. Typically, each wholesaler has a continuing arrangement with a group of farmers to dispose of vegetables they send to him. Based on mutual trust and long-established links, this relationship frequently involves the wholesaler in supplying credit to the growers, sometimes in cash but mostly as fertilisers and insecticides. The wholesaler takes a commission of between 5 and 10 per cent of the reported sale price, which is based on an average determined by him in the light of the day's trading; he also deducts repayments of credit before passing the net proceeds back to the grower. Cabbages are sent fom the Highlands to Kuala Lumpur every day except Sunday. Usually, those destined for the capital are harvested early in the morning, generally before 8 a.m., and packed in bamboo baskets. These are taken by hired landrover or jeep to collecting centres in the Highlands where they are loaded on to the lorries of specialist transport companies. The lorries leave for Kuala Lumpur early in the afternoon and begin to arrive at Pasar Borong at about 5 p.m; the cost of this transport is borne by the producers. Most wholesalers dispose of cabbage to second-level wholesalers or retailers within twenty-four hours of its arrival and these lesser traders attempt to pass it on equally quickly. The supply chain for Cameron Highland vegetables, particularly for cabbage, is thus both simple and effective.

A quarter of respondents in the Wholesale Market, together with the major dealers in Pasar Besar, handled imported vegetables, generally in addition to their trade in local varieties. This is most common among those selling cabbages who find it necessary to use imports to supplement domestic production when this is low. The imported cabbage comes from China, Taiwan and Indonesia, with the contribution of each varying annually. Imports from China and Taiwan are greatest between December and April and for the most part they are acquired through importers in Singapore and transported to Kuala Lumpur by road. Supplies of Indonesian cabbages, from around Berastagi, a hill-station in North Sumatra, are less seasonal; these go by sea from Belawan, the port of Medan, to Prai and thence by lorry to Kuala Lumpur. Despite its proximity to the capital, few vegetable imports pass through Port Kelang because of slowness in handling caused by congestion and frequent labour disputes.

The supply system for lowland vegetables is more diffuse. These vegetables are essentially of two types. First, there are those produced by specialist market gardeners: these include leafy vegetables, which lose moisture and weight quickly once harvested, and fruit vegetables. Second, there are many vegetables and leaves used particularly by Malays for flavouring, cooking or in side-dishes accompanying the main meal. For the most part these are collected wild in the forest or from plants growing in village house lots. Although much of the lowland produce consumed in the capital also passes through Pasar Borong, the fact that many of these vegetables are available within a short distance of the city opens up possibilities of direct supply to retailers or of producers selling their own vegetables in the markets.

All except two of the wholesalers in Pasar Borong selling lowland vegetables received their stocks direct from producing areas. Virtually all the perishable lowland leafy vegetables handled by these wholesalers, together with some legumes and fruit vegetables, came from growers in Selangor located within seventy kilometres of the market. Slightly over half of these wholesalers also obtained some supplies, mainly of fruit vegetables, from other parts of the peninsula, particularly from the neighbouring States of Perak and Pahang. In both cases, most received these stocks from regular suppliers in the producing areas who usually arrange for transport to the city in hired lorries. Thus, although a few of those selling Selangor produce use their own transport to make collections from growers, three-fifths are supplied direct by producers. This also occurs with vegetables from other States, but more often these are forwarded by agents or assemblers in the areas concerned.

It is a measure of the degree to which the supply of lowland vegetables is controlled by Pasar Borong wholesalers that only 16 per cent of all vendors interviewed in the public markets received stock direct from producing areas or sold their own produce. Most of these dealt in vegetables coming from a relatively short distance by way of two different supply chains. First, small-scale Chinese market vendors, mostly female, bring in vegetables daily by bicycle or on foot either from their own plots or from market gardens in nearby areas. Second, the rapid growth of the city's Malay population has given rise to a system whereby vegetables specifically demanded by Malays are channelled to Raja Bot market. Generally,

this involves Malay village collectors, chiefly women, who acquire
small supplies in rural areas of Selangor and transport these to
Kuala Lumpur by bus early in the morning.

There is one additional channel through which lowland vegetables enter the city's market system. Most vendors operating
from temporary pitches within the Pasar Borong compound specialise
in the vegetable trade. These are termed *market gardeners* in
official publications (Dewan Bandaraya Kuala Lumpur, 1973), but in
reality they fall into two different categories. First, over two-
thirds of those interviewed acquired their stock from wholesalers
in Pasar Borong who apparently have no desire to subdivide the
large consignments they receive into the tiny quantities required
by the kind of customers using these pitches. These vendors constitute mediators in the wholesale marketing chain and perform an
important break-of-bulk function. The rest, however, do channel
local produce directly into the city's food supply system. Of
these, over one-third sell their own produce. These vendors
operate market gardens within a maximum radius of nine kilometres
of Pasar Borong and use their own transport, principally motor-
cycles, to convey their produce to the market. The remainder drew
their supplies, mainly leafy vegetables, directly from producers
located almost entirely in Selangor. About half collect these
vegetables from producers, usually the previous evening, in their
own transport; the others receive supplies sent to them by producers
in hired trucks and lorries.

In total, therefore, although the wholesale supply chain for
fresh vegetables extends to most parts of the peninsula, there is
heavy reliance on two principal source areas: the Cameron Highlands for temperate vegetables and adjacent parts of Selangor for
the more perishable lowland varieties. The majority of the produce
from these areas, as well as most imports, now passes through the
Wholesale Market although Pasar Besar, once the city's major supply
point, remains important as a secondary focus. Considering both
the strong consumer preference for freshness and the significance
of Selangor as a supply area, and particularly the role of market
gardens in the vicinity of Kuala Lumpur, a remarkably small proportion of the vegetables consumed in the city passes directly from
producers to market retailers. In essence, the supply chain for
vegetables is controlled by a relatively small number of major
wholesalers, mostly operating in the Wholesale Market, to whom are
directed bulk consignments of the output of myriads of small-scale
producers and who initiate the process of reducing and redistribut-
ing these consignments.

Almost 70 per cent of those interviewed in Pasar Borong,
principally those dealing in Cameron Highlands produce, reported
some sales to other wholesalers in Kuala Lumpur whether these
operated in Pasar Borong itself or had businesses in the city's
largest 'public' markets (Fig. 2.3B). Over a quarter also reported
sales to *contract buyers* such as schools, supermarkets and restaurants. But that more than three-quarters sent stock, generally
as re-consignments in response to telephone enquiries, to dealers
in other parts of the country reveals the national importance of
Pasar Borong as a distributing point for this commodity. Indeed,
although the main destinations for these extra-city sales were
other towns in Selangor, Negeri Sembilan and Melaka, vegetables,

and especially cabbages, are distributed by Pasar Borong wholesalers
to all parts of the peninsula.   The largest of these operators,
therefore, are first-level wholesalers concerned primarily with
arranging the movement of large quantities of vegetables on a
national basis.   Nonetheless, Pasar Borong is also the focal point
for the distribution of vegetables to the city's retailers and
three-quarters of all respondents in this market reported regular
sales to hawkers and almost all supplied local market retailers.

The structure of the city's internal vegetable distributing
system is explicable in terms of these comments (Fig. 2.3C).   Over
three-fifths of all retailers acquired their stock from the Wholesale Market which was the sole source for vendors in six smaller
markets; it was also the principal supply point for the three
largest markets and was used by traders in six others.   Most of
these retailers go personally each day to Pasar Borong to make their
selections, usually between 5 a.m. and 6 a.m.   However, some
respondents in six markets, including that at Jalan Pasar Baharu,
amounting to 13 per cent of all retailers interviewed, reported
Pasar Besar as their source of stock.   Superficially, the Jalan
Pasar Baharu market also seems important in this respect but, in
reality, it only supplies pitches in its own compound and the
occasional trader from the nearby Jalan Menteri market.   Similarly,
the role of Raja Bot market as a supply point for vegetable
retailers is strictly limited.

(ii)   The supply of meat

There is no Wholesale Market in Kuala Lumpur for meat.   By
law, all livestock, excluding poultry, intended for human consumption in the Federal Territory must be slaughtered at the Syah Alam
abattoir.   Opened in 1973, this abattoir is operated by the
National Livestock Development Authority (*Lembaga Kemajuan Ternakan
Negara* or, more usually, *Majuternak*).   The Authority purchases
livestock which it slaughters then sells to retailers, acting in
this case as both assembler and distributor.   It also slaughters
the animals of others for a fee.   The occasional illegal disposal
of pigs does occur, but virtually all fresh meat sold in public
markets has passed through the abattoir and carries the appropriate
distinguishing mark.   Although inward movements of livestock are
recorded, details are not kept of the destinations of meat.   Nonetheless, it is clear from the survey that the extent to which supply
chains for each type of meat focus on the abattoir depends on the
proportion of imported chilled or frozen produce in overall consumption.

Pork.   Over nine-tenths of the pork traders interviewed sell fresh
meat and the rest deal in roast pork which they have prepared themselves; in both cases the meat is derived solely from locally-reared
pigs.   Not surprisingly, therefore, in view of legal requirements,
84 per cent of respondents reported receiving their supplies
directly from the abattoir.   The others claimed to be supplied by
wholesalers in Kuala Lumpur and, while it is possible that some
were concealing illegal purchases, this had probably also passed
through Syah Alam.   The pigs destined for Federal Territory markets
are mainly from farms in Selangor, with additional supplies coming
from Negeri Sembilan and Province Wellesley.   Typically, these are

channelled to groups of dealers registered with *Majuternak* who act
as assemblers and wholesalers.   These have the pigs slaughtered at
the abattoir for a fee and distribute the meat, by van or lorry, to
market traders who place their orders daily by telephone.   Thus,
although these dealers have premises elsewhere, in reality, the
system by which fresh pork reaches the public markets focuses almost
entirely on the abattoir.

Beef.   Malaysia imports only small amounts of chilled and frozen
beef, mainly from Australia and New Zealand.   There are no specialised beef farms in the country, yet about 90 per cent of total consumption comprises fresh meat from animals reared locally.   The
bulk of these are buffaloes and oxen from the rice-growing areas of
Kelantan, Terengganu and Kedah; some are beasts culled from local
Indian dairy herds, and bull calves are fattened on the western
coastal plains.   *Majuternak* buys live animals from these sources,
together with a few from southern Thailand and Indonesia.   These
are kept in its holding yards at Syah Alam or on its farms near
Kuala Lumpur until required for slaughter and fresh beef is distributed daily to market traders by truck and lorry on the basis of
standing orders which retailers can vary at a day's notice.   Vendors
specialising in fresh beef, as do the majority, thus receive their
supplies direct from the abattoir.   The single respondent selling
imported beef, which is more usually found in supermarkets, obtained
his stock from a dealer in Pasar Besar.

Mutton.   Slightly over half the mutton consumed in Peninsular
Malaysia is imported chilled or frozen, chiefly from Australia.
Almost three-quarters of the vendors interviewed dealt wholly or
partly in such imported meat.   These obtain stocks by telephoning
their orders to a major supplier in Pasar Besar or to specialist
importers in the city, such as the long-established firm of S.V.K.
Patchee Brothers now located in Bungsar Baharu, and the meat is
usually delivered to them by van in the late afternoon.   There are
few sheep in the country and most of the fresh mutton on sale in
markets comes from local goats; a little is also from sheep imported
live from Australia.   As with beef animals, where the meat is destined for Kuala Lumpur consumers, these are slaughtered at Syah
Alam which then supplies those traders selling fresh mutton.

Primarily because of legal requirements relating to slaughter,
the general preference for fresh rather than frozen produce, and
the low per-capita consumption, the supply chains for meat in Kuala
Lumpur are thus simple and compact.

(iii) The supply of poultry

Poultry, principally chicken, is relatively cheap and acceptable to almost the entire Malaysian population and total consumption is satisfied by local production of broiler birds from modern
poultry farms and free-range traditional *kampung* fowl.   Since
Malaysian consumers believe that fresh birds have superior flavour,
only small quantities of oven-ready chilled birds are sold, usually
in supermarkets.   About 90 per cent of total consumption comprises
live birds and it is in this form that chickens, and to a lesser
extent ducks, are available in public markets.   Usually the customer

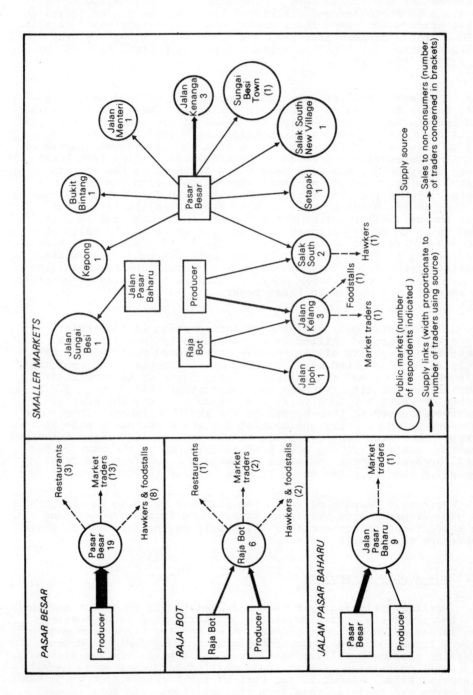

Fig. 2.4: The marketing chain for poultry.

selects one of these caged birds on the basis of appearance and feel.   This selection is weighed and priced and the customer either takes the bird home live or, more commonly, it is killed and dressed on the spot.   Poultry sellers must, therefore, ensure that they have sufficient birds in the market to meet daily and seasonal fluctuations in demand and particularly the sharp rises which occur before and during major festivals.

As with meat, there is no Wholesale Market for poultry in Kuala Lumpur and 54 per cent of all respondents received their stocks direct from producing areas (Fig. 2.4).   The most frequently reported point of supply was Bukit Mertajam in Province Wellesley, but poultry from there go direct only to Pasar Besar and Raja Bot market.   Bukit Mertajam possesses a specialised poultry market and is the location of several national-level dealers; it is the assembly point for one of the peninsula's main areas of table-bird production and distributes poultry to markets in all the larger towns.   Having estimated their needs to replenish stock, vendors in Kuala Lumpur's largest markets telephone their orders in the afternoon to regular suppliers in Bukit Mertajam.   These arrange to despatch the appropriate number of live birds by lorry so that they will arrive in Kuala Lumpur early next morning.   Some traders both in the two largest and in two smaller markets acquire stock regularly from poultry farms in Selangor, mostly within fifteen kilometres of the city centre, but when chickens from elsewhere are in short supply more go direct to these local producers.

Approximately 70 per cent of traders receiving supplies direct from producing areas operate in Pasar Besar and 15 per cent are in Raja Bot market.   Within Kuala Lumpur, therefore, Pasar Besar is the major point of distribution for poultry, supplying retailers at Pasar Jalan, Pasar Baharu and in eight smaller markets.   Typically, these telephone their orders daily to wholesalers in Pasar Besar who arrange for delivery by lorry or truck.   Over 80 per cent of the poultry sellers in this market sell to non-consumers, 68 per cent sell regularly to market traders, and some of the largest operators send birds to dealers elsewhere in the country.   This pattern is repeated, on a smaller scale, in Raja Bot market.   Thus, although it differs from those for other commodities, mainly because of the need for regular deliveries of live birds, the supply chain for poultry is relatively simple.   Chickens sold in Kuala Lumpur's markets come from distant sources in the northwest or from nearby farms; for the most part, these are channelled to retailers through dealers in Pasar Besar.

(iv)   **The supply of groceries**

This is the least homogeneous of all the trade categories. The mixed inventory of most grocery traders includes a variety of bottled, canned and packaged foods, loose condiments, spices and flavouring requisites, dried and preserved vegetables and fish, *dry* vegetables, such as potatoes and onions, and rice.   A few small-scale vendors, however, specialise in lines such as preserved vegetables or ingredients for traditional Malay cooking.   Many of these items are imported and some are produced by local manufacturers. The majority are handled by specialist wholesale shops which cluster near Pasar Besar and it is from these that 91 per cent of all

grocery vendors in the markets obtained their stocks, often by
placing telephone orders or, with branded products, by letting sales
representatives who call on them know their needs.   The only market
traders who do not adhere to this pattern are those who specialise.
A few elderly Chinese women, for example, sell preserved vegetables,
mainly imported, which they purchase in Pasar Borong.   There is
also the occasional small-scale Malay vendor who concentrates on
spices, *belacan* (shrimp paste), and *kerupuk* (prawn crackers) which
are acquired from the Wholesale Market or from producers.

5.   TOWARDS A HIERARCHY OF TRADERS

The systems described above do display many of the characteristics
identified by Geertz (1963).   They are concerned with commodities
typified by easy divisability, lack of processing or standardisa-
tion, and relatively low unit-value, which are not readily amenable
to large-scale trading methods.   At all stages of distribution
turnover is high and transactions occur through a process of bargaining; moreover, vendors are individualistic, specialisation by
type of goods and role is marked, and the average length of involvement by each trade is high indicating considerable stability*.   But
they also diverge from Geertz' 'bazaar' trading pattern in two
important respects.   First, these food supply chains are more
organised, more compact, and seemingly more sophisticated than the
Modjokuto marketing system and each has its own distinctive characteristics.   Second, as the foods involved move through space from
producer to consumer they are handled by varying numbers of intermediaries.   Concurrently, however, they are also moving through a
hierarchy of traders who differ sharply in their role as breakers
of bulk; in their relations with the rest of the urban, and indeed
the national, economy; in the scale of their operations; and in
their place in the network of credit.

Although it was impossible in the survey to secure sufficiently reliable data on several potentially valuable measures of
size, the information collected did reveal that market traders in
Kuala Lumpur varied substantially in the scale and nature of their
operations.   For vendors in the public markets a broad three-fold
classification was devised.   First, 67 per cent of all respondents
in these markets were classed as small-scale or petty operators.
Typically, these rent only one stall or pitch, possess the basic
minimum equipment necessary for their trade, and are either single-
person enterprises or have only one assistant.   They sell only to
domestic consumers who buy in tiny amounts and their purchases of
stock are small; all vegetable traders in this category, for
example, acquired less than one hundred *katis* daily and most obtained
only from forty to eighty *katis***.   This level of operation is most

---

*   The median length of operation for all traders in the public
markets was ten years; almost one-quarter had operated for over
twenty years and only 27.9 per cent were defined as 'new entrants'
who had been in business for under five years.   The degree of stability among wholesalers in Pasar Borong was also high; over three-
fifths of the vegetable and fish dealers and half of the fruit
traders interviewed had been in operation since the market opened in
1964.

**   1 *kati* = $1^{1}/_{3}$ lb. or 626 grams.

common in the fish, vegetable, and pork trades, the foods in greatest daily demand.   Second, a quarter of these vendors were classed
as medium-scale operators.   Most of these also rent a single stall
or pitch and have a minimum of equipment, but they all employ two
or three assistants.   In addition to their retail sales, operators
of this type supply hawkers, food stalls, and eating shops, and
they purchase their stock regularly in larger quantities, in the
case of vegetable traders amounting to 100 to 350 *katis* per day.
However, units of this size are most frequent in the coconut,
grocery, poultry and egg trades.   Finally, almost 7 per cent of
respondents in these markets were categorised as large-scale.   Most
of these rent more than one stall or pitch, employ at least four
assistants, possess additional equipment, and frequently admit to
keeping accounts.   Their sales are more diversified, including
provision of supplies to lesser market traders, and they buy stocks
in greater quantities.   All large-scale vegetable traders, for
instance, reported purchasing over 350 *katis* daily and most claimed
a total in excess of 500 *katis*.   This level of operation is most
common in the poultry, egg, grocery and coconut trades.

      Each trade in the public markets, therefore, is structured
differently in terms of scale and nature of operations.   The
majority of businesses dealing in poultry, eggs and coconuts are
medium or large in scale and frequently undertake some combination
of wholesaling and retailing.   On the other hand, the vending of
vegetables, fish and pork is typically small-scale, although, for
reasons indicated earlier, vegetable traders in these markets range
from a mass of petty operators to a restricted number of large-scale
traders.   The latter were located particularly in Pasar Besar and
had a significant involvement in wholesaling.   That these structural differences are related directly to another dimension of
variation, lends further support to the suggestion that the hierarchy of traders is critically important.   Over two-thirds of all
public market traders interviewed were male, but the extent of
female participation varied greatly between the trades and there
was a strong correlation between scale of operations and the sex of
traders.   Female vendors were most heavily concentrated in the
smaller-scale enterprises and there was a marked tendency for
progressively greater male dominance with increasing size so that
the largest units, which are those most involved in wholesaling,
were almost exclusively run by men.   Significantly, the largest
groups of female traders were those who had been widowed, divorced
or deserted and those whose husbands were unemployed or in casual
irregular employment.   Faced with the need to support their
families, these women seem to have entered market trading in a
small way, generally as petty vegetable sellers working mainly from
pitches, because of their lack of skills and capital and the shortage of alternative means of making a living.   Their prime object is
to make sufficient from each day's trading to provide for immediate
family requirements and they often take unsold stock home for
domestic consumption or use part of their minute profits to buy
other foods in the market when these are cheapest late in the day.
Traders at this level, whom Szanton (1972) has aptly termed *subsistence vendors*, differ greatly from the overwhelmingly male large-
scale operators in some of these markets whose commercial activities
embrace varying degrees of wholesaling.

      As the earlier discussion of supply chains suggests, in the
fish, fruit and vegetable trades this hierarchy extends upwards

into the Wholesale Market where it is also possible to distinguish
broad categories of operators according to the scale and nature of
their activities.   A third or more of the wholesalers in each of
these trades were classed as small-scale and approximately half as
medium-scale.   Like the largest vendors in the public markets,
these had diversified sales supplying mainly market retailers,
hawkers, food stalls and the like but sometimes also selling to
other wholesalers.   Large-scale wholesalers, on the other hand,
who accounted for almost 10 per cent of respondents in the vegetable trade, 11 per cent in the fruit trade, and 16 per cent in the
fish trade, are significantly different.   They all claimed that
the majority of their sales were to other wholesalers and almost
all forwarded supplies to other parts of the country.   These then
are the first-level wholesalers who dominate the distribution of
their respective commodities.   They include the so-called 'kings'
of each trade who hold senior positions in the guilds or associations regulating the commercial behaviour of market wholesalers in
that trade.   Their prime function is to organise the flow of goods
to supply other wholesalers both in Kuala Lumpur and elsewhere and,
if they do engage in the trade, only a small proportion of their
business is with retailers since this would entail subdivision of
their bulk stocks.   Indeed, one of the largest vegetable wholesalers insisted that he made no sales to retailers because it was
not worth his while.   Clearly, therefore, the marketing chains
through which these various foods reach Kuala Lumpur's consumers
incorporate a hierarchy of traders which is paralleled at success-
ively higher levels by progressively greater involvement in pure
wholesaling and thus in the quantities handled.

        The applicability of Geertz' (1963) generalisations to Kuala
Lumpur's fresh food supply system thus depends very largely on the
specific level referred to in this hierarchy.   At the apex are
large-scale wholesalers whose turnover may be high, but who
frequently avoid selling in small amounts; goods do flow through
their hands as 'broad torrents', they mostly rely on regular suppliers, and, as organisers and manipulators of trade in bulk, they
are heavily involved in a nation-wide system of distribution.   The
multitude of petty vendors at the base of the hierarchy, on the
other hand, resemble more closely the traders of Modjokuto.
Undoubtedly, these differences are due principally to the vastly
greater size and functional complexity of Kuala Lumpur and to its
primacy in the nation's distributive network*.   Recognition of
this trader hierarchy, and full elaboration of its nature and
implications, is of extreme importance both theoretically and
practically since generalisations or policies applicable at one
level may be totally inappropriate at other levels.

---

*   Kuala Lumpur is the focal point in the peninsula's distribution
networks for commodities other than food.   Thus, about four-fifths
of all textile cloth wholesalers in Peninsular Malaysia have their
headquarters in the capital (see Yong, 1969-70).

REFERENCES

Agarwal, M.C. (1966),   'Marketing Margins for Malayan Cabbage',
                             Journal of Agricultural Economics,
                             17(1), pp. 91-8.

Bromley, R.J. (1977),   Organization, regulation and exploita-
                             tion in the so-called "urban informal
                             sector": the street traders of Cali,
                             Colombia, prepared for Institute of
                             British Geographers Symposium on The
                             Urban Informal Sector in the Third
                             World, School of Oriental and African
                             Studies, University of London, London.

Chye, Kooi Onn and   'The Cabbage Industry in West Malaysia
  Loh, Wee Yet. (n.d.),   - An Economic Study', *Review of Agri-
                             cultural Economics Malaysia*, 4(2),
                             pp. 15-28.

Department of Statistics,   *Household Budget Survey of the Federa-
  Kuala Lumpur (1960),   tion of Malaya, 1957-1958*, Kuala Lumpur.

Dewan Bandaraya Kuala   *Lapuran Tahunan bagi Pejabat Kesihatan
  Lumpur (1973),   Bandaraya 1973*, Kuala Lumpur.

Elliston, G.R. (1967),   'The Role of Middlemen in the Fishing
                             Industry of West Malaysia', *Review of
                             Agricultural Economics Malaysia*, 1(2),
                             pp. 1-18.

Federal Agricultural   *A Survey Report of English Cabbage
  Marketing Authority   Production and Marketing, Cameron
  (1974),   Highlands*, Petaling Jaya.

Fei, J.C.H. and   *Development of the Labour Surplus
  Ranis, G. (1964),   Economy: Theory and Policy*, Homewood,
                             Illinois.

Friedmann, J. and   'The Absorption of Labor in the Urban
  Sullivan, F. (1974),   Economy: The Case of Developing
                             Countries', *Economic Development and
                             Cultural Change*, 22(3), pp. 385-413.

Geertz, C. (1963),   *Peddlers and Princes: Social Change and
                             Economic Modernization in Two Indonesian
                             Towns*, University of Chicago Press,
                             Chicago.

Harriss, B. (1977),   Quasi-formal employment structures and
                             behaviour in the unorganized urban
                             economy and the reverse: some evidence
                             from South India, prepared for Insti-

	tute of British Geographers Symposium on The Urban Informal Sector in the Third World, School of Oriental and African Studies, University of London, London.
Hauser, P.M. (1965),	'Observations on the Urban-Folk and Urban-Rural Dichotomies as Forms of Western Ethnocentrism' in P.M. Hauser and L.F. Schnore (eds), *The Study of Urbanization*, Wiley, New York, pp. 503-517.
International Labour Office (1972),	*Employment, Incomes and Equality: A Strategy for Increasing Productive Employment in Kenya*, Geneva.
Jabatan Perangkaan (1975),	*Consumer Price Index for Peninsular Malaysia, May, 1975*, Kuala Lumpur.
Jackson, J.C. (1975),	'The Chinatowns of Southeast Asia: Traditional Components of the City's Central Area', *Pacific Viewpoint*, 16(1), pp. 45-77.
Jackson, J.C. (1976),	*Marketing Chains: The Case of Fresh Food Supplies in Kuala Lumpur*, Final Report to the Social Science Research Council, Hull.
Lai Kwok Kong, Andrew (n.d.),	'A Comment on the Marketing Pattern of Local Fruits: the Pajak or Lease System', *Review of Agricultural Economics Malaysia*, 5(2), pp. 27-9.
Lewis, W.A. (1958),	'Economic Development with Unlimited Supplies of Labour' in A.N. Agarwal and S.P. Singh (eds), *The Economics of Underdevelopment*, Bombay, pp. 400-99.
Low Wan Kim (1967),	'Fish Marketing in Malaysia', *Review of Agricultural Economics Malaysia*, 1(1), pp. 28-33.
Malaysian Government (1971),	*Second Malaysia Plan, 1971-1975*, Government Printer, Kuala Lumpur.
McGee, T.G. (1967),	*The Southeast Asian City: A Social Geography of the Primate Cities of Southeast Asia*, London.
McGee, T.G. (1973),	'Peasants in the Cities, a Paradox, a Paradox, a Most Ingenious Paradox', *Human Organization*, 32(2), pp. 135-42.

McGee, T.G. (1975),   *Hawkers in Selected Southeast Asian
                             Cities: The Comparative Research Study
                             Outline, Findings and Policy Recommenda-
                             tions*, Report presented to the Confer-
                             ence on Hawkers and Vendors and the
                             Development of Asian Cities, sponsored
                             jointly by City Hall, Kuala Lumpur and
                             the International Development Research
                             Centre of Canada, Kuala Lumpur.

McGee, T.G. (1976),   'The Persistence of the Proto-prolet-
                             ariat: Occupational Structures and
                             Planning the Future of Third World
                             Cities', *Progress in Geography*, 9,
                             pp. 1-38.

Pryor, R.J. (1973),   'The Changing Settlement System of West
                             Malaysia', *Journal of Tropical
                             Geography*, 37, pp. 53-67.

Santos, M. (1971),   *Les Villes du Tiers Monde*, Librairies
                             Techniques, Paris.

Sethuraman, S.V. (1976),   'The Urban Informal Sector: Concept,
                             Measurement and Policy', *International
                             Labour Review*, 114(1), pp. 69-81.

Smith, W. and Associates   *Urban Transport and Planning Study for
(1974),   Metropolitan Kuala Lumpur: Final Report*,
                             prepared for the Government of Malaysia
                             and the International Bank for Recon-
                             struction and Development, New Haven,
                             Connecticut.

Szanton, M.C.B. (1972),   *A Right to Survive: Subsistence Market-
                             ing in a Lowland Philippine Town*, Penn-
                             sylvania State University Press,
                             University Park, Pennsylvania.

Yap Chan Ling (n.d.),   'Fish Marketing Mechanism with Special
                             Reference to the Dindings (landing
                             stage) and the Kuala Lumpur Wholesale
                             Market', *Review of Agricultural Econ-
                             omics Malaysia*, 4(1), pp. 22-33.

Yeung Yue-man (1973),   *National Development and Urban Trans-
                             formation in Singapore: A Study of
                             Public Housing and the Marketing System*,
                             Department of Geography, University of
                             Chicago, Research Paper No. 149,
                             Chicago.

Yong Ching Hee (1969-70),   *The Wholesale Distribution of Textile
                             Cloth in West Malaysia*, unpublished
                             Graduation Exercise, Faculty of
                             Economics and Administration, University
                             of Malaya, Kuala Lumpur.

CHAPTER 3

MARKETING DISTRIBUTION SYSTEMS IN THE SOLOMON ISLANDS:

THE SUPPLY OF FOOD TO HONIARA[*]

MURRAY A. BATHGATE[**]

1. INTRODUCTION

The steady growth of economic influence exerted by the main urban centres on the surrounding rural communities has been one of the most important post-Second World War developments in the southwest Pacific. In particular, there has been a substantial movement to the towns which has resulted in such problems as housing shortages and unemployment. On the other hand, as roads have been extended outwards and transport services improved, an increasing number of villagers have been able to sell food and earn money in the towns. In many Pacific countries the supply of food to the towns has been actively encouraged by the government to lessen the reliance on imports. Market buildings have been constructed, some assistance has been given to set up marketing co-operatives and the various departments of agriculture have distributed planting material. Most of the urban centres and semi-urban settlements in the southwest Pacific now have a market place — the larger centres having several — and with the continual increase of urban populations, marketing has assumed considerable importance as a source of income for many rural communities. This is particularly true in the case of the Solomon Islands.

The Solomons had a population of 161,000 in 1970, of which 98 per cent were Solomon Islanders — Melanesians, Polynesians and Micronesians — 94 per cent of whom lived in villages. (The remaining 2 per cent of the population were expatriates most of whom lived in Honiara, the capital of the Solomons.) Life in the villages centres around gardening, fishing, the exchange of food, feasting, store-keeping, cash cropping, and intermittent movement into wage employment either in Honiara or in the expatriate-owned coconut plantations. Apart from wage employment and cash cropping village activities do not feature in the national income accounts, and can be allocated to the economy's informal sector.

The most important informal sector activity practised by villagers is the sale of food and there are many flourishing market places throughout the territory. These market places vary in size and type and there is a distinguishable continuum.

---

[*] This chapter is a much shorter version of the paper presented at the Seminar.

[**] Dr Murray A. Bathgate is a Research Fellow in the Papua New Guinea Institute of Applied Social and Economic Research, Waigani, Port Moresby, Papua New Guinea.

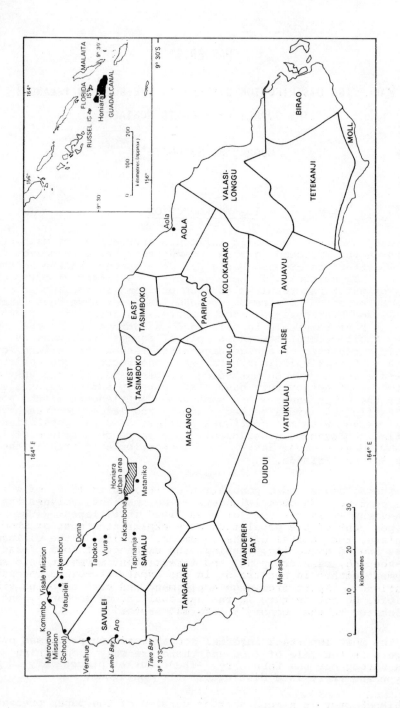

Fig. 3.1: Guadalcanal council wards; location of villages in Western Guadalcanal; and inset showing location of Guadalcanal in Solomon Islands.

At one end of the continuum there are the small traditional food markets along the west, north and northeast coasts of Malaita Island.   For centuries the people dwelling in the interior have exchanged pigs, taro, possum and *Canarium* nut for fish caught by the coastal or 'salt-water' communities.   This exchange has always been based on the occupance and exploitation of different environments.   However, there have been two changes since the early 1950s — money has become the medium of exchange and the morphology of some of the traditional marketing areas has altered following the provision of market buildings.

At the other end of the continuum is the large market place in Honiara (see Fig. 3.1).   A survey of rural supply to the Honiara market was made by the author in 1971 and 1972 in conjunction with the collection of social and economic data in two Ndi-Nggai villages in the western part of Guadalcanal (Bathgate, 1975).   The first of these, Taboko, is characterised by a high degree of involvement in marketing, the second, Verahue, by only limited involvement.

This chapter describes the development of rural supply to Honiara, the spatial and temporal structure of the marketing system in 1971 and 1972, and the nature of vendor economic behaviour.   It is divided into four parts.   In dealing with the development of marketing, the first part draws attention to the manner in which the urban centre progressively shifted from a dependence on local expatriate agents with a heavy reliance on imported foods to a growing dependence on supply from villagers.   Second, there is a brief account of the organisation and patronage of the Honiara market in 1971.   In the third part a broader perspective is adopted. Through a series of surveys covering total supply to the Honiara market, the relative pattern of marketing is established.   Throughout the section the differences between the areas of supply are emphasised in order to define the stages of involvement in marketing and to highlight in particular the fact that within the overall structure some areas simply provide surplus food whilst others have moved into specialised production.   The fourth part has an entirely different focus and attempts to give some idea of the role of traditional exchange practices in central place market trade.   Finally, although the chapter is essentially concerned with outlining the development and current nature of marketing and some of the major problems which have arisen, an assessment is made of some of the deleterious side effects in the villages surveyed.

2.   THE DEVELOPMENT OF RURAL FOOD SUPPLY

TO HONIARA MARKET

Until the late 1940s there was no place on Guadalcanal where villagers could regularly sell surplus garden produce.   European-owned plantations were established along the north coast of the island between the mid 1890s and 1920, but the labourers were supplied with rations consisting of imported rice, biscuits and fresh meat — a few supplemented their diet by maintaining gardens. In consequence, supply from the local villages to the plantations never developed.   Nor was there any demand for produce at the Government station established at Aola in the northeast part of the island.   Occasionally, the District Officer did purchase produce with stick tobacco, but only when food supplies at the station were

temporarily short.   Otherwise, the station was entirely self-
sufficient for the District Officer, the police, the prisoners, the
labourers and the native clerks maintained gardens and the station
received a quota of imported food.   The Roman Catholic and Anglican
mission stations established at regular intervals around the coast
of Guadalcanal between about 1890 and 1915 were also self-sufficient
with those in Western Guadalcanal (at Visale and Marovovo) purchasing food from villagers only during the foundation period (Fig. 3.1).

        In 1941 Guadalcanal was invaded by the Japanese and later by
the Americans, and it was in the aftermath of these events that the
sale of food by villagers began in earnest.   The Americans established camps and military installations at most of the plantations
to the east of the Visale mission.   Although the government declared
these places to be off-limits for villagers, trade with the Marines
soon commenced, largely in fruits which were paid for in dollars.
This trade did not last long because the Americans departed from the
Solomons in 1946.   However, in that short period of time infrastructure was created which was to be of long-term importance to
villagers.   When hostilities ceased on Guadalcanal in 1943 the
Americans established a supply and transit base at Point Cruz.
Besides the base itself, the Americans also built a road extending
about twenty miles east and seventeen miles west from the centre —
the first road in the Solomons.   In preference to returning to the
pre-war capital of Tulagi in the Florida Islands, the government
decided to make use of the complex of roads, buildings, wharves and
airfields, and in 1946 they transferred their headquarters to
Honiara.   The Americans valued the settlement complex at more than
$US10,000,000 and this was probably the amount the British govern-
ment paid for the pre-made town before allocating further funds for
the development of more facilities.   Chinese traders also moved in
and by 1948 a Chinatown was established.   Early population figures
are not available but the town grew at a steady rate between 1952
and 1970 (Table 3.1).

TABLE 3.1:   RACIAL ADMIXTURE OF HONIARA AT
VARYING DATES BETWEEN 1952 AND 1970

| Race | Population | | | | |
	1952	1954	1959	1965	1970
Melanesian) Polynesian)	1600	1800	2618 185	5460	8621 630
European	250	400	365	624	796
Chinese	150	200	266	414	482
Fijian) Other)	40	n.a.	24 78	177	140 522
Total	2040	2400	3536	6675	11,191

Source: B.S.I.P. Department of Statistics, Honiara.

After the War the Administration saw the need to develop internal marketing in the Solomons. Two alternatives were postulated; either villagers could be forced to join co-operatives and market their produce jointly, or open markets could be established. Ultimately, the idea of co-operative marketing was set aside because the people were considered to be 'essentially individualistic and for the most part unable to act in unison on a common purpose for an appreciable time' (Western Pacific High Commission Archives, 1948). Free marketing was thus preferred and it was hoped that a number of market centres might be established throughout the Solomons to which people in the local area could take both their copra and their surplus garden produce. Cash would be paid and the produce would be stored for subsequent transport to one of the new, emerging centres. This idea was extended in June 1947 when the Secretary to the Government proposed that the Administration should purchase root crops in order to save on imported rice rations supplied to government and plantation workers. It was suggested that villagers might pay their taxes in root crops with the government undertaking to sell the produce to expatriate employers. However, this scheme depended on shipping facilities which were unavailable. In addition, there was a shortage of funds to establish an integrated territory-wide marketing system and it was decided instead to establish food markets at the main government centres and foster the development of rural supply to them. Specifically, this meant the establishment of marketing in Honiara.

The first Solomon islander hawkers, arriving on foot or by canoe, were already established in Honiara by 1947. A few villagers living close to the centre were selling surplus root crops to labourers in the town. However, the dependence of Honiara on rural supply was minimal at this time. Instead, Honiara relied largely upon imported rice and meats, with vegetables supplied from the town prison garden and the government-owned farm at Ilu, east of Honiara.

The Honiara market centre proposed by the Commissioner for the Central District in 1950 was not constructed until 1952. It was sited near the District Commissioner's office so that he could keep an eye on the operations, and on the beach front for easy access by canoe. Enclosed by a fence, the centre consisted of several leaf houses with tables. Marketing only occurred on Wednesdays and selling lasted less than two hours because of under-supply and keen competition among the buyers. While the District Commissioner helped to run the market, a policeman was seconded for duty each market day. After allowing vendors into the market to lay out their wares he would blow a whistle to signify to the towns-men that the market was open. He was also there to prevent disputes between sellers and buyers over prices and to ensure that no hawkers, Chinese or Solomon islanders, were selling produce around the town on the market day. If they were, they were rounded up and taken to the market-place. The object in centralising the produce sales was to set an example and stimulate, or enforce, villager interest in market-place trade so that Solomon islanders in the town might be better and more equally served. With the government departments who supplied produce operating on a system of fixed prices, villagers, after a few months, were forced to adjust to the prevailing rates.

Between 1952 and 1956 there was a steady increase in rural supply to the central market and a widening of the area from which it came.   Within Western Guadalcanal, Mataniko and Kakambona remained the main villages supplying produce because of their proximity to Honiara and poor access from more distant areas.   In 1953, after the road was extended up the Poha Valley, Tapinanja villagers started to supply a small but increasing amount of food.   Further westwards, Vura and Taboko villagers also began selling produce in the central market from 1952 onwards but on a much smaller and more intermittent scale.   Westwards again, the early hawking activities of several villagers who resided in the vicinity of the Visale mission did not lead to any subsequent expansion in participation. Instead, villagers in the area opted for the production of copra. With the commencement of launch services in the area in the early 1950s, it was this commodity, not garden produce, which was transported for sale.   However, some households at Takemboru occasionally hired a Chinese truck to take crops to the market.

By 1956 the central market was operating on Wednesdays and Saturdays.   Although the twice-weekly market was made to assist the townspeople it also reflected an increase in supply.   A greater volume and variety of introduced vegetables were now being provided, bringing diversity to the supply.   Ilu Farm was sold to an expatriate in 1955 but a farm for the training of extension assistants, and for local demonstration, had been established at Kukum. Because there was a heavy demand for exotic vegetables among the expatriates living in Honiara, and there was no comparable farm on Guadalcanal, supplies from Kukum were sold in the market.   In 1956 vegetable seed was distributed to a number of villagers in Western Guadalcanal, particularly to those of Mataniko and Kakambona, while several householders in Honiara also gave seeds to the people of Tapinanja.

Between 1959 and 1970 the increase in the population of Honiara from 3500 to 11,200, and the near obsolescence of the practice of giving rations facilitated a sharp increase in cash income from food supply.   Of all the areas providing produce, Western Guadalcanal was the one in which the growth of marketing was most pronounced.   In 1961 it was reported that every village as far as the Visale mission was interested in growing vegetables for the Honiara market (Department of Agriculture, 1962).   The region was on the doorstep of Honiara and was rapidly being opened up by road development and the Department of Agriculture ultimately realised that Western Guadalcanal held great promise as an area of supply.   To promote marketing, small exotic vegetable demonstration farms were established at several villages near the Visale mission.   Some of their produce was sold in Honiara, but it was not until 1965 that intensive extension work commenced.   Large demonstration farms were established at Komimbo (Visale) and Vatakola (Kakambona) and people from the neighbouring villages were taken to these to see new types of crops and to receive planting material and advice on the most hygienic way to parcel produce for sale in the market.   As part of their extension work the Department of Agriculture also made an unsuccessful attempt to establish vegetable marketing co-operatives in Western Guadalcanal.

3. HONIARA MARKET IN 1971: PATRONAGE AND ORGANISATION

Honiara market in 1971 was of vital importance to townspeople.
While one or two Chinese trade stores in Honiara imported apples,
oranges, onions, potatoes and cabbages from Australia, most of the
expatriate households purchased fruits and vegetables in the market
at least twice a week.   Solomon islanders, however, were numer-
ically dominant as buyers and they depended to a much greater extent
on the market for essential staples.   Only a few government departments (principally the Ports Authority) provided rations in full or
part in 1971.   Although some Solomon islander households, especially
those of the lower income group, had gardens in town in which they
grew sweet potato, cassava, leafy vegetables and banana, these
gardens were too small to be able to meet all food requirements. A
survey carried out in 1970 showed that the all-male households, and
those comprising family units, spent respectively some 23.4 and 29.5
per cent of their food expenditure in the market itself.   The
remaining food expenditure went on such items as rice, biscuits,
bread, tinned meats, tea and sugar which were purchased in the trade
stores (B.S.I.P. Department of Statistics, 1970, p. 14).

From the villagers' viewpoint, the Honiara central market was
but one of several outlets open to those who wished to earn money
by selling food.   Among the others were missions and schools in
the local area, road-side stalls, contracts with government departments and other concerns in Honiara, the Chinese trade stores and
the market set up by the Honiara Town Council at Kukum — a suburb
where there are a number of labour lines.   Collectively though, these
outlets were of marginal importance for the majority of the villagers
of Guadalcanal compared with the central market.

Apart from the three buildings and the ever present market-
master whose main task was to collect a monthly rate of twenty cents
from each vendor, the Honiara market in 1971 showed very little
evidence that it had been established by the Department of Agriculture, nor any obvious sign that it was controlled by the Honiara
Town Council.   All of the vendors were Solomon islanders who produced betel nut, coconuts and chickens in bulk at lower rates for
resale in their own stores.   No scales were used and the vendors,
although using baskets, parcels and piles as standard measures, were
able to vary their prices.

While the market's main function was a place for the sale of
produce, it was also a community centre — a meeting place visited
by Solomon islanders during the lunch break and in the evening after
work to find friends and *wantoks* (people from their own language
area) as much as to buy coconuts, cooked fish, puddings and fruit
for immediate sustenance, and root crops and vegetables for meals
cooked in their own homes.   Through the market messages were passed
by people arriving from various islands, and at night the market was
a sleeping place, not only for those vendors who were on a two or
three day selling trip but also for those people who arrived in town
and were unable to find accommodation.

There was then a distinctly Melanesian flavour to the market.
As also noted by Ward and Drakakis-Smith (1976) in the New Hebrides,
one of the most revealing aspects of this flavour is that the market

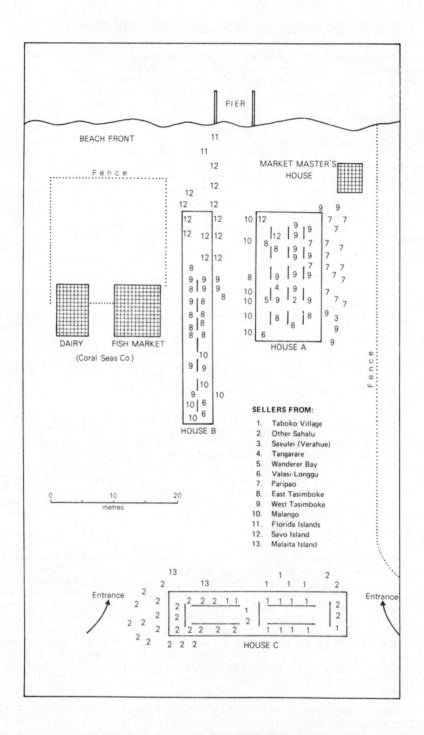

Fig. 3.2: Location of sellers in Honiara central market, 1971.

compound was divided up into discrete social territories (Fig. 3.2).
There were always some differences in the specific area occupied in
or around the houses, since late arrivals had to take up the vacant
spaces, but the vendors from Malaita, Valasi-Longgu, Paripao, Tasimboko, Malango, Savulei, Tangarare and Wanderer Bay, all of whom
spoke different languages, always laid out their produce either in
House 'A' or House 'B' (Fig. 3.2).   Coming in groups, vendors from
each of these districts usually stayed close to one another in the
market so it was not uncommon to see people arriving from a particular area congregate in one place rather than separate and occupy
the smaller vacant but dispersed spaces.   This was recognised as
being their territory.

        Essentially, houses 'A' and 'B' and the area around the pier
constituted the 'native market', and House 'C' represented the
vegetable market which expatriates patronised.   This broad distinction meant that vendors took up positions which, according to
the items they provided, reflected their particular trading interest
— a pattern that they themselves had created through time.

4.   SURVEYS OF THE HONIARA MARKET, 1971-1972

In 1966 Lasaqa (1969) carried out ten surveys of the Honiara market,
these being made on the days when workers in town received their
fortnightly pay.   At that time the attendance of vendors at the
market was highest on these days and this was still noticeable in
1971, although there were vendors present every day of the week.   In
order to allow comparison the same procedures as those adopted by
Lasaqa were applied to surveys in 1971 and 1972.   The primary
objectives in carrying out bi-weekly surveys were: first, to
isolate the longitudinal dimension of the market in respect to the
seasonal availability of particular commodities and the way this
affected vendor participation and income; and second, to establish
the pattern of supply as accurately as possible by recording events
over an extended period of time.

        Twenty-five bi-weekly surveys were carried out between April
1971 and April 1972. Data were collected from 6 a.m. through to
6.30 p.m.   Early each morning before selling had commenced, the
value was estimated of all the produce belonging to those vendors
who had arrived the previous day and had stayed overnight.   During
the day as further vendors arrived and laid out their wares, their
stocks were valued at the prices they had set.   No records were
kept on sales during these surveys, the emphasis being totally on
supply; thus the data are not wholly comparable with those collected
by Lasaqa.

        A second survey was undertaken between 5 November and 6 December
1971.   On this occasion recording was carried out on thirty-two
consecutive days with two objectives in mind.   First, the aim was
to obtain a second set of data to cross-check the pattern of vendor
attendance by area, which had been recorded in the first survey, to
detect any bias in supplier origins on pay days.   Second, the aim
was to establish the differences between areas in the interval between market trips according to distance from the centre.   In addition, a record was kept of the income of each vendor so that the

TABLE 3.2: VENDORS AT THE HONIARA MARKET DURING ANNUAL AND MONTHLY SURVEYS

Area	Population[a]	Bi-weekly Surveys April 1971 - April 1972			Monthly Survey 5 November - 6 December 1971		
		Number	Per cent[c]	Trips/capita	Number	Per cent[c]	Trips/capita
Taboko	192[b]	161	8.2	0.83	112	8.9	0.58
Other Sahalu	1948	514	26.3	0.26	499	39.9	0.31
West Tasimboko	1408	427	21.8	0.30	245	19.6	0.17
East Tasimboko	1759	236	12.1	0.13	142	11.3	0.08
Malango	1290	146	7.5	0.11	59	4.7	0.05
Paripao	651	109	5.6	0.17	14	1.1	0.02
Savo Island	1352	89	4.6	0.07	19	1.5	0.01
Florida Islands	5293	88	4.5	0.02	45	3.6	0.01
Wanderer Bay	1004	75	3.8	0.07	29	2.3	0.03
Aola	1185	27	1.4	0.02	18	1.4	0.01
Savulei	603	26	1.3	0.04	8	0.6	0.01
Valasi-Longgu	1550	16	0.8	0.01	13	1.0	0.01
Malaita Island	50504	13	0.7	-	6	0.5	-
Duidui	1290	12	0.6	0.01	24	1.9	0.01
Tangarare	851	10	0.5	0.01	5	0.4	0.01
Vatukulau	1188	3	0.2	0.00	10	0.8	0.01
Birao	1091	3	0.2	0.00	1	0.1	0.00
Russell Islands	8602	2	0.1	-	-	-	-
Talise	633	-	-	-	3	0.2	0.01

a Unofficial figures exclusive of institutional population with that for Sahalu excluding the 1971 population of Taboko.

b Official 1970 Solomon islanders population.

c Refers to total market attendance.

total turnover could be calculated.   Commodity sales and income
were established by ascertaining the value of the produce of the
vendors immediately after they entered the market; visiting them
every two hours during the day to check off what they had sold and
what was left; asking them the amount of money they had made as they
were about to depart, and noting the various unsold items which
were either dumped or taken home.   To ensure accuracy over the
determination of incomes the recording period was lengthened to
8.30 p.m. and the next day those vendors who had stayed overnight
were asked if they had made any late night sales.   Finally,
although priority was given to establishing turnover some note was
taken of the purchases made by the various racial groups patronising
the market.

Vendors at the market: factors behind participation

During the course of the annual and monthly surveys the greatest number of vendors at the Honiara market came from Sahalu ward,
West and East Tasimboko (Table 3.2).   Particularly revealing is the
fact that Taboko, contributing over 8 per cent of the vendors in
both surveys, had a considerably higher per capita participation
rate than the remainder of Sahalu and all the other areas.   Within
Western Guadalcanal itself there was a noticeable relationship between participation and distance (Table 3.3).   The highest number
of trips per capita were recorded for villages in the zone up to
nineteen miles (thirty-one kilometres) from Honiara.   Towards the
end of the range, at between sixty-five and eighty-four miles (105-
135 kilometres), participation rates have been raised because of
the availability of government shipping services.   One vessel
called at several anchorages in that area specifically to transport
villagers and their produce to the market.

Besides distance and linkage, another important factor in
participation was that villagers in some areas were more tied than
others to making a trip to the market on a pay day.   Figure 3.3
shows that Taboko villagers were present at the market two or three
days a week during the monthly survey, but for the remaining Sahalu
villages, and those in other areas, most of the vendors made the
trip to Honiara for the two pay days.   This defines a pattern of
continuous or regular marketing on the one hand and discontinuous
marketing on the other.   Essentially, this pattern correlates with
distance.

The orientation of the outer areas to pay day trips is a
reflection of the dependence on the sale of surplus produce
invariably of a type for which there is a Solomon islander, rather
than a European or Chinese, demand.   By virtue of the greatest
number of Solomon islander buyers present, the greatest sales opportunities are on pay day.   This pattern is reinforced by higher
transport costs in the outer zone which demand that a large   amount
of produce be brought into the market.   For example, from Marasa in
Wanderer Bay, a personal charge of $A4 return to Honiara and $A0.20
per basket, against a selling price of $A1, meant that a man had to
bring in five baskets to break even and ten to make a net profit of
$A4.   Because much time is required to bring produce down to the
anchorages from the bush villages and the trip requires a number of
days absence, villagers do not consider it worthwhile to bring in
small amounts and so look to the pay days as the periods of greatest

TABLE 3.3: MARKET PARTICIPATION BY DISTANCE FROM HONIARA, WESTERN GUADALCANAL VILLAGES, 5 NOVEMBER – 6 DECEMBER, 1971 (SAHALU, SAVULEI, TANGARARE AND WANDERER BAY)

| Distance from Honiara | | Partici- pating villages | Popula- tion 1970 | Total vendors | Trips per capita | Average vendors per day | Percentage Western Guadalcanal vendors | Average number of vendors on pay day and day after |
Miles	(Kilometres)	Number	Number	Number	Ratio	Number	Per cent	Ratio
1 – 4	(1 – 7)	2	408	137	0.34	4.28	21.11	0.50
5 – 9	(8 – 15)	3	146	96	0.66	3.00	14.79	2.50
10 – 14[a]	(16 – 23)	3	310	176	0.57	5.50	27.12	5.75
15 – 19	(24 – 31)	7	93	62	0.67	1.94	9.55	3.50
20 – 24	(32 – 39)	13	271	90	0.33	2.81	13.87	7.75
25 – 29	(40 – 47)	10	168	28	0.17	0.87	4.31	2.50
30 – 34	(48 – 55)	2	90	20	0.22	0.62	3.08	0.75
35 – 39[b]	(56 – 63)	1	122	3	0.02	0.09	0.46	0.50
40 – 44	(64 – 71)	1	52	3	0.06	0.09	0.46	0.25
45 – 64	(72 – 104)	4	148	6	0.04	0.18	0.93	1.50
65 – 84	(105 – 135)	7	220	28	0.13	0.87	4.32	6.75

a Includes Taboko.

b Verahue.

sales.   Closer to Honiara the more frequent participation of
Taboko and neighbouring villages was only partly explained by lower
transport costs — $A1.50 per family trip regardless of the number
of baskets taken to market.   More important was the fact that vegetables supplied to the market had to be harvested regularly.

Because of the pay day orientation of vendors in the areas
more distant from Honiara, their simultaneous arrival invariably
meant that the market was over-supplied and competition was greater.
Thus, workers in town had a wide variety of choice and many vendors
from the outer areas often returned to their village with unsold
baskets.   In the Sahalu area however, a type of market ring existed
with the major villages supplying produce on different days of the
week.   Thus, Takemboru and Vatupilei mainly marketed on Monday;
Taboko villagers sold on Tuesday, Friday and Saturday morning; Vuru
villagers on Wednesday, Thursday and Friday; and Kakambona on
Friday, Saturday and Tuesday.   This pattern initially developed as
a local response to the shortage of transport but in 1971, in view
of the increase in the amount of produce supplied, the ring served
to reduce competition and ensured that everyone had the chance of
making sales.   At the same time the residents of Honiara were
provided with greater continuity in the supply of fruits and vegetables.

The supply of commodities to the Honiara market: changes since 1966

Produce supplied to the market during the annual survey
averaged $A854 per pay day compared with an average daily turnover
of $A427 during the monthly survey.   However, if the month of
January 1972, when cyclone Carlotta disrupted marketing activities,
is excluded from the annual survey then the average value of supply
per day over the remainder of the year was almost $A916.   In 1966
Lasaqa (1969) noted an average value of supply per pay day of $A965.
The different values for the annual and monthly surveys stem
largely from an overall change in the pattern of marketing.   Villagers had become less confined to pay day trips than previously and
this probably explains the flattening of the marked pay day peak
which was apparent, but not measured, in 1966.   Another change was
that the dominance of the Tasimboko people in marketing had declined
since 1966 and there had been a large increase in the supply contribution of other areas (Table 3.4).

By 1971 then, the improvement in linkage to Honiara had
resulted in a widening of the area of supply and an increase in the
importance of the market to a much larger population.   In the perspective of the monthly survey, Sahalu ward had become the dominant
area of supply, providing 33 per cent of the produce with Taboko
village accounting for one-quarter.

There had also been a change in the various commodities supplied
to the market (Table 3.5).   The most marked difference was that in
1971 root crops, cooked foods and stimulants were less ubiquitous in
the total supply, each having declined in importance. Conversely,
there had been an increase in the relative share of fruits, exotic
leafy vegetables and other exotic vegetables and nuts.   The change
in the types of commodities supplied is even more apparent from the

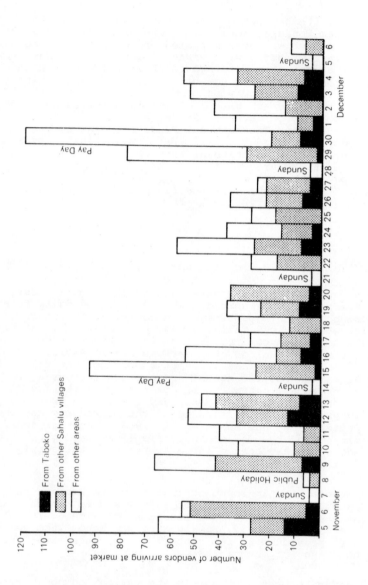

Fig. 3.3:   Vendor attendance at Honiara market from 5 November
1971 to 6 December 1971.

TABLE 3.4: AREAL CONTRIBUTION TO THE HONIARA CENTRAL
MARKET, 1966 AND 1971-1972

Area	Lasaqa Survey 1966 Per cent	Annual Survey April 1971 - April 1972 Per cent	Monthly Survey 5 November - 6 December, 1971 Per cent
Taboko village	)	7.6	8.0
Other Sahalu	) 16.7	16.7	24.7
Savulei	)	1.5	0.5
West Tasimboko	66.4	19.5	17.3
East Tasimboko	7.1	12.4	11.2
Aola	3.2	2.2	3.5
Malango	2.1	10.0	5.5
Paripao	1.8	4.4	1.3
Duidui	) 1.7	0.9	4.5
Vatukulau	)	0.2	1.3
Florida Islands	0.9	6.0	4.3
Kukum Agric. Stn	0.1	-	-
Wanderer Bay	-	5.9	7.7
Savo Island	-	5.9	5.5
Malaita Island	-	4.0	2.6
Valasi-Longgu	-	1.9	1.2
Tangarare	-	0.8	0.8
Birao	-	0.1	0.1
Russell Islands	-	-	-
Total	100.0	100.0	100.0

Source: Lasaqa, 1969; Fieldwork.

TABLE 3.5: MAJOR COMMODITIES SUPPLIED TO THE
HONIARA CENTRAL MARKET, 1966 AND 1971-1972

Category	Lasaqa Survey 1966 Per cent	Annual Survey April 1971 - April 1972 Per cent	Monthly Survey 5 November - 6 December, 1971 Per cent
Traditional root crops	) 67.3	5.1	5.0
Sweet potato	)	48.0	35.9
Native vegetables	1.1	1.1	2.6
Exotic leafy vegetables	) 1.8	3.7	1.7
Other exotic vegetables	)	6.2	10.2
Fruits	5.7	15.4	23.3
Nuts	4.8	8.1	7.4
Cooked foods	8.1	3.5	2.4
Uncooked meats	3.0	3.6	6.4
Stimulants	8.0	5.0	5.0
Handicrafts and other	0.2	0.3	0.1
Total	100.0	100.0	100.0

Source: Lasaqa, 1969; Bathgate, 1975.

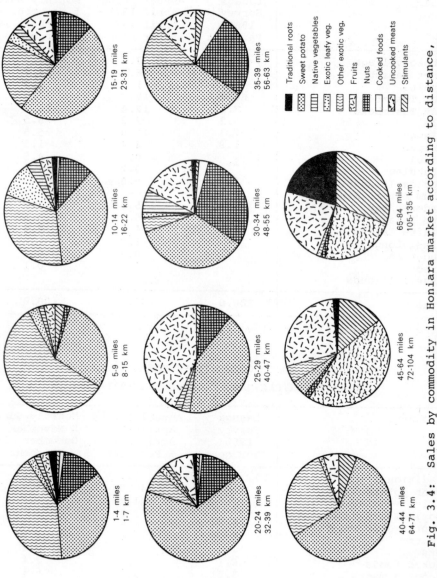

Fig. 3.4: Sales by commodity in Honiara market according to distance, Western Guadalcanal, from 5 November 1971 to 6 December 1971.

monthly survey where fruits and exotic vegetables accounted for 35
per cent of the total value of sales.

To some extent the differences reflect seasonality.   Mangoes,
pineapples and water-melons are mainly supplied from September onwards and they were in full supply when the monthly survey was
carried out.   But overall, it has been the increased participation
from Sahalu in particular and the emphasis on the production of
exotic vegetables and fruits by villages such as Taboko, Vura and
Kakambona which has reshaped the pattern of market supply.

There are also sharp differences between areas in their relative contributions of various commodities and the degree to which
they are dependent on particular items. The differences result
from distance to the market *vis-a-vis* the perishability of items,
transport costs, the racial groups to whom vendors direct their
supply, and seasonality.   The interplay of these factors has led
to a spatial pattern of rural supply which in many ways approxi-
mates Von Thunen's model of rural land use.

The monthly survey data shown in Figure 3.4 reveal a pronounced change in the relative dependence on various commodities as
distance from Honiara decreases.   Between 65 and 84 miles (105-135
kilometres) pigs and stimulants form the bulk of the supply and
traditional root crops and sweet potato the remainder.   However,
between 45 and 64 miles (72-104 kilometres) dependence on pigs and
sweet potato is greater than in the first zone while nuts, fruits
and exotic vegetables of a type locally consumable and which keep
their quality for several days are also supplied.   The latter
include plantains, pineapples, oranges and corn.   Between 40 and
44 miles (64-71 kilometres) one has moved into the zone where traditional roots and pigs barely feature in sales.   Exotic vegetables
however, become more important, particularly beans, shallots and
corn.   Although the overall dependence on fruits increases, in
terms of the total income per vendor, these items are not as
important as they are to the people of the two outer zones.   From
39 miles (63 kilometres) onwards coconuts become a major item in
the supply, this being an area where large plantations have been
established.   The first cooked foods, fish and puddings, also make
their appearance at this point.   The supply from the area between
30 and 34 miles (48-53 kilometres) distant from Honiara is similar
and it is not until 24 miles (39 kilometres) from Honiara that major
differences start to emerge.   The dependence on, and income from,
sweet potato sales declines sharply; the dependence on fruits and
nuts tends to fluctuate as one moves closer to the centre whilst
the supply of exotic vegetables increases.

Monthly variation in the supply of commodities to the market

The amount of each type of produce supplied to the market on
any one pay day is determined by the number of vendors present and
the seasonal availability of the commodities.   In 1966, from ten
surveys covering the dry season, Lasaqa (1969) reported that there
was no marked variation in the supply of various commodities to the
market, but in 1971, with surveys extended to cover a full year,
the author found striking seasonal differences.

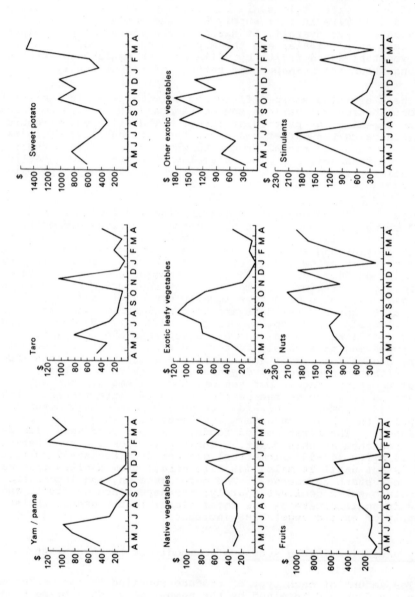

Fig. 3.5:   Monthly variation in the supply of major commodities to the Honiara market between April 1971 and April 1972.

Variation in the supply of some of the main commodities during the year is shown in Figure 3.5. Peaks and troughs are noticeable but not all were determined by the seasonal availability of items to the vendors: in some instances they reflect the changing number of vendors at the market.

Yam, *panna* and taro were mainly provided in the wet season from November to April. Sweet potato and native vegetables were supplied to the market throughout the year but tended to have a wet season bias. In contrast, exotic leafy vegetables, other exotic vegetables and fruits were mainly supplied in the dry season.

Obviously, the seasonality of supply affects vendor participation and income. In 1971 the most important month for trips from Duidui and Wanderer Bay for example was November when the traditional root crops were available. With this being the case, the provision of traditional stimulants also increased at this time since villagers brought in these items to vary their supply. At the other extreme, the participation of people living in a group of villages near the Visale mission in Western Guadalcanal was highest during the fruit season. In this area only Tsavuna, Tsapuru, Veravalou and Vatupilei villagers visited the market regularly during the year, but from October onwards as pineapples, watermelons, *Canarium* nut and mangoes ripened their participation for a short time rapidly increased. In the month's survey these items formed 57 per cent of the income of villagers living in the Visale area.

Vendor-consumer relationships

Purchases for each ethnic group shown in Table 3.6 reflect their relative importance in Honiara's population in 1970. However, in accounting for 80 per cent of the purchases it is clear that in focusing attention on vendor-consumer relationships the market is essentially a Solomon islander domain.

TABLE 3.6: VALUE OF PURCHASES IN THE HONIARA MARKET

ACCORDING TO ETHNIC GROUP, 5 NOVEMBER TO 6 DECEMBER, 1971

Buyers	Honiara population Per cent	Total value of purchases Dollars	Per cent
Solomon islanders[a]	87.9	4440	79.8
Europeans	6.8	529	9.5
Chinese	4.1	356	6.4
Fijians)	1.2	203	3.7
Indians)		36	0.6
Total	100.0	5565	100.0

a Includes Melanesians, Polynesians, Gilbertese and mixed races.

Source: Department of Statistics, Honiara.

Vendor-consumer relationships were of more interest and importance in the pattern of market participation. During the surveys it became increasingly apparent that although linkage to Honiara is initially important in enabling a surplus to be sold, the very infrequency of visits to the market by the people of the outer areas meant that they felt more comfortable selling to fellow Solomon islanders. Once established, patronage relationships enforced a stabilisation in the types of produce supplied and an unwillingness, notwithstanding transport difficulties, to cultivate and provide other crops such as exotic vegetables. This conservatism was most noticeable among the people of Tasimboko. Although they have good linkage to Honiara and could supply a wider variety of perishable produce in greater amounts their main response to date has been to expand their root crop area instead. Stabilisation in the type of commodities supplied was also typical of the villages in the areas of Western Guadalcanal more peripheral to Honiara than Taboko.

One conclusion that is reached is that the change from the sale of local consumables to the supply of a wider variety depends largely on the ability or willingness of vendors to move into selling relationships with other groups. Taboko vendors always gave the impression that they were equally at home in selling to Chinese and Europeans as they were to Solomon islanders. Having moved to this stage, the range of crops villagers have been cultivating must expand to meet the known demands of each group. The income gained from various crops is assessed and followed by a particular course in planting strategy: new crops known to be purchased by a particular group are grown on a very small scale until the demand is such that the income potential is recognised.

Incomes from marketing

In the early 1960s most of the money earned in the market went to the villagers living within twenty-four kilometres of Honiara. Since then however, road extension and the improvement in transport services has resulted in a more widespread flow of money from the market. The pattern related to the period 5 November to 6 December 1971 is indicated in Table 3.7.

TABLE 3.7: DIFFUSION OF MONEY EARNED IN THE MARKET ACCORDING TO DISTANCE FROM HONIARA, 5 NOVEMBER TO 6 DECEMBER, 1971

Distance from Honiara miles (kilometres)	Amount (dollars)	Percentage
0 - 9 0 - 15	1228	10.2
10 - 19 16 - 31	3455	28.8
20 - 29 32 - 47	3244	27.0
30 - 39 48 - 63	1724	14.4
40 - 49 64 - 79	232	1.9
50 - 59 80 - 96	189	1.6
60 - 69 97 - 111	372	3.1
70 - 79 113 - 128	764	6.4
80 - 89 129 - 144	565	4.7
90 - 99 145 - 160	232	1.9

There is a general falling off in per capita marketing income
with increasing distance.   This is especially noticeable between
12 and 39 miles (19-63 kilometres) and the progressive decline would
continue to about 57 miles (92 kilometres) were Savulei not an
anomolous case.   From 70 miles (113 kilometres) onwards there is an
increase in per capita income — this reflects the special provision
of government shipping for Wanderer Bay and Duidui wards and the
lack of any major alternative village-based source of cash income.

The importance of the Honiara market is such that in 1971 it
provided Guadalcanal villagers with more money than that which they
earned from the sale of copra and cocoa.   However, because of
varying access to Honiara marketing assumes more importance as a
source of cash in some areas than in others.   Between 5 November
and 6 December 1971 a record was kept of the place of origin of all
the copra and cocoa sold in Honiara by Guadalcanal villagers.   The
data did not include copra sold by villagers to visiting Chinese and
European traders, but the results still gave a reasonably accurate
picture of the varying dependence on copra, cocoa and the sale of
food. Specifically, it was found that per capita incomes from copra
are low in the main marketing zone within 19 miles (31 kilometres)
of Honiara, but rise thereafter as income from the sale of food
decreases.   The pattern suggests that the villagers close to
Honiara have made a conscious decision to concentrate on the regular
sale of food produce, and that those further distant have opted for
export cash-crop production.

It must also be borne in mind that the market is of value to
transporters as well as to vendors.   Between 5 November and 6
December 1971 the marketers paid out $A1627 — 12 per cent of their
earnings — to get themselves and their produce to Honiara; an
amount which represented nearly 50 per cent of the total income the
operators earned.   Most of this money went into the hands of the
Melanesian transporters based in West Tasimboko and Sahalu, although
expatriates and the government ship operating between 40 and 109
miles (64-175 kilometres) also earned a sizeable amount.

5.   MARKET BEHAVIOUR

In the preceding sections a statistical picture of marketing has
been presented.   In this section the main features of vendor
behaviour in the market are considered.

Prices in the market

Prices in the market have been based on multiples of ten cent
units since 1948.   This practice enabled transactions to be carried
out easily and fairly quickly.   At the beginning of fieldwork all
the baskets of sweet potato sold for $A1 each and the individual
piles of vegetables and small fruits for $A0.10.

In themselves the baskets, bundles and piles represent standard units, all with standard prices which are acknowledged by both
vendors and buyers alike.   However, the actual weight of the
bundles, piles and baskets varies quite considerably across the

market as a whole.   There are several reasons for this and since
the degree of weight or number difference against the standard unit
price is more pronounced for some items than others, the salient
features of the way in which prices are established may best be
described by looking at each of the main items in turn.

The items which displayed the greatest fixity in price across
the market throughout the year, and for which there was no, or very
little, variation in the amount offered for ten cents and one dollar,
were betel nut, pepper leaf, coconuts, *Canarium* nut, *ghola* puddings
and chickens.   The reasons why these items have a fairly uniform
weight or number against a standard market price appear, at first
sight, to be obvious.   They are supplied by vendors from most
areas and there is no seasonal shortage of supply to the market to
create excessive demand and the potential for fluctuating prices;
betel nut and pepper stick are easily counted and measured, and
villagers cook and cut *ghola* into portions of what seems to be a
universal meal size.   Yet there is an element of custom here.   For
most of the groups of Solomon islanders patronising the Honiara
market the use of fixed exchange rates has been, or still is, a
feature of their internal trading.   This has been well documented
for the Lau, To'ambaita and Langalanga people of Malaita (Ivens,
1930; Cooper, 1972; Frazer, 1973; Maranda, n.d.).   Ivens (1930,
p. 261) for example, noted that in the Lau periodic markets in the
late 1920s ten large porpoise teeth could buy ten coconuts or ten
sticks of tobacco, or one or two large fish, five smaller fish or
one hundred taro.   Although no formal periodic marketing existed
in Western Guadalcanal on the same scale as it did, and still does,
in Malaita, various foods could be acquired from others at an
acknowledged rate.   One hundred taro for instance, are said to
have cost one string of red shell valuables.   The important thing
about fixed exchange rates is that they were necessary because the
trading partners usually belonged to different language groups
who, outside normal trade, might be hostile to each other or even
at war.   Haggling and confusion over prices, or dispute about
underweight produce against the fixed exchange rates, could therefore lead to open confrontation.   This was particularly true of
the markets in Malaita and the system of fixed exchange rates has
been carried through into modern day marketing there, as well as
into the market in Honiara where Guadalcanal vendors follow their
own customary precedent for standard unit price exchange.

Generally, the collective weight of items sold in such units
as bundles and baskets can vary quite considerably.   The lack of
scales and the impracticability of purchasing by number means that
the buyers are prepared to accept a degree of variability in weight
from one bundle or basket to another.   This was particularly
marked with sweet potato.   As it was sold by the basket — or sometimes in rice bags — this item displayed greater variability in
weight against the universal asking price of $A1 than either yam,
panna or taro.   However, as with these items, it was the difference
in the weight of sweet potato offered for $A1 on any particular day
and across the market as a whole, which was more evident than any
noticeable seasonal or monthly change in price according to the
availability and supply of the crop.   Then too, there was considerable variability in the weight of baskets supplied by individual
vendors.   Such variability is determined by several factors, the
two which are the most important being the desire or otherwise of
vendors to make quick sales by supplying baskets larger than the

average, or *vice versa* the desire to obtain a higher income from
the same amount of produce over a longer period of time.   In this
respect some people from the outer areas such as the Florida Islands
and the South Coast of Guadalcanal often provided larger baskets
than villagers from places closer to the market because in bringing
in a greater number per vendor — sometimes up to twenty due to
higher personal transport costs and the irregularity of trips —
there was always the possibility that some of the produce would lose
its freshness and thus be difficult to sell on the third or fourth
day of the trip.   By the same token, a few vendors from these areas
brought in baskets smaller than the average in the hope of gaining a
higher income, reducing their prices so to speak by filling up
baskets from others only after it had become apparent that not all
would be sold before leaving the market.   Then again, a number of
vendors who provided baskets below average weight and did not sell
all of these were more prepared to pay an additional charge for
transporting their baskets back to the village rather than increasing the size of some of them.

While on any day there is variability across the market in
the weight of the baskets of sweet potato offered for sale, there
has in fact been very little major change in the average market
price since 1948.   From then until 1961 sweet potato had an average
price of 1.5 cents per pound (3.3 cents per kg), yam and *panna* 2.5
cents per pound (5.5 cents per kg) and taro 2 cents per pound (4.4
cents per kg).   By the early part of 1971 these prices had increased only slightly to 2.1 cents per pound (4.6 cents per kg), up
to 4 cents per pound (8.8 cents per kg) and 3 cents per pound (6.6
cents per kg) respectively.   Given rising transport costs and continually increasing prices for the imported foods vendors buy with
their earnings, the relative stability in the average price of root
crops sold in the market is remarkable.

Most villagers consider that they do not have the freedom to
raise the price of staples and many believe that even if they had
this right it would be improper to take advantage of it.   To en-
large on the first point; whilst vendors *do* have the right to set
any price they wish, the fact that the Department of Agriculture
and the Guadalcanal Council have sometimes made recommendations concerning prices has created the situation whereby villagers believe
that these two bodies control the market.   Invariably, the advice
given by both bodies is that prices should be fair and that vendors
should work them out in consultation with the buyers.   Yet many
villagers still believe that if they started to supply less than
the average for one dollar the Department of Agriculture would step
in and force them to sell at a certain rate.   On the second point,
villagers regard sweet potato, *panna* and taro as 'food nomoa' and
so do the Solomon islander buyers.   In other words, because these
items form a large part of the diet of town dwellers, the vendors
consider it unethical to overall markedly reduce the size of
baskets or increase the asking price for individual fruit of yam
and taro because this would adversely affect fellow Solomon islanders.
Clearly, it is important to record the influence of custom, for
until recently constancy in prices through time has been one of the
important and essential characteristics of traditional-type purchasing.   Seen in the context of the fact that in Western Guadalcanal
and in most other districts the 'price' of canoes and other valued
products against the number of shell valuables or pigs required
remained fairly stable until the early 1960s when the various

valuables were rescaled upwards in value against Australian currency;
then the relative constancy in the average monetary price for staple
crops sold in the Honiara market is another example of an exchange
system operating independently of the reduction in the value of the
Australian dollar — even though this currency was incorporated as
the medium for transaction.

Until the early part of 1971 vendors seemed to have overcome
the problem of the declining purchasing power of the Australian
dollar by increasing their total supply.   This expansion seems to
have been the natural consequence of vendors realising that there
is an opportunity for gaining more money from the sale of staples
to a continually growing town population rather than any planned
effort to overcome the fact that less and less rice, biscuits,
tinned meats and other imported commodities can be purchased with
each dollar they earn in the market.   However, vendors are sensi-
tive to increasing prices for these commodities and in 1971, for
the first time, villagers made a major and general adjustment by
raising the price for a basket or a rice bag of sweet potato to
between $A1.30 and $A1.50.   This occurred in June and although
villagers in Western Guadalcanal discussed the possibility of selling at higher prices it was the people of Savo, the Florida Islands,
the Weather Coast and East and West Tasimboko, for whom sweet potato
is a major market item, who initiated the price increase.   This
adjustment was a direct response to the doubling of the price of
Australian rice which was caused by the government increasing the
import duty.

Early in June only a few vendors were selling sweet potato
for $A1.30 or $A1.50.   Most were reluctant to increase the price
at which they had been selling because of their sympathy for towns-
men and their belief in the need to adhere to the accepted practice
of holding asking prices, if not weight, constant for the main
selling units of baskets and piles.   By the end of the month however, after a meeting in Honiara at which officials of the Department of Agriculture and representatives from the various wards of
Guadalcanal agreed that the average price should increase to a
maximum of three cents a pound, more vendors began to follow the
lead of others.   By August nearly all the vendors were selling
sweet potato at a higher asking price than before, some providing
smaller baskets for one dollar — the average weight being 34 pounds
(15.5 kg) — and others supplying heavier ones with asking prices
grading upwards to $A1.50.   Over a relatively short period of time
what happened was that the overall marked variability in the weight
of baskets against the constant price of one dollar became much
less pronounced and prices began to display a greater relationship
to weight.

Of all the commodities supplied to the market in 1971, fruits
and vegetables displayed the greatest variability in weight or
number against the standard asking price of ten cents for a pile or
bundle.   In the case of Taboko villagers for whom these commodities
made up the bulk of the supply, a wide range of factors conditioned
the variability.   First, since most fruits and vegetables are not
staples, and a high proportion of them are purchased by expatriates,
villagers feel freer to vary the weight of the parcels or the
number of items in each pile.

Second, nearly all the bundles of vegetables are made up in
the village at night, so there is no possibility of changing the
size of them once in the market.   However, whenever there is a
desire to earn a greater than average amount of cash from a market
trip, villagers do sometimes make their bundles smaller, especially
when they do not have very much for supply.   A third factor is
flush and seasonal availability.   Householders whose gardens are
producing a flush of vegetables and fruits usually make up larger
bundles and piles than at other times or compared with other vendors.

While bundles of vegetables are made up in the village, piles
of tomatoes, cucumbers and citrus fruits are made up shortly after
arrival in the market and there is greater potential for varying
the size of these according to demand as affected by total market
supply.   Although the great majority of the villagers do not
take advantage of this opportunity, two householders who were said
to be 'fighting for the dollar' always took a quick look around the
market to see how much of a particular item had been supplied and
what the size of the piles were, making their own bigger or smaller
to attract more buyers or gain more from an item in short supply.
One of these householders, whenever selling oranges, *tangkwa* or
water-melon, was astute enough to inform prospective buyers of the
price according to how he appraised their desire to purchase the
particular item.   In his own words, '*mi luk long ae bulong man an
mi savvy sapose hemi wannim tumus mi putem prais hae*' ('I look into
the eye of the man. If I think that he really wants to buy, then I
put the price up').   However, he was more willing to take advantage of an expatriate than a fellow Solomon islander because '*hemi
olseme mi, hemi no garem sileni olseme wait man*' ('we are both the
same, we do not have money like Europeans').

Other than pigs and turtles which are invariably sold later
in the day at below the initial asking price, there are only two
important items which are sold under a system of sliding prices.
These are water-melons, for which the practice is especially
noticeable, and *tangkwa*.   Both items are supplied by Taboko
villagers, the latter exclusively, and householders always mark
prices on the fruit soon after they arrive.   During the day those
which have not been sold are graded to a lower price, this occurring
perhaps three times before they are eventually sold.

Selling patterns

Despite the variability of prices in the market there is a
passive tone to the selling.   Villagers do not openly compete
amongst themselves through price-cutting, nor, with one or two
exceptions, do they attempt to attract buyers by indicating to them
that they have a good bargain and better quality produce.   Instead,
even though everyone is keen to earn money, vendors sit quietly ——
or even sleep part of the day —— looking as though they are not
interested in selling their wares.   To understand this feature,
the Ndi-Nggai practice of *tsabiri* and *voli* will be discussed.

In earlier times *tsabiri* was seldom pre-arranged: rather, it
came about when those persons requiring certain goods at a particular
time made a visit to their normal trading partners.   The items
offered for exchange would be displayed and the parties would select

those they wanted.   The same pattern is followed today in the
Honiara market: villagers lay out their wares and wait for someone
to exchange these for cash.   The Ndi-Nggai do not have a word for
'selling' — indeed the Western concept of a 'sale' is an alien
notion.   Besides *tsabiri* the only other word the Ndi-Nggai have to
denote formal exchange is *voli* and this means 'purchase'.   Thus,
although the word *sellum* is now occasionally used this in fact is
interchanged with the term *voli*, and 'sale' is conceived of as
'purchase'.   The absence of a language word and concept for selling
reflects traditional practice.   Today, as in the past, the 'sale'
of such items as pigs occurs only when a person needing them searches
for a seller.   Buyers then always make the approach and pig owners,
or persons who make good mats and other handicrafts, never go out
propositioning people to buy.   This practice of passive selling and
active buying repeats itself in central market-place trade: it is
the people of the town who *voli*.   Yet, there is an important
difference between *voli* in the village and *voli* in the market.
Quite obviously, a pig owner or a person who wants someone to purchase his produce can speed up the process of exchange by presenting
his produce at the market since this place is frequented by a greater
number of potential buyers.

There is one other feature which explains the passive selling
tone in the market.   *Tsabiri* is essentially seen in terms of a
food exchange.   Although there is a desire to exchange the items
supplied for cash so that other foods may be purchased, vendors
enter the market knowing that they have only transport costs to pay
and can always eat or feed to the pigs that which they do not sell,
or dump some in the waste bins in the market and depend on their
own gardens when they return home.   This means that villagers are
more prepared to accept the labour cost and put up with a less
varied, more monotonous diet rather than adopt active selling
tactics or sell at well below the accepted market price.

In a passive vending system all sales are considered to be a
matter of good fortune.   A person who brings in an item which is
unknowingly under-supplied and manages to sell it quickly is considered to have been 'lucky'.   The same is said of those who are
able to sell more produce than others and earn a higher income for
the outing.   To enhance their 'luck' the people of Taboko have
adopted two strategies.   First, whenever householders arrive in the
market, most of them scramble their produce, placing some on display in one part of the market house and some a little further away.
By doing this they increase their selling chances because a buyer
who passed one lot of produce might stop at the second.   Related
to this, the more alert elders always try to get a position near
to one of the entrances into the market house where produce can not
only be more conspicuously displayed but is more accessible to the
buyers.   The enticing of buyers — which appears to represent a
considerable change from customary practice — is the second tactic
adopted.   One or two of the Taboko elders who have engaged
in marketing for some fifteen years have established a joking relationship with certain Chinese buyers.   Whenever these people
visited the market the elders adopted an approach which they described as '*olsem way bulong oloketer Siena*' — the Chinese way.
'Number one Chinese cabbage, *tangkwa* here', they would cry out,
directing the Chinese to the cabbage and *tangkwa* melons which they
were selling — sometimes offering coconuts in bulk at below the
market price as well.   These proceedings were usually watched with

bemused interest by the other Taboko vendors who did not agree with
the vociferous approach, and felt that the elders were making fools
of themselves.   They considered that the display of items preferred
by the Chinese was alone sufficient to establish a market relationship, even if they were disappointed when not all of the produce
supplied was purchased.

Trading partners and contract sales

Although villagers sell the bulk of their produce to a population with whom they have no close social relationship and vending is
a formal affair, some villagers involved in marketing have established a selling relationship with certain townsmen which works to
the benefit of both parties.   Trading partnerships were a feature
of traditional *tsabiri* in Western Guadalcanal and indeed of trade in
most other parts of the Solomons.   The essential characteristics
are that the two parties would exchange visits on a regular basis;
certain members would trade with particular persons known to them
from previous visits; people would be accommodated by their trading
partner, and small gifts might be given to cement as well as express
the relationship.   Where villagers held back produce in their
baskets for a Melanesian 'friend' in town they conformed to the
partnership pattern of *tsabiri*.

The normal course in the development of these partnerships is
as follows.   Through constantly coming into the market on a particular day a villager might strike up an acquaintance with a townsman who regularly buys from him.   Gradually the two parties might
come to rely on each other: the villager, always expecting the
buyer to arrive, is assured that he will sell at least a certain
and known amount, with the townsman in turn being assured that he
can always get what he wants.   Other than on the basis of recognition alone, a townsman who observes that a particular villager is
providing larger baskets of sweet potato or better quality produce,
might make a binding agreement by asking the villager to bring in a
certain amount for him each week.   Later, as the partnership
develops, the villager might start bestowing favours on his counterpart, such as providing extra amounts of produce without cost,
whilst the townsman might ask for items not normally supplied to the
market or which are difficult to obtain such as sago palm leaf, used
for thatching houses.

Among the partnerships established by the Ndi-Nggai, one of
the most developed involved a villager from near the Visale mission,
and a Malaitan.   Each week the villager brought in several baskets
of sweet potato, selling these to his friend at well below the
average market price.   Another partnership between a Ndi-Nggai and
a Malaitan was even more developed and conformed in the strictest
sense to traditional *tsabiri* practice.   By arrangement the two men
would meet in the market once a week and in return for the baskets
of sweet potato provided, the Malaitan gave his *wale lau* ('my
friend') half a bag of rice and some tinned meat.   Since these were
the commodities the villager would have purchased before returning
home, the partnership worked well.   Then one night the relationship
was put on a more social footing.   Unable to find transport to get
back home the villager was taken by the Malaitan to his own house
and provided with food and shelter (F. Saemala, pers. comm.).

As for Taboko villagers, the very fact that they provide a variety of items preferred by each of the racial groups in town clearly indicates that from their point of view they have in effect entered into trading partnerships of a particular kind.   One or two, it has already been noted, have established more personal selling relationships with certain Chinese.   However, in neither case is there any obligation on the part of the purchasers to buy from particular vendors.   Unsure as to whether they can obtain a reasonable income on a market trip, many villagers would like to establish an acknowledged clientele.   In this respect, it is noteworthy that when one European woman in 1971 asked a villager who was at the market to supply her with vegetables of the same type in the same amounts once a week, he quickly took advantage of the opportunity to do so.   Each Tuesday when he and his wife visited the market they would keep a look-out for 'our lady' and when she arrived they would hand over to her a basket of vegetables, the parcels themselves being much bulkier than those normally sold at the rate of ten cents for one.

Sellers as buyers

While the Honiara market provides a place where villagers sell produce to the people of the town, the vendors do in fact purchase various items from each other.   Although this accounts for less than 1 per cent of total sales the market provides an important opportunity to purchase items which are not available in their own area or which may be in short supply.   There are differences in the supply from various areas and with regional specialities being purchased by some vendors the market has become something of a minor central point in intra-island *voli*.   The transport of various items to Honiara from fairly distant and widely separated areas has thus given certain villagers access to a much wider range of goods than before — this is particularly true for the people of Taboko.

The item most frequently purchased by Taboko vendors is betel nut.   Betel palms are grown in the village but if the fruit is not yet ripe householders are forced to meet the deficit through the market.   This reliance on the market is enforced for other reasons as well.   Betel is freely given away in the village, with people often demanding the item from each other, but over-asking is considered to be impolite and sometimes a person might refuse to give away nuts on the pretext that he has none.   Furthermore, most of the mature palms are owned by elders and quite often they place *kastom* in their groves.   This is usually a stone over which incantations are made to a powerful spirit.   Since those who break the *tambu* are liable to become sick, this is an effective way of preventing people from climbing the palms and helping themselves. It is the younger married men who are affected by this practice so that they tend to buy the most betel nut in the market.

Besides betel nut, vendors from Taboko purchase a number of other foods such as pineapples, puddings, baked tarc and fresh fish, either for sustenance during the day or to take home for the evening meal.   With no trees in the village, they also spend heavily on mangoes supplied by the villagers living near the Visale mission. Many households also purchase water-melons in order to obtain seed for planting.   There is also a keen demand for the shellfish provided by the vendors from Nggela and Savo islands, and the

megapode eggs from East Tasimboko and Savo. *Colocasia* provided by
the vendors from Paripao, Wanderer Bay and Duidui is also purchased
by those households who maintain very few plants.

Whenever they are in the market, Taboko villagers always keep
a look-out for a group of articles which they themselves do not
manufacture.   The most important is coral lime supplied by the
people of Aola, Wanderer Bay and Duidui.   The burning of coral to
make lime used to be undertaken about once every three years but
Taboko villagers now prefer to buy the commodity because it takes
too long to prepare.   Villagers also purchase kapok pillows and
woven baskets made by the Aola people, and the cured tobacco supplied
by vendors from the south coast of Guadalcanal*.

A feature of the purchase of non-food items is that not only
have Taboko villagers come to rely on market purchases rather than
self-manufacture, but they also rely less now on *sivo* and local *voli*.
Before they became fully involved in marketing, villagers usually
obtained rolls of tobacco and bamboo containers of lime from relatives living in other districts.   Several men used to make regular
trips to Tiaro Bay taking with them items to *sivo* and receiving
lime and tobacco in return, or sometimes purchasing these items
with cash.   While it is still cheaper to go to Tiaro Bay where
tobacco can be purchased at well below market prices, trips have
become fewer in recent years because they take about three days to
complete and interfere with the increasingly important cash-cropping
activities.   Simultaneously, there has been an overall decline in
the production of lime with only the more traditional but least
accessible villages still keeping up the industry and satisfying
their own needs rather than catering for people in other areas as
well.   In view of these difficulties and changes, Taboko people now
find it much easier to satisfy their demand for lime and tobacco by
purchasing from other people in the market.   In effect, therefore,
they have taken advantage of a new channel and in doing so have
substituted their previous dependence on *sivo* and local *voli* for
central place *voli*.

Summary

By considering the total pattern of supply and sales it has
been possible to demonstrate that participation in the market is
largely conditioned by distance and linkage to Honiara, and that as
one moves outwards there are perceptible changes in the nature of
involvement.   Thus, for Guadalcanal as a whole and within Western
Guadalcanal in particular, as distance from the market decreases
trips become more frequent; the sale of a surplus over subsistence
needs gives way to the supply of items grown or produced specifically for the market; there is a change in the seasonal pattern of
supply, especially within Western Guadalcanal; the patronage of
persons other than Solomon islanders broadens out as a wider or
different range of items is supplied (this again being a feature of

---

* This tobacco is often purchased by the 'businessmen' of Florida
Island and Tasimboko who use it to buy coconuts or copra from fellow
villagers.   A $A2 bundle is usually cut into thirty pieces, each
costing ten cents.

Western Guadalcanal in particular); and finally, total income
increases.   What has happened in Western Guadalcanal through time
is that as more trucks have been purchased there has been an outward acceleration of change.   The villages earliest involved in
the selling of surpluses have now moved into specialised production
and regular marketing whilst the outer areas, as they have become
better serviced, have increasingly provided those types of items
which once made up the bulk of the supply from the villages closest
to town.   However, this pattern of change has not occurred every-
where.   Some areas, such as West Tasimboko, still concentrate on
providing the same items supplied in the early 1960s.   In addition,
overall stabilisation in the type and range of commodities supplied
does occur once a certain distance from the market is reached.
Thus, the continuum, isolated in respect of the types of commodities
supplied, only partially represents a developmental sequence.
Although in future, as transport services improve, villagers from
more distant wards will undoubtedly become more involved in marketing, it remains to be seen whether they will opt for increasing the
production of Melanesian-type foods above the current subsistence
surplus level or whether they will begin to adopt a range of exotic
crops for sale to a wider clientele.

6. CONCLUSION: SOME LEADING ISSUES

Although the Honiara market is the most successful of all the
informal agricultural enterprises in the Solomon Islands, there are,
nevertheless, some problems concerning supply.   To the Solomon
islander residents of the town the most basic problem is that the
villagers are beginning to raise the price of food whenever there
is a major increase in the cost of imported foods and transport.
The fundamental issue is whether the standards of an open market
should be allowed to persist.   Rather anachronistically, the issue
arises not through the simple process of villagers supplying towns-
men with food, but of villagers buying imported foods in ever
greater amounts, thereby finding it increasingly necessary to
transfer the imported inflation to the townsmen who are on fixed
wages.   In 1971 when workers for the Ports Authority threatened to
go out on strike if their wages were not raised to accommodate the
increase in food costs, the Department of Labour suggested that
there should be some form of price control in the market.   The
Guadalcanal Council too, which has several times stated that it has
no authority to control prices, came out in favour of the idea,
suggesting that a market board should be established.   Although, as
yet, there has been no major outside interference in price setting,
there is growing concern over the matter and it is felt that scales
should be introduced to ensure that the sale of food on a weight-for-
price basis does not disadvantage the Solomon islanders living in
town.

Another problem is that too much food is offered on pay days
and too little over the remainder of the month.   The Department of
Agriculture would like to see vendors space out their trips, and
one suggested way of gearing supply to demand is to inaugurate a
radio service to inform villagers of the state of the market each
day.   Although villagers do possess radios, it is unlikely that
this measure would do much to improve the situation.   It would
take villagers two or more days to respond to the call for increased

supply because they would have to harvest produce and make travel arrangements.

Even more important is the fact that there are insufficient ships, launches, canoes and trucks operating in the outer areas. Transporters are not able to regularly visit each village to collect produce, and because of the extra fuel costs it would be quite un-economic for them to service villages in districts adjoining their own where only a handful of vendors were wanting to take a small amount of produce to Honiara on any one particular day. While the purchase of more vessels and vehicles might ease the problem in the years ahead, the onset of regular supply to the market and the reduction in the glut of staples on pay days will depend on how the vendors themselves assess the situation. At present, despite the large wastage, they are able to earn more on pay day trips. In addition to an improvement in transport services, it would require an increase in the number of market consumers at times other than pay days, before the vendors could make adjustments to their visit-ing pattern. Perhaps this is the most critical point because if there is an increase in the number of vessels and trucks being operated without a change in the visiting pattern, then over-supply on pay days will become even more pronounced. What is ultimately required is the establishment of a rational system of transport in which produce is collected from one set of villages in one of the outer areas at one time of the week, and from another set later on. Each transport system should in turn be synchronised with those in the other areas to avoid periodic supply.

With an increase in supply now taking place there is also con-siderable scope for the development of a food export trade with the nearby Nauru, Gilbert and Ellice islands. Besides providing an outlet for some of the surplus produce and bringing in money to the Solomons, the trade would be of great benefit to the Micronesian countries because the atolls, in contrast to the volcanic islands of the Solomons, have few agricultural resources and the people depend heavily on fish and coconuts.

The development of a food export trade was mooted in the early 1960s but it was not until 1968 that the first steps were taken to sell food abroad. In that year the Department of Agriculture pur-chased fruits and vegetables from Guadalcanal farmers and sent a trial shipment to Tarawa in the Gilbert Islands. The produce sold very quickly when it arrived but unfortunately no refrigerated or ventilated cargo space was available on the ship and much of the food perished. Further transport difficulties prevented the sub-sequent shipment of food to the Micronesian islands but prospects for the development of an export trade did improve in 1971 when Nauru opened up an air link with Honiara. One load of produce was sent by air to Nauru in 1975 and high hopes are now held that the export of food on a regular basis will soon be inaugurated. Nauru, in particular, is eager to buy exotic vegetables and it is antici-pated that when transport services improve the Gilbert and Ellice islands will also begin to purchase sizeable amounts of taro, yam and sweet potato.

It is possible, therefore, that within a few years Guadalcanal producers could have both a local and international clientele. Supply to the Micronesian islands will require intervention and

organisation on the part of the Administration but as yet no guide-
lines have been established.   The current line of thinking is that
the producers in Western Guadalcanal, from where the bulk of the
exotic vegetables will come, should be encouraged to form an export-
orientated marketing co-operative, but it remains to be seen whether
villagers will go along with this idea and be willing, or able, to
provide produce in sufficient amounts to permit the development of
regular exports.   Certainly, it would be wise for the Administration to recognise that villagers like to sell produce in the Honiara
market so that they can keep abreast of town affairs and escape
from the monotony of village life for a day; that the amount they
provide is geared to household cash needs at a particular time; and
that all but one of the five producer co-operatives set up in
Western Guadalcanal in the 1960s failed, as have many of the unofficial joint-selling enterprises or *kompanis* which villagers themselves have inaugurated.

        The mention of co-operative marketing opens up another topic:
the development of a class of middlemen buyers.   At present the
only true middlemen operators are the Chinese who buy produce in
the market and then re-sell it in their own trade stores.   Sometimes villagers do sell food belonging to those who were unable to
make the trip to Honiara but because they invariably hand over all
the money earned they qualify as replacement sellers, not middlemen.
In the case of Taboko, however, there are some operations which fit
the usual definition of middlemen enterprise.   Two villagers had
contracts to supply a set amount of produce once a week to the Ports
Authority and the Police Department.   Often, when their gardens
were not in flush, they made up their order by buying the largest
bundles of beans and cabbage in the market, opening them up and
making a larger number of smaller bundles from them.   The respective institutions were only a few blocks from the market and since
food was purchased on a price-weight basis, both men always secured
a small profit for their efforts.   One of the men, if he thought
he might not be able to supplement his order through the market,
sometimes asked relatives if they had any surplus left over from a
market trip.   If they did, then he took this to the Police Department the next day and paid his relatives at the end of the month
after he himself had been paid.   Seldom did he extract a 'fee' for
he considered this inappropriate where relatives were involved.

        If middlemen did become more prominent then several of the
current problems associated with marketing might be solved.   If
villagers sold their produce to middlemen buyers then it would not
be necessary for them to spend several days in the market.   This
would be an advantage for the people of the outer areas in particular, for at present they have to bring in large amounts of food to
cover transport costs and be prepared to sleep in exposed conditions.   Furthermore, all the trips from the peripheral villages
are undertaken by men, and they are always concerned that their
wives may be subject to sexual harassment during their absence.
Besides minimising these two problems another advantage of the
emergence of middlemen could be the onset of more regular supplies
from the fringe area.

        However, it does appear that middlemen buyers are
emerge in the years ahead.   There are several reasons for this.
First, producers prefer to sell their produce in the market

themselves because this not only affords them their main opportunity
to get away from the village to see what is happening and changing
in Honiara, but enables them to meet and chat with *wantoks* as well.
Second, the emergence of middlemen buyers is intimately tied up with
transport.   As services improve more people are able to take their
own food into Honiara and the necessity for a middleman diminishes.

Another consideration is that during the 1960s those persons
who purchased food locally and then resold it in Honiara did not
always pay the suppliers.   Because of this villagers are now reluctant to hand produce over to others.   Villagers are also keen to
sell their own food in Honiara so that they can buy goods at the
Chinese trade stores.   Most of these goods are much cheaper than
those sold in the village stores, many being obtainable only in town.

Potential middlemen themselves, also face numerous problems.
For instance, they would have to be able to give cash on the spot
to the sellers because villagers want to purchase items for the
household as soon as they have disposed of their produce.   They
would also have to calculate buying prices on imperfect information
on market turnover and the amount of wastage, and villagers may not
be willing to sell food at the rates offered.   Finally, they would
have difficulty obtaining a profit because, apart from all the other
factors, the amount available for purchase from villagers would not
be large.

While personal marketing will remain dominant in the future,
there are some changes emerging in the selling system.   The first
concerns the exchange of food in the village sector itself.   At
Taboko, the area growing most specialised crops, it is common for
people who have an abundance of a particular crop to allow others
not cultivating it or whose gardens are not in full production, to
harvest some for sale in Honiara.   In most cases this is a reciprocal arrangement which is an extension of the food gift or *sau
vaniho* system beyond its purely subsistence function.   But increasingly, those people who are *not* close relatives are allowed to take
some of the surplus in return for cash payment after their trip
to the market.   In essence, formality is now being introduced into
the village sector and it can be expected that the use of money as
a medium of exchange in supply transactions for the market will
become more pronounced in the next decade.

The other change is that the villagers of Vura, Lambi and
Sugu in Western Guadalcanal are interested in setting up communally-
owned and operated stores in Honiara.   In one way they wish to
imitate the Chinese, but the real reason for their interest is that
with the increase in total supply to the market the time required
to sell produce has doubled.   The people of Vura, in particular,
are alert to the fact that over-supply will occur in a few years
and they hope to set up their own vegetable store in town.   The
village leaders say that if they opened up a retail outlet they
would buy food at below the market price but redistribute part of
the profits to the member producers at the end of each year.
Whether villagers can put their plans into operation is another
matter.   They will require money to buy a plot of land in town and
will have to acquire an insight into commercial practice before
they can expect to successfully engage in the retail trade.

This chapter has concentrated on the manner in which rural supply has been harnessed to cater for urban needs, and a picture of success has been painted.   However, when the viewpoint is reversed, it cannot be said that involvement in marketing has been entirely beneficial to the villagers.   On the contrary, marketing is not the most efficient of the cash-earning opportunities open to the rural people and involvement in it has resulted in a number of deleterious changes.

First, it is necessary to emphasise the fact that inputs into market gardening have risen in the last twenty years.   In 1971 and 1972 the married men and women of Verahue, in a traditional-crop area, devoted only eight and twelve hours per week to subsistence gardening.   Those at Taboko, which was highly orientated to market sales, were spending between twenty-two and twenty-three hours a week in their gardens, plus another seven and eleven hours preparing for market trips and selling produce.   Taboko villagers have willingly made inroads into their leisure time in order to buy imported foods, but they are beginning to feel the strain of the longer hours.   In 1971, many householders claimed that they would gradually phase out of marketing and concentrate on the production of export cash crops instead.   Such a course of action makes sense: the return per hour from a market trip was about the same as that from producing copra but lower than the return from the sale of wet cacao beans.   In fact, during 1971 when the drying of cacao beans was instituted, returns increased by 450 per cent, and some of the leading cacao growers promptly began to cut more beans and rely less on the sale of food.   They also expanded their groves and it would appear that in the long-term, where people have several alternative sources of income, their interest in marketing will fluctuate according to changes in the price for export cash crops.   It was quite marked in 1972 that those persons at Taboko who had the largest groves of cacao and coconuts, sold less garden produce than others, while in 1973 when copra prices tripled, the majority of the villagers made more regular harvests from their palms and reduced the supply of food.   It is also likely that, in the long-term, supply from Western Guadalcanal and the area to the immediate east of Honiara could stabilise, or even fall, because of a short-age of labour.   Each year the villagers along the north coast of the island are spending more time expanding their groves, and the amount of copra being sold is progressively increasing.

Another way of considering the efficiency of marketing as an occupation is to compare the amount of time villagers spend producing and selling food to buy imported produce, *vis-à-vis* the time needed to meet food needs through subsistence production.   The people of Verahue are subsistence gardeners and depend very little on imported food compared with their counterparts at Taboko, thus data collected in the two villages can be used to calculate the efficiency of the transition.   Table 3.8 indicates the value of the items consumed in the two villages and whether they were produced locally or purchased.

Whereas for Verahue only 9 per cent of all consumed foods had been purchased, the figure reached 76 per cent at Taboko.   However, of more importance is the fact that of the 772 hours required to meet sustenance needs at Verahue only 2 per cent were spent in cash-earning activities, but at Taboko cash-earning activities leading to the purchase of food took up 59 per cent of the 1004 hours, with the amount of time devoted to growing, harvesting and selling market crops accounting for most of the total. As most of the money earned by Taboko villagers to buy food came from marketing, it is clear that the system of meeting sustenance needs through the sale of food is *not* efficient in terms of the time involved compared with subsistence production. In short, Taboko villagers are now spending more time meeting their food requirements than their traditional counterparts.

TABLE 3.8: MONETARY VALUE OF LOCAL PRODUCE CONSUMED AND CASH OUTLAY ON FOOD, VERAHUE AND TABOKO, 1971-1972

| Produced for Consumption | Value per Consumption Unit | | | |
| | Verahue[a] | | Taboko[b] | |
	dollars	per cent	dollars	per cent
Root crops	0.82	56.5	0.14	9.4
Coconuts	0.08	5.5	0.05	3.3
Traditional vegetables	0.11	7.6	0.03	2.0
Exotic vegetables	0.02	1.4	0.05	3.3
Fruits	0.08	5.5	0.08	5.4
Fish, shellfish	0.21	14.5	-	0.0
Sub-total	1.32	91.0	0.35	23.4
Purchased food				
Rice	0.02	1.4	0.23	15.4
Biscuits, bread	0.03	2.0	0.29	19.5
Tinned meat, fish	0.01	0.7	0.15	10.1
Tea, sugar	0.01	0.7	0.16	10.7
Traditional foods	0.01	0.7	0.04	2.7
Salt, dripping	0.02	1.4	0.01	0.7
Onions	0.00	0.0	0.01	0.7
Confectionery	0.00	0.0	0.01	0.7
Beverages	0.01	0.7	0.14	9.4
Tobacco	0.02	1.4	0.10	6.7
Sub-total	0.13	9.0	1.14	76.6
Total	1.45	100.0	1.49	100.0

a Average of surveys carried out between 2-8 July 1971 and 21 February - 21 March 1972. Data cover twelve households.

b Average of surveys carried out between 1-7 May, 4-10 June and 11-17 June 1971. Data cover eight households.

Source: Bathgate (1975, pp. 587-91).

As to the deleterious consequences of involvement in marketing, one of the important social costs has been the decline in
reciprocity.   Compared with Verahue, subsistence staples are now
hardly ever redistributed between households at Taboko because each
unit has barely sufficient to meet its own requirements.   This
situation has arisen through a combination of factors, the leading
one being that in order to grow vegetables for the market, the root
crop area has been reduced.   To compensate, Taboko villagers now
rely heavily on rice, bread and biscuits purchased from their
market income — a feature brought out in Table 3.9.

TABLE 3.9:   MAIN SOURCES OF CARBOHYDRATE IN THE DIET,
VERAHUE AND TABOKO, 1971-1972

Items	Frequency in all Meals	
	Verahue per cent	Taboko per cent
Locally grown food		
Sweet potato	68.0	26.8
Yam, *panna*	11.9	5.5
Cassava	9.2	4.0
Purchased foods		
Rice	7.0	30.6
Biscuits	2.8	26.3
Bread	2.1	12.5

Source: Bathgate (1975, pp. 576-91).

Besides the reduction in the root crop area, and the switch
to a dependence on imported foods, the decline in reciprocity at
Taboko is also due to the desire to sell what little surplus there
is in the market.   In addition, the exotic vegetables cultivated
in the village are seldom consumed there because they are alien to
the local palate.   As a result of this decline in food reciprocity
several other unsatisfactory changes have been set in motion.
First, household units seldom co-operate in activities of common
interest and there has been a breakdown of the overall social
cohesion of the village.   Disputes over land rights are a serious
problem at Taboko and the growing self-reliance of each household
in particular is exacerbating the problem.   The people of Taboko
also are no longer able to cope with a food crisis.   This was
revealed in January 1972 when Cyclone Carlotta destroyed several
gardens in the village.   Those households whose gardens had not
been seriously damaged refused to give root crops and vegetables to
others on the grounds that by doing so their cash earnings would be
reduced once it was possible to take food into Honiara again.   On
the other hand, a number of households at Verahue did provide small
amounts of food to those people who suffered the misfortune of having
their gardens affected by slips and excessive rainfall.   A further
problem is that because of the diminution of the root crop area

villagers sometimes have very little to eat whenever heavy rains
cause the rivers to flood and prevent trips to Honiara.

All of these changes mean that, in the case of Taboko at
least, involvement in marketing has led to a deterioration in the
quality of village life.   Even worse, there has been a deterioration in the standard of nutrition and health as well.   Although no
survey was carried out to establish the nutritive value of the
present diet, it is obvious that polished rice, bread and biscuits
are inferior to yam, *panna* and sweet potato.   Dental caries are
becoming more prevalent among the younger children, whilst villagers
claim that a number of them, especially the women, suffer from
'weak blood' (anaemia).   As early as 1958, when the village was
being visited by a truck from the hospital to collect fruits and
vegetables the District Officer received reports about 'sick men
and ailing wives' at Taboko.   Although the village is located on
low-lying land surrounded by small swamps and courses of stagnant
water which provide conditions conducive to the breeding of malaria-
carrying mosquitoes, it appears that 'weak blood' results from the
combination of a changed diet and the considerably longer hours
villagers are spending in gardening and marketing.   The results of
a private survey carried out in the Visale area in 1971 support
this contention (V. Phillips, pers. comm.).   The Visale families who
were involved in marketing were far less healthy than those who did
not engage in the activity.   Sickness was more prevalent because
the women had to sleep in open conditions at the market; also, the
prolonged absence meant that they were not able to attend to the
complaints of their children; and because of their marketing
schedule they found it easier to provide meals of bread, rice and
biscuits, rather than locally-grown foods.

Before they became fully involved in marketing Taboko
villagers were considered to be healthy and adequately nourished
although not much concerned with cash and progress.   It is indeed
ironic that the promotion of marketing by the Department of Agriculture to ensure that the people of Honiara have fresh fruits,
vegetables and root crops, has been matched by a deterioration in
the diet and health of the people of the nearby rural area who
supply these crops.   The moral from this paradox seems clear.   No
Administration in the Pacific should determine the efficiency of a
food marketing system solely in terms of the way in which rural
supply is catering for urban needs (see also Chapter 11).   It
should also look at the impact of marketing on the social and
physical welfare of the suppliers.

REFERENCES

Bathgate, M.A. (1975),   Fight for the dollar: a study of the
                             Ndi-Nggai of West Guadalcanal and their
                             involvement in the Solomon Islands cash
                             economy, unpublished Ph.D. thesis in
                             Geography, Victoria University of
                             Wellington, Wellington.

BSIP British Solomon   File XT 22. Extension Work, Visale.
Islands Protectorate
Department of Agricul-
ture, (1962),

BSIP British Solomon   Nutritional and budgetary survey,
Islands Protectorate   unpublished paper, Department of
Department of Statistics,   Statistics, Honiara.
(1970),

Cooper, M. (1972),   'The Economic Context of Shell Money
                             Production in Malaita', *Oceania*, 41,
                             pp. 266-76.

Frazer, I.L. (1973),   To'ambaita Report, Department of
                             Geography, Victoria University of
                             Wellington, Wellington.

Ivens, W.G. (1930),   *The Island Builders of the Pacific*,
                             London.

Lasaqa, I.Q. (1969),   'Honiara Market and the Suppliers from
                             Tasimboko West', in H.C. Brookfield,
                             *Pacific Market-places: A Collection of
                             Essays*, Canberra, pp. 48-96.

Maranda, P. (n.d.),   Lau markets: a sketch, unpublished
                             paper.

Ward, R.G. and   Vila market - January-February, 1976,
Drakakis-Smith, D.W.   Preliminary Report No. 1, New Hebrides
(1976),   Food Distribution Study, Canberra.

Western Pacific High   File 8/I (BSIP).
Commission Archives,
Suva (1948),

PART II

SHELTER: OVERVIEW

D.W. DRAKAKIS-SMITH*

Most studies of housing provision in the Third World have suffered
from three principal drawbacks. First, they were descriptive
rather than analytical in nature, a consequence of past roots in
physical planning and land use studies. Second, assumptions on
the homogeneity of the urban poor had resulted in similar conclusions on the nature of their housing needs. Third, the research
tended to be pursued in isolation from other facets of the development process. The result of these conceptual inadequacies is that
although such studies have added to the stock of descriptive, and
sometimes statistical, knowledge, there has been little contribution to greater understanding of the problems posed in housing the
urban poor.

Typically, studies of housing provision in the Third World
are plagued by the lax use of terminology. 'Low cost housing' is
almost invariably employed to describe accommodation which is
seldom occupied by the urban poor. On the other hand all types of
makeshift housing are usually labelled as squatter dwellings irrespective of their legal status. There is also a trend in most
studies to search for a single universal remedy to what is regarded
as a uniform problem. In the past, the provision of mass, high-
rise estates fell into this category. This has currently been
replaced by aided self-help housing, particularly in the form of
site and service schemes.

The most urgent research need in the field of housing provision
is for a more thorough approach to structural conceptualisation.
The main sources of housing provision for the urban poor need to be
clearly distinguished, together with the nature of their interrela-
tionship. This structure must then be put into a developmental
perspective in order to examine its linkages with the wider
economic, social and political systems of the city and/or nation.
Implicit in this operation is the identification of ways in which
such linkages have been, and can be, changed. Thus, attention is
directed to conceptual development incorporating this praxis.

Structural frameworks

A basic structural framework which identifies the major
sources of housing open to the urban poor in most Third World cities

* Dr D.W. Drakakis-Smith is Research Fellow, Department of Human
Geography, Research School of Pacific Studies, The Australian
National University, Canberra.

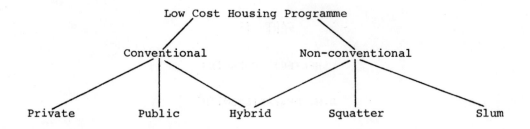

This model adopts the following definitions:

Public housing: units constructed by the government (national or urban) for sale or rent.

Private housing: that which is obtained on the open market and is constructed by commercial builders or developers.

Squatter housing: any housing which contravenes existing legislation on the occupation of land or the construction of dwellings. This juridical definition is preferred to currently fashionable neologisms, such as 'spontaneous' or 'uncontrolled' urban settlements, because the illegal nature of such housing strongly affects all aspects of life in the squatter community, from the physical environment, through types of economic activity to relations with the urban authorities (see McGee, 1977; Drakakis-Smith, 1977 for further discussion).

Slums: are legal dwellings which have been rendered substandard (according to local criteria) by age, neglect and/or internal subdivision.

Hybrid: those dwellings that are a combination of conventional and non-conventional attributes, for example, units built by small conventional firms for which no occupation permits have been obtained, or houses built in ignorance or contravention of existing legislation which are officially 'tolerated'.

Fig. II.1: Structural model of housing sources for the urban poor.

has been outlined by Drakakis-Smith (1975, 1976).   In Figure II.1,
however, the contentious formal/informal dichotomy has been replaced by a more suitable conventional/non-conventional nomenclature.   'Conventional' has been defined as 'being in accordance
with accepted artificial standards' (Garmondsway, 1965, p. 157)
making it a particularly apt term to apply in the context of
developing countries.

This model is not intended to reconstruct reality for any
individual city, it is conceived simply as an aid to understanding
the structural sources of housing provision for the urban poor.
Nor does the model indicate the relative importance of the component
parts, although in most Third World cities the conventional sector,
whilst holding most resources, constructs very little housing for
the lower income groups.

The model may be elaborated in two main ways.   First, by the
addition of components or continuums which permit it to approach
reality.   This is more appropriate for individual countries and
cities where structural elaborations are necessary for better understanding of the processes in operation.   Examples of such phenomena are the pavement dwellers in Calcutta and Jakarta, or the
company dormitories of Japan.   The second elaboration is of a more
general nature and concerns the incorporation of the agents of
production into the model.   It would be true to say that most
model building to date has been more related to housing as a consumer good than as a function of specific production modes.   Market
supply and demand relationships are undoubtedly inadequate to explain the shortages in housing for the urban poor and several
production-based models have emerged in recent years which offer
valuable insights into the current situation in the Third World.
One of the most useful is that of Burgess (1977).

The three modes of production in Burgess' model are the
industrial, the manufactured and the artisanal.   Industrial production covers construction activity in which the relationship between
consumption and production is governed by commercial exchange and
market values.   The second category, manufacturing, refers to
activity in which small groups of hired workers undertake housing
construction for an architect or builder.   It is characterised by
a mixture of capital investment and intensive labour usage.
Artisanal construction covers situations in which the producer and
consumer are one and the same.   Only rudimentary technology is
involved in the construction process which is also characterised by
its use of recycled materials and large amounts of labour.

Burgess' classification, like most neo-Marxist theory, tends
to romanticise the self-sufficiency of the urban poor.   It assumes
without justification that most squatter housing is self-built.
This may well prove to be the case but at present the evidence for
such a statement is contradictory and much more research is needed
on the operations of this type of petty capitalism before firm conclusions can be reached.   In addition to this criticism, there
seems to be no place in Burgess' model for government housing construction, the production of which is usually industrial in nature
but whose distribution is sometimes affected by forces other than
market values, for example if rents are subsidised or allocations
made to certain categories of population.

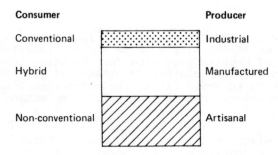

Fig. II.2:   Housing types available for the urban poor: the
             consumer and producer approaches.

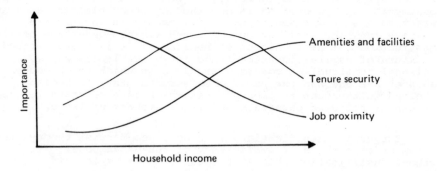

Fig. II.3:   Housing priorities and income change.

Despite these criticisms Burgess' model does offer a useful
structural framework in which to examine the characteristics of low
cost housing production and as such it complements existing conceptual theories which are largely consumer-based.   However, many neo-
Marxists would have consumer oriented models completely replaced
with those based on various forms of production.   Yet there are
many elements within the present situation which cannot be explained
solely by reference to production characteristics — the pavement
dwellers in Jakarta are a case in point since no physical production
is involved.   A structural model which incorporates both consumption and production therefore seems to be more useful.   Figure II.2
illustrates one possible combination in which the basic consumption
elements outlined earlier are fused with Burgess' tripartite division of production agents.

Structure and the development process

The place of individual households within any particular
structural framework is obviously not static.   As their socio-
economic circumstances change, so do their demands and preferences
in relation to housing (Fig. II.3).   In contrast, national or
urban policies, which should in theory reflect the cumulation of
these changes, tend to be cataleptic for long periods of time
pursuing one type of programme which is rarely suited to any of
those for whom it is intended.

It might be expected that longer-term changes in resource
allocation to the urban poor would be a function of the development
philosophy followed by particular cities or states (Fig. II.4).
However, in practice, investment in most Third World countries is
more conditioned by the operations of capitalism and peripheral
capitalism (Gerry, 1977; McGee, 1977) — in the field of housing
provision this means that investment is channelled through the
conventional sector.

If the structural framework is merged with resource allocation (Fig. II.5) it is evident that apparent increases in housing
investment for the urban poor are made through a system in which
the real benefits are siphoned away before the lower income groups
are reached.   This results in the familiar situation in which most
'low cost' housing is occupied by middle income households, particularly those employed in the civil or military services (see
Morell and Morell, 1972; and Abrahams, 1975 for examples of this
process).

Any direct benefits received by the urban poor are usually
considerably modified by their simultaneous incorporation into the
conventional sector with its associated regularity of payments and
adherence to regulations.   Viewed in this light even aided self-
help programmes can be recognised for what, in many cities, they
undoubtedly are, i.e. a *placebo* whereby the established elites maintain their *status quo* in relation to the urban poor.   At best,
aided self-help merely lifts the restrictions on the poor helping
themselves and, in doing so, appears to incorporate and accept
former law-breakers (squatters) into conventional urban society.
Without parallel changes in the redistribution of income or in
access to increased incomes, such programmes are largely of illu-
sionary benefit to the urban poor whose real position in relation

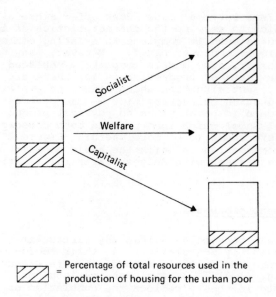

Socialist

Welfare

Capitalist

= Percentage of total resources used in the production of housing for the urban poor

Fig. II.4:   Low cost housing resource allocation and development
             philosophy.

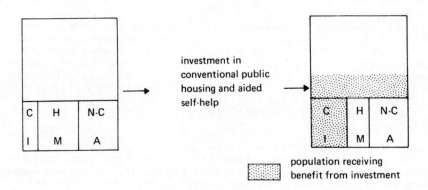

investment in
conventional public
housing and aided
self-help

C	H	N-C
I	M	A

population receiving
benefit from investment

Fig. II.5: Effects of current low cost housing investment.

to the established capitalist elites remains unchanged (see Ashton, 1976 for a Colombian example of the pressures which relocation to a site and service project can place on poor families). To many cynics the recent increase in funds from multinational organisations specifically for site and service projects has confirmed this criticism (Drakakis-Smith, 1975; Gerry, 1977).

Conclusions

Changes in conceptual methodology are of little value unless they result in policy amendments that bring real benefits to the urban poor. Whilst the neo-Marxist school is very adept at critical analyses of existing approaches in the field of housing provision, as yet it offers few immediate, pragmatic programme improvements. However, the notion of emphasising production modes does provide a very fruitful area in which useful research might be undertaken.

At the general level there is a great need for information on current cost factors in a wide variety of production components, such as building materials, land, labour and credit facilities, and in particular on how these costs can be lowered. Reduced dependency on overseas standards, technology and materials is one obvious area for investigation. At the more specific level, there has been very little research on the mechanics of the production agents themselves to determine the ways in which they operate and how they can be induced to increase their output of genuinely low cost housing. There is, for example, almost no information on commercial builders within squatter settlements despite the scale and importance of their activities*. Nor is very much known of the small legal builders who operate at the interface between the conventional and non-conventional sectors, meeting the demands of the former but drawing most of their labour and some of their resources from the latter. Even the larger private developers may have some role to play in housing the 'rising poor' — families with stable incomes but which are ineligible for, or do not want, government housing (Drakakis-Smith, 1977).

In all of these possibilities, perhaps one final point is worthy of note — no matter what improvements are suggested in the present production process almost all involve increased activity by the petty-capitalist elements within the non-conventional sector. The fact that the squatter commercial builder operates at lower profit margins than his larger and more legal counterparts makes him no less of a capitalist and exploiter of those he supplies.

The four chapters in this section on shelter make varied but important contributions to the study of housing the urban poor.

---

* For example, in Ipoh, Malaysia during the 1976 Hari Raya holiday, over 100 squatter huts were erected and sold within three or four days. The selling prices were between $M700 and $M1300 — very much cheaper than conventional government housing. Obviously the builders were experienced and had good connections with material suppliers.

Michael Johnstone (Chapter 4) and Lea Jellinek (Chapter 5) both
elaborate on the basic structural model in their descriptions of
particular housing features in Malaysia and Indonesia respectively
— variations which have hitherto received little attention in the
formulation of national programmes.

Johnstone's chapter on Malaysia is valuable on two counts.
First, it indicates the enormous conceptual problems involved in
defining squatter populations and the ways in which government
attitudes on this question have influenced the statistical input to
national housing programmes.   Second, he illustrates that in
Malaysia, as a consequence of such conceptual limitations, the size
of squatter populations outside the capital city of Kuala Lumpur
has been grossly underestimated.   In drawing our attention away
from the metropolis to the problems of the middle and small cities,
this chapter ventures into an area for which many assumptions are
made but little practical knowledge exists.

Whilst Jellinek's contribution on *pondoks* in Jakarta also
examines a structural aspect of housing supply, she adopts a completely different approach from that of Chapter 4, investigating
the relationships between *tauke* and lodgers through anthropological
methods.   In addition to providing information on an unusual type
of housing provision, the author also analyses the linkages between
pondok and the countryside, thereby adding an important dimension
to her detailed structural study.

The paper by Alan Stretton (Chapter 6) presents one of the
few attempts to examine the production aspect of housing provision.
The author has chosen for his subject the independent foremen in
Manila who assemble their own labour gangs in response to contracts
from architects or owners.   Paralleling, as it does, a similar study
in Mexico by Lomnitz (1977), this investigation offers valuable
insight into operations at the interface between the conventional
and non-conventional sectors.   It studies linkages at various
levels within the structural system — particularly the relationships between employers and foremen, and between foremen and their
labourers — in the process shattering several widely held assumptions on the nature of employment in the construction industry.

Richard Jackson's examination of 'housing trends' in Papua
New Guinea (Chapter 7), differs substantially from the other
chapters in this section by directing its attention specifically at
policy formulation — examining it through the medium of traditional
geographical methodology.   In this respect it is less innovative
but is more concerned with the pragmatic problem of translating
conceptual advances into real programmes.   Papua New Guinea provides a good setting in which to critically examine public housing
policies because the private property market is not well developed
and the government is landlord for a wide range of the urban
community.

These varied approaches to the problem of providing
adequate shelter for the urban poor illustrate clearly that housing
research is beginning to break away from the routine descriptive
investigations of government housing programmes and is seeking
fresh and more rewarding alternatives.   There is much still to be

discovered about structural relationships within the residential construction industry, but these new studies by young researchers augur well for the future.

REFERENCES

Abrahams, C.E.R. (1975),   'The Impact of Low-cost Housing on the Employment and Social Structure of Urban Communities in Penang' in *Aspects of Housing in Malaysia*, Southeast Asian Low Cost Housing Monograph, International Development Research Centre, Kuala Lumpur, pp. 380-475.

Ashton, G.T. (1976),   'Slum Housing Attrition: A Positive Twist from Cali, Colombia', *Human Organization*, 35(1), pp. 47-53.

Burgess, R. (1977),   Informal sector housing? A critique of the Turner school, paper prepared for Institute of British Geographers Symposium on The Urban Informal Sector in the Third World, School of Oriental and African Studies, University of London, London.

Drakakis-Smith, D.W. (1975),   Perspectives on urban housing problems in developing countries, paper prepared for Work-in-Progress Seminar at Department of Human Geography, Research School of Pacific Studies, Australian National University, Canberra.

Drakakis-Smith, D.W. (1976),   'Urban Renewal in an Asian Context: a Case Study in Hong Kong', *Urban Studies*, 13(3), pp. 295-306.

Drakakis-Smith, D.W. (1977),   'Low cost Housing Provision and Development Planning in West Malaysia', *Habitat*, [in press].

Garmondsway, G.N. (1965),   *The Penguin English Dictionary*, Harmondsworth.

Gerry, C. (1977),

Shantytown production and shantytown producers: some reflections on macro- and micro-linkages, paper prepared for Burg Wartenstein Symposium No. 73 on Shantytowns in Developing Nations, Wenner-Gren Foundation, New York.

McGee, T.G. (1977),

Conservation and dissolution in the Third World city, paper prepared for Burg Wartenstein Symposium No. 73 on Shantytowns in Developing Nations, Wenner-Gren Foundation, New York.

Morell, S. and Morell, D. (1972),

Six Slums in Bangkok: Problems of Life and Options for Action, United Nations Childrens Fund, Bangkok.

CHAPTER 4

UNCONVENTIONAL HOUSING IN WEST MALAYSIAN CITIES:

A PRELIMINARY INQUIRY

M.A. JOHNSTONE[*]

1. INTRODUCTION

Squatter settlements are one of the most spectacular manifestations of poverty, rapid population growth and housing shortage in Third World cities.   Until recently it has been generally assumed that the gravest housing problems exist in the largest cities where squatters are far more evident (World Bank, 1975, p. 13).   Yet, smaller cities are not entirely free from such problems as a study in the Philippines has indicated (United Nations, 1973, p. 29).

In the Malaysian context the preoccupation with the primate city is reflected in the overwhelming amount of research on Kuala Lumpur and a concomitant lack of data and studies on squatters and housing in other cities.   Of the eighteen individual studies or reports on squatters in West Malaysia, seventeen refer to Kuala Lumpur.   Even those studies which attempt a broader perspective do so more as an afterthought and always with Kuala Lumpur as the main focus.   Thus, for example, Wegelin (1975, p. 4) claimed that 'squatting is most prevalent in Kuala Lumpur...In other urban centres this phenomenon seems to be of much lesser importance', but did little to substantiate the claim.

This chapter examines three aspects of the squatter phenomenon. First, the validity of currently used concepts and housing typologies will be questioned in the light of several other unconventional housing forms.   In this regard, the problem of defining squatters is particularly important and will be examined in some detail.   Second, preliminary data on the extent of squatter settlements in fifteen West Malaysian cities will be presented to indicate that squatter settlements exist to some degree in almost all cities.   Third, some of the forces affecting the evolution, mode of construction and physical character of squatter settlements, and other unconventional housing forms, will be examined.

In the framework of current Third World urbanisation theory the paradigm of a dichotomous division between 'formal' and 'informal' urban sectors (Hart, 1973; McGee, 1974 and Sethuraman, 1976) is not suitable when applied to housing because it does not reflect the variety of housing forms which exist.   The importance of this is

---

[*] M.A. Johnstone is a Scholar, Department of Human Geography, Research School of Pacific Studies, The Australian National University, Canberra.

TABLE 4.1: SOME CHARACTERISTICS OF CONVENTIONAL AND
           UNCONVENTIONAL HOUSING FORMS

| | Unconventional | | Conventional |
	Squatter	Vernacular	
Juridical			
Legal tenure	None	Some	All
Legal standards	None met	Some met	All met
Construction			
Producer - user	High degree	Some-medium	None
Builder (firm)	Some	Considerable	All
Materials	Scrap - purchase	Purchase - supplied	Supplied
Manufactured products	Little	Some	Most
Modern technology	None	Some (limited)	Medium to high level
Use of wage labour	None	Some	All
Modern style	No	No	Yes
Standards			
Health	Not met	Some met	All (most) met
Land use	Uncontrolled	Limited control	Controlled
Densities	Self-regulation	Some administrative regulation	All regulated
Building	None (own)	Own (self-regulated)	Fully regulated
Institutional Involvement			
Planning authority	No	Little	Always
Land alienation	No	Occasionally	Always
Banking system	No	Rare	Always
Real estate system	No	Rare	Always
Socio-economic			
Socially acceptable	No	Some	Yes (elites)
Income flexibility	High	High	Low

twofold.   On the one hand, the existence of several forms of unconventional housing means that the term 'squatter' can no longer be
applied to all housing used by the urban poor.   On the other hand,
it is not possible to fully isolate unconventional housing from the
conventional housing subsystem, because the latter affects the
extent and limits of the former.   Thus, while this paper essentially describes the occurrence of unconventional housing (including
squatters) in West Malaysian cities, it also is critical of some of
the assumptions made regarding such housing.

2.   ANALYTICAL FRAMEWORK

Note should be taken of the nomenclature to be used in the ensuing
discussion (Table 4.1).   The term unconventional is used here to
mean housing that is not developed through established legal and/or
socially acceptable channels; does not utilise the recognised institutions of housing, i.e. planning and licensing authorities, land
alienation and purchase, commercial banking and real estate systems;
and does not conform to modern (often Western) standards (of construction and health), styles and tastes.   Burgess (1977) has
called such housing 'petty commodity housing', thus emphasising its
mode of production and role in the 'commodity process' of national
economies.   However, because of its more general coverage, the
term unconventional will be used in this chapter.   Within this
broad and general grouping two main subgroups can be identified.
First, squatter housing which in Malaysia refers to housing
illegally built on land for which the owners have no title, and
second, vernacular housing which is essentially traditional-based
housing with some degree of legitimacy.   The structural-functional
relationships between the two broad groups of unconventional housing
(and their relation to conventional housing) are summarised in
Table 4.1.   Housing is differentiated by five main groups of
factors and the degree of involvement or significance of each set
is reflected in a different housing form.   Each form can be seen
as a point along a continuum which ranges between totally illegal
squatters and large-scale speculative housing development.   In
between the two extremes, particularly within the unconventional
sector, lie a variety of housing forms which previously have not
been recognised or examined.   Both forms of unconventional housing
allow the low income family greater flexibility in the use of income
than does conventional housing.   Both allow the urban poor to
select (within the constraints superimposed by the national socio-
economic system) forms of land use, building standards and density
levels which are less restrictive than those governing the conventional sector and which simultaneously provide an urban habitat
conducive to the economic and social *milieu* that characterise this
group.   In this respect the main difference between squatter and
vernacular housing is that some varieties of the latter are subject
to certain administrative controls which regulate layout, building
standards and densities.   Finally, both forms can be the result of
a more highly personalised form of construction where the owner-
occupier is often the builder.   As such they represent residential
development motivated by need rather than profit, as is the case
with conventional commercial residential construction.

        Surveys in nine squatter areas indicate that in general home
ownership is extensive, ranging from 68 to 91 per cent of the total

(Table 4.2).   In addition the number of owner-occupiers who built
rather than purchased their dwelling was, in all settlements but
one, over 70 per cent.   Moreover, although the data indicate that
the degree to which squatter housing was self-built varied between
the three cities surveyed, in all cases it represented 75 per cent
or more of the total owner-occupied houses that were constructed by
or for the owner.

TABLE 4.2:   HOME OWNERSHIP AND SELF-BUILT HOUSING IN NINE
WEST MALAYSIAN SQUATTER SETTLEMENTS

City - settlement Number	Owner-occupied Per cent	Built Per cent	Self-built Per cent	Total respondents (N=100%)
Kuala Lumpur 1	85	91	88	52
Kuala Lumpur 2	82	58	81	52
Kuala Lumpur 3	74	73	89	53
Kuantan 1	70	70	87	60
Kuantan 2	68	86	78	53
Kuantan 3	91	92	89	53
Alor Setar 1	77	77	79	56
Alor Setar 2	76	72	76	54
Alor Setar 3	90	85	75	51

Source: Fieldwork 1976-7.

These data contrast markedly with those from other surveys*.
For example, Sen (1975) reported only 34 per cent home ownership,
Wegelin (1975) 57 per cent, Urban Development Authority (1975) 66
per cent and Ng (1976) 66 per cent.   However, similar data pertaining to the type of construction are available only in one study
(Pirie, 1976) which reports on 75 per cent, 70 per cent, 67 per
cent and 80 per cent self-built houses respectively in each of four
surveyed squatter settlements.

While comparable data on vernacular housing are not available,
observation and personal communications with residents indicate
that while levels of home ownership are similar to the squatters,

---

* Existing statistics relating to squatters are often confused, inconsistent and contradictory.   Much of the difficulty in comparing
such data is due to the variance in the terms of reference and urban
boundaries used in each study, the pecularities of the sample used
or under enumeration.   Thus, for example, Sen (1975) gives no
indication of the size or type of sample used, Wegelin (1975) bases
his surveys on a sample of 1538 households in the Federal Territory
(hence a 1.14 percentage sample) but from twelve settlements, nine
of which are in the same general geographical location, and Wehbring
(1976) used aerial photographic analysis which is open to errors in
enumeration.

the proportion of self-built housing is much lower.   This is probably due to the more widespread use of semi-permanent materials
(official terminology) in the construction of vernacular housing
forms and the need for a higher level of labour and skills.   Thus,
while vernacular housing is generally constructed by a builder on
request for an individual, and, therefore, involves profit realisation, the essential purpose of production is the user's need.   Thus,
while squatter and vernacular forms of housing are similar in many
respects, the differences are greatest in relation to two elements.
First, the general method of construction, whereby squatter housing
is largely self-built while vernacular housing is more likely to be
built by a petty capitalist unit of production (Gerry, 1974;
Burgess, 1977).   Second, vernacular housing is usually regulated
to some extent by established planning and building authorities
while squatter housing purposefully operates outside these regulations.

Two salient points have emerged in this section.   First,
squatting is considered illegal because it violates laws of property
— one of the inalienable institutions of capitalist economies.
This clearly places squatters in direct conflict with the objectives of the politico-economic elites and it is not surprising,
therefore, that the administrative response to squatter activity is
often their eviction and the demolition of their houses.   Moreover,
the extra-legal nature of squatter activity influences not only the
physical character of the settlements, but also their location and
land use patterns (Johnstone, 1976).

The second point to be emphasised is that as a result of
administrative preoccupation with the legal aspects of squatter
activity there has been a restricted and narrow attitude to what
constitutes the 'housing problem' and a failure to see squatter
housing as but one of a range of unconventional forms, each of
which is to some degree extra-legal.   In view of this the use of
the term 'squatter' should be avoided when dealing with all the
housing responses of the urban poor in the Third World.   It must be
clearly understood that the term relates to only one, albeit a
significant, specific response.   Turner (1968, p. 107) has suggested
use of the term 'uncontrolled urban settlement' when dealing with
unconventional housing but there are unconventional housing forms
in some West Malaysian cities which are controlled by the authorities, although not fully sanctioned because they are considered
substandard.   Indeed, it is the very existence of such administrative controls which permit the construction of unconventional
housing in certain cities, with the result that many of the urban
poor have no need to circumvent legal procedure and become squatters.

3.   THE OCCURRENCE OF UNCONVENTIONAL HOUSING

Examination of historical records reveals that squatters have been in
evidence in Kuala Lumpur since the early 1930s, but most observers
agree that it was the combined effects of the Japanese occupation
(1942-45) and war-induced food shortages that resulted in the first
really rapid expansion of squatters in the city (McGee, 1968; Friel-
Simon, 1976).   While the records of other cities in West Malaysia
(shown in Fig. 4.1) are not as thorough, readily accessible or
available, they reveal that squatters existed in many cities before

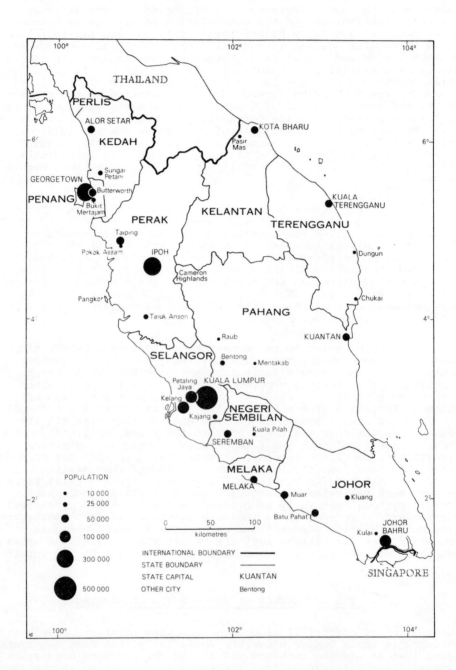

Fig. 4.1:   West Malaysia 1971.

1940, such as Ipoh, Taiping, Kota Bharu, Kuantan and Alor Setar
(Advisory Council of the Malayan Union, 1946; Kota Bharu Town
Board Annual Report, 1949; Kuantan Town Council, 1976; District
and Town Council Kota Setar, 1976).   Two main points emerge from
an historical examination of the growth of squatter settlements.
First, they developed in smaller cities at approximately the same
time as in Kuala Lumpur and appear also to have grown rapidly in
the postwar years.   Second, squatter settlements in all West
Malaysian cities were the product of the same forces — namely the
socio-economic and spatial effects of colonial and neo-colonial
forms of economic activity.   However, the impact of local forces
ensured variation in the manner of their evolution and operation.

        In Malaysia there is little evidence of any organised mass
invasion of land by squatters such as has occurred in parts of
Latin America (Mangin, 1967; Turner, 1967).   Thus, in Kuala Lumpur
squatter areas evolved basically as an 'illegal' occupation of
vacant public (and later private) land by individuals or small
groups followed by the construction of 'illegal' houses.   While
this process has also occurred in smaller cities it is possible to
identify a wider range of squatting forms.   Such settlements are
equally 'illegal' in the eyes of the public authorities but involve
various forms of land tenure and planning authorisation.   For
example, one squatter area examined in Kuantan began as a legal
Malay settlement but all of the early residents were ex-squatters
who had been evicted from their original homes.   Many of the legal
residents were subsequently regarded as squatters because they
failed to pay land fees.   In essence, the 'legal' settlers were
never recognised as owners of the land but paid an annual fee which
gave them rights to live on state land for that year.   The licence
was renewable annually and the authorities regarded houses without
a current temporary occupation licence (T.O.L) as illegal.   As a
result the official view of this settlement was that the 'intended
"Model Malay Settlement" had degenerated into a jumble of no man's
land...and the majority of the present occupants have erected semi-
permanent buildings' (Pahang Executive Council Paper No. 51/61
[Confidential - not dated but approximately 1949] #(6) in District
Office Kuantan 84/49).   Groups of newcomers later settled on
adjoining land, some of which is tidal swamp, and built 'purely'
illegal squatter houses.

        It is difficult to obtain historical or even contemporary
statistics relating to the occurrence of squatters in secondary
urban centres.   However, Table 4.3 illustrates official squatter
statistics for fifteen urban centres (i.e. settlements of over
10,000 people).   The data suggest that in Kuala Lumpur squatters
are the single most important component in the city's housing
system.   However, apart from Kuala Lumpur and Kelang, which can be
considered as one metropolitan entity (Aiken and Leigh, 1975),
squatters did not account for more than 20 per cent of the total
housing stock in any one city.   In fact a proportion of between
5 to 10 per cent was common in most cities surveyed, irrespective
of population size.

        This is true, however, only if two assumptions are accepted.
First, that the narrow, but generally utilised, official definition
of squatter is sufficient for a real understanding of the phenomenon.
Second, that housing markets can be divided into three submarkets —

TABLE 4.3:   ESTIMATED NUMBERS OF SQUATTER AND OTHER
UNCONVENTIONAL HOUSING IN SELECTED WEST MALAYSIAN CITIES

City	Total dwelling units				
	Squatter structures on public land Number	Squatters units Per cent	Make-shift housing[a] Per cent	Unconventional housing[b] Per cent	Dwelling units of very low quality materials[c] Per cent
Johor Bahru	2218[d]	8.4	1.5	34.6	1.8
Batu Pahat	423	5.1	2.4	46.8	10.8
Kluang	400	5.4	1.1	53.6	8.8
Kelang	7000	37.3	7.3	46.3	12.0
Kuala Lumpur	27000[d]	37.0	8.6	42.3	2.2
Kota Bharu	1000	9.3	1.8	51.4	7.5
Kuala Terengganu	465	4.2	1.5	56.7	12.0
Kuantan	1200[d]	12.8	1.7	62.3	9.7
Bentong	136	3.7	1.4	71.6	0.3
Melaka	700	6.0	0.5	33.5	7.5
Ipoh	3480	9.2	2.1	40.2	1.9
Georgetown (Penang)	3000	7.2	3.6	26.1	8.8
Butterworth	1050	9.7	2.0	64.2	26.9
Alor Setar	2150	20.0	1.2	60.7	20.2
Sungai Petani	605	9.4	2.4	60.4	13.4

a   An undefined classification used in the 1970 Census of Housing.

b   Housing built with walls of attap, plank, zinc or other materials and with a roof of iron, zinc or attap (includes c).

c   Housing built with walls of attap, zinc or scrap and with a
roof of attap or scrap.

d   Includes squatters on private land.

Source: Fieldwork (1976), Government of Malaysia (1972a, 1972b).

squatter, government and commercial — as suggested by Vernez (1976, p. 9). Squatter housing is generally associated with the 'informal' or 'popular' sector and the other two with the 'formal' sector. However, neither assumption is acceptable because each fails to comprehend the role of housing as a constituent of the dominant capitalist economy and the fact that the preferences of the bulk of the urban poor are subjugated by the operation and extent of the 'formal' housing market. Moreover, such assumptions ignore the existence of the vernacular housing subsystem, the extent of which is evident in Table 4.4.

Two facts pertaining to the relative proportions of squatter and vernacular housing need to be considered. First, the only national level enumeration of dwellings (Government of Malaysia, 1972a) does not show any significant occurrence of squatter housing in any city, even Kuala Lumpur. It is possible to assume that the classification 'makeshift housing' used in the census is a surrogate for squatter housing. However, the data presented indicate a high degree of deviation from the officially reported squatter housing data collected by postal survey. For example, the squatter numbers reported for Kuala Lumpur, Kelang, Kuantan and Alor Setar, which can be considered very reliable since they have been collected from field counts, are considerably larger than the houses enumerated as 'makeshift' by the census. Most squatter houses, therefore, must appear in the census under another classification.

For a more realistic estimate of squatter numbers it is possible to use the type of construction materials as an indicator. Using the category of housing classified as being of very low quality materials it is possible to see a closer correlation with the observed number of squatter units. This is not surprising, however, given the low incomes of most squatters which force them to minimise housing cost and hence quality of building materials. The use of this category as an indicator is appropriate except that it does not take account of legality. However, given the unavailability of nation-wide squatter statistics, it does offer a useful surrogate.

Second, there exist in almost all Malaysian cities large proportions of dwellings, built of low quality materials, which correspond closely to the rural *kampong* style house with its wooden walls and *attap* or corrugated iron roof. Their incidence ranges from 26 per cent of the total in Georgetown to almost 72 per cent in Bentong. The significance of this form of housing (which generally corresponds to the unconventional sector), lies in its intrinsic extra-legal status. Until 1974, and even later in some states, building and planning by-laws did not permit the construction of timber houses in most cities. The *Street, Drainage and Building Act* (1974) sought to alter this by amending and consolidating all provisions relating to buildings, streets and drains found in the various government legislations under which local authorities operate. Part of this Act controls the whole process of building construction from planning approval to the issuing of the certificate of fitness for occupation. Prior to the introduction of the new law, which places fewer restrictions on the use of timber as a building material, there was no uniformity in the by-laws relating to residential construction. Thus, if timber houses were illegal then most of the dwellings built of low quality materials — often called

TABLE 4.4:   ESTIMATED PROPORTIONS OF HOUSING TYPES IN
SELECTED WEST MALAYSIAN CITIES

City	Total housing units			
	Unconventional		Conventional	
	Squatter Per cent	Vernacular[a] Per cent	Modern[b] Per cent	Transitional[c] Per cent
Johor Bahru	8.4	26.2	50.52	14.9
Batu Pahat	5.1	41.7	45.2	8.0
Kluang	5.4	48.2	31.9	14.6
Kelang	37.3	9.0	40.2	13.5
Kuala Lumpur	37.0	5.4	52.5	5.1
Kota Bharu	9.3	42.0	38.0	10.7
Kuala Terengganu	4.2	52.5	37.0	6.4
Kuantan	12.8	49.5	27.1	10.6
Bentong	3.7	67.9	19.8	8.6
Melaka	6.0	27.5	55.8	10.7
Ipoh	9.2	31.0	47.4	12.4
Georgetown (Penang)	7.2	18.9	66.9	7.0
Butterworth	9.7	54.5	31.2	4.7
Alor Setar	20.0	40.7	28.0	11.3
Sungai Petani	9.4	51.0	30.4	9.2

a   Includes all units constructed of wood, attap, zinc and scrap
other than officially declared squatter housing.

b   Housing constructed of permanent, manufactured materials, i.e.
brick, concrete and tiles.

c   Housing constructed of less permanent materials, such as wood
or asbestos, but also brick and concrete.

Source: Fieldwork (1976), Government of Malaysia (1972b).

temporary or semi-permanent by local authorities — must be classified the same way.   Yet this is not reflected in the numbers of
officially reported squatters.   The explanation for underenumera-
tion is relatively simple, the accepted definition of squatter
relates to illegal occupation of land, usually public land, but not
to the contravention of building or planning laws.

Thus, it is possible to view squatter housing in a broader
context and it becomes apparent that the numbers of squatters are
considerably higher than those reported.   Moreover, if we assume
that dwellings built of wood are also illegal a totally different
pattern of distribution of squatter, i.e. illegal and unconventional,
housing emerges in which the medium and smaller sized cities have
higher proportions than the large cities.   However, not all unconventional housing is illegal, different methods of construction are
used and administrative reactions to the variant forms differ.

Whilst it is important to distinguish between two general
housing forms — squatter and vernacular — it should be recognised
that each is part of a broader unconventional category and has
functional and structural similarities.   Vernacular housing emerges
as the single most important component in the housing system of
many cities and when combined with squatter housing dominates the
urban residential ecology.

4.   FORCES AFFECTING UNCONVENTIONAL HOUSING

In searching for explanations for the occurrence of squatting and
other unconventional housing in various cities two sets of forces
can be identified.   First, those that operate on a national level
and establish the basic socio-economic parameters of general development but do not explain local variations.   Second, those forms
that operate within individual states and cities.   It is not
intended to discuss in any detail the first set of variables since
there has been widespread discussion on why squatters emerge in
Third World cities (Johnstone, 1975a, 1975b).   Suffice it to say
that throughout most of the Third World urban squatters emerge under
conditions of accelerating urbanisation in economies characterised
by peripheral capitalism (Amin, 1974; Obregon, 1974), where large
elements of the population are disadvantaged in relation to the
governing and socio-economic elites.   Under such conditions, and
where land is used for profit rather than need, conventional housing
is not available to the bulk of the urban poor and the disparity
between the latter's need for housing and the ability of the conventional system to meet this need is widening.   The result is that
groups of the urban poor are forced outside the system to seek their
own unconventional housing solutions at costs they can afford.
Many of these 'solutions' involve some form of squatting.

The complex set of forces that interact to produce a city's
local and regional character are also too numerous to analyse in
detail here.   However, three elements are pertinent in a discussion
of unconventional housing.

Demographic forces

     Available data suggest that cities characterised by high
national growth rates, rapid immigration and a significant proportion of immigrants from other states, have large numbers of unconventional housing.   Continued population increase will result in
greater pressure on existing housing stock and highlights the
inability of the conventional housing market to produce new housing
at prices the poor can afford.   The example of Kuantan illustrates
the effect of these demographic forces.   Between 1970 and 1975
some 2500 new households were added to the city's population, of
which an estimated 55 per cent were immigrants (Pahang State Government, 1975, p. 6).   During the same period 2000 new housing units
were built, of which only 11 per cent were priced within the income
range of low income families (Table 4.5).   Detailed studies
revealed that a high proportion of squatters in Kuantan were immigrants many of whom were employed in informal sector activities
(particularly fishing and *beca* riding).   Average monthly household
incomes in the squatter settlements were below $M250 compared to the
city average of $M515 and highlight the difficulty of obtaining
conventional housing.

Housing markets and construction

     The inability of housing markets to provide housing at costs
the poor can afford is illustrated with data from Kuantan (Table
4.5) where, of the housing built since 1970, 89 per cent of the
total is priced within the range of only 10-15 per cent of the
population.   This situation is typical in all cities of West
Malaysia but there are factors which exacerbate the difficulties in
secondary centres.   Indeed, the operation and structure of the
residential construction sector provides good examples of the distortions that exist between 'core' and 'periphery' in developing
capitalist economies (for general discussion of 'core-periphery
spatial distortions' see Santos, 1975a, 1976b; Friedmann and
Douglas, 1975).

     The dominance of the conventional housing market defines and
limits the quantity and type of housing to be built in smaller
cities and in turn the quantity and type of housing available to
the urban poor.   In other words, essential to any explanation of
the existence of unconventional housing, particularly squatting, is
the understanding that the structure of the residential construction
industry mitigates against the provision of low cost houses.   It is
not the purpose of this chapter to discuss this important topic in
detail (see Johnstone, 1977) but two characteristics should be noted.
First, a structural and spatial concentration of residential construction firms in Selangor, particularly in the Federal Territory
— Kelang Valley region.   There were 1123 residential construction
firms in West Malaysia in 1973 of which 68 per cent were small firms
(output valued at less than $M100,000 annually) whose output
equalled only 8.5 per cent of the total value (Government of
Malaysia, 1976).   Of the large firms, 33 per cent were based in
Selangor.   These produced 56 per cent of the total output and 55
per cent of the profits generated by the industry.   Moreover, the
thirty-five largest firms in Selangor, representing 7.5 per cent of
the national total, produced 40 per cent of all housing units built

by private developers in the period 1969 to 1976 (Ministry of
Housing and New Villages, 1976).

TABLE 4.5:   RESIDENTIAL CONSTRUCTION AND HOUSING
COSTS IN KUANTAN 1970-1975

Housing types	Built		Average cost $M	Monthly repayments $M	Population[a]
	Number	Per cent			Per cent
High cost:					
bungalow	250	12.8	50-70,000	600+	
semi-detached	294	15.0	25-35,000	350+	4-6
shop houses	337	17.2	60-90,000	700+	
Medium cost:					
terrace	852	43.5	15-25,000	220+	10-12
Low cost:					
wooden[b]	223	11.4	1-4000	18-35	60

a   Population able to afford.
b   Semi-permanent.
Source: Fieldwork (1976), Kuantan Town Council Building Registers
(1970-75).

Second, the largest residential developers are an integral
component of Malaysia's capitalist economy and generally are owned
and/or controlled and financed by large corporations whose prime
interests are the major export sectors of the economy.   Of the
twenty largest developers fifteen are partly or wholly-owned sub-
sidiaries of large corporations and of these thirteen are more than
30 per cent foreign-owned — five of which are almost totally
foreign-owned (Register of Companies, 1976).   This ownership structure creates contradictions in the housing system to the extent that
the flow of investment is determined by the relationship between
rates of profit in the housing sector and those in other sectors in
which the parent companies have a prime interest.   High profits
from other economic sectors are 'pumped' into speculative housing
development, such as occurred in the 1973-75 period, to reproduce
quickly even higher profits, which are then redirected back into
the export oriented enterprises.

The structural imbalance in the residential construction
industry places smaller cities at a competitive disadvantage to the
larger centres.   Thus Pahang, with 4 per cent of Malaysia's urban
population and 3.6 per cent of the licensed housing developers (88
per cent located in Kuantan) had only 1 per cent of the total urban
housing constructed between 1969 and 1976.   A similar picture is
seen in Alor Setar (Kedah) with 4.7 per cent of the national urban
population and 2.7 per cent of the developers but only 0.7 per cent
of the dwelling units (Ministry of Housing and New Villages, Private
Developers Files, 1976).   These patterns are reflected in almost

all secondary cities.   One result of the overconcentration in both
the numbers of developers and the amount of residential construction in the larger cities, especially in Kuala Lumpur, is that
developers located in other cities cannot meet the growing demand
for medium and high cost housing, let alone consider building lower
cost dwellings.

        Building costs in secondary centres are also considerably
higher than in large cities due to the lack of skilled tradesmen
and the high net 'imports' of building materials which raise transport costs.   Despite the high and growing demand for housing in
secondary cities, such as Kuantan and Alor Setar, risk factors are
considered greater and as a result profit margins tend to be higher.
It is estimated that both actual building costs and increases
in costs were 40 per cent higher in Kuantan than in Kuala Lumpur in
the period 1973-75 (Manager, Malaysian Building Society Berhad,
Kuantan, pers. comm. 1976).   The effect of these cost and price
differentials is to force many middle-class families into housing
which might normally be occupied by lower income groups; hence the
observed large demand for 'lower' cost terrace houses.   Given the
structural character of conventional housing production it becomes
less surprising to find a relatively larger proportion of the population in secondary cities living in unconventional housing forms.

Administrative arrangements

        The two factors discussed above help to explain why conven-
tional housing provision in smaller cities is even less adequate
than in larger cities.   However, perhaps more than any other factor
it is the local administration, control and regulation of residential construction that affect the availability of housing, particularly unconventional forms.   Local government legislation (*Town
Boards Enactment, 1937*) enabled town and municipal councils to
modify the building and planning by-laws to suit local conditions.
This fact has meant that while legal construction of wooden houses
is not permitted in most large cities, particularly Kuala Lumpur*,
there are arrangements which make it possible in many other cities.
Often the existence of such procedures is more the result of historical development than of purposeful design.   Typical examples
are the more 'traditional' east coast cities, such as Kuala
Terengganu, Dungun, Chukai and Pasir Mas, and cities to which New
Villages were 'attached', such as Segamat and Bentong**.   In the
former case the cities are largely an amalgam of rural style Malay
kampungs and mainly non-Malay town centres and other 'modern' urban
elements.   In the latter, the New Villages were encapsulated as
the cities grew to become an integral component of the urban structure.   In both cases the residential areas consisted of predominantly wooden structures most of which did not meet design, health,
safety or building standards and therefore have posed a dilemma to
local authorities bent on 'modernising' their cities.

---

* There are of course several areas of legal wooden housing in
Kuala Lumpur which are mainly either low cost public housing schemes
such as Kampung Data Keramat and Pandan, or government authorised
settlements such as Kampung Baru.

** Little is known about the role and development of smaller cities
despite several case studies undertaken (McTaggart, 1969; Jackson,
1974).

In some cities the decision was made to recognise wooden houses as semi-permanent structures and authorise them. This was done for four reasons: to control the 'illegal' housing that existed and was still being built; to enable the enforcement of basic health and safety standards; to permit town council registration and assessment; and to provide a legitimate alternative to expensive conventional housing.

Hence, by-laws permitting the construction of wooden dwellings were established in many secondary urban centres and continue to operate today. In almost all respects the planning procedures involved are the same as those for conventional structures. Plans have to be submitted and approved, and a certificate confirming fitness for occupation has to be issued. However, certain building and design standards are minimised, less stringently enforced or, in some instances, waived altogether. Planning standards, such as distance from nearest structure, and building standards, such as window space or height of rooms, are still kept for safety and health reasons but standards relating to structural quality, reinforcing, window materials, type of drainage and toilet facilities have been modified, as have certain planning procedures relating to land subdivision and conversion. The result for low income families is that adequate low cost housing ($M1000-4000) can be constructed providing they have a land plot. For the public authorities involved this has meant better development control and fewer potential squatters.

The manner in which this system operates varies in each city. Alor Setar and Kuantan demonstrate marked differences despite the fact that both cities have similar proportions of the total housing stock built of wood — 60 per cent and 62 per cent respectively. Two-thirds of these are registered as temporary dwellings, i.e. authorised wooden structures (Registers of Temporary Buildings, Kuantan Town Council and District and Town Council Kota Setar,1976). In Alor Setar the process of 'legalising' wooden houses is little more than a registration of temporary (wooden) dwellings for control and assessment purposes, rather than a desire to authorise new construction. This is seen in Table 4.6 which shows the small number of new wooden houses issued with certification in that city between 1958 and 1976, particularly in comparison to Kuantan. It appears that in Alor Setar one consequence of the slow authorisation rate of new wooden dwellings has been the marked increase in the rate of illegal squatter construction. Less than 100 authorised wooden dwelling units were built between 1970 and 1976 compared with at least 500 to 600 squatter dwellings.

TABLE 4.6:   CONSTRUCTION OF WOODEN HOUSES IN ALOR SETAR
AND KUANTAN 1958-1976

City	1958-59 Number	1960-64 Number	1965-69 Number	1970-76 Number	Total
Alor Setar	50	129	99	87	365
Kuantan		1600	1630	350	3580

Source: Register of New Buildings District and Town Council Kota Setar, 1977; Register of Temporary Buildings Kuantan Town Council, 1976.

In contrast, Kuantan's public authorities display a more progressive policy which, while largely pragmatic in orientation in
terms of the town council's development control objectives, is
blended with the desire to reduce the institutional barriers facing
the urban poor.   Since Kuantan became a town council in 1959 some
3000 'temporary' wooden houses (mainly Malay *kampung* style) have
been registered and have become a major component in the city's
residential ecology (Table 4.6).   Since 1965 the town council has
simplified the procedures involved and improved the opportunity for
low income families to build and own a house.   This has been done
by introducing three standard wooden house plans which are sold
very cheaply to interested persons, thus helping to avoid expensive
architect fees.   The chosen plan needs to be submitted only with a
simple sketch plan of layout and site and, providing basic standards
of construction are met, the structure is authorised.   These standard plans permit a free choice of materials, reduce service fees
and provide a house which a high proportion of low income families
can afford ($M1000-4000).

In these cities, therefore, whilst the housing stock may be
substandard in terms of official conventional criteria, the existence of such administrative procedures has undoubtedly resulted in
fewer illegal squatter houses.   Kuala Lumpur, on the other hand,
with the highest proportion of squatter housing in West Malaysia,
provides no mechanism for the poor to build legally sanctioned low
cost dwellings.

Given that legally sanctioned mechanisms exist for building
unconventional housing, why then do cities such as Kuantan still
have considerable numbers of squatters?   Although there is still
incomplete understanding of the search mechanisms used by the urban
poor, several tentative answers can be offered.

First, and most obvious, there are still those among the
urban population who cannot afford even the cheapest legally
authorised wooden house and thus squatting releases them from the
burden of continual or continued expenditure on housing.   Second,
there are people who do not have access to land even if they could
afford to build a cheap wooden house.   Thus, squatting as already
suggested, is a question of land availability and its distribution.
This question of land and squatting is highlighted in many cities
where land is legally reserved for Malay occupation only (Malay
Reservations).   Third, there are individuals, called alternatively
'opportunist' or 'speculator' squatters by Sen (1975, p. 341), who
squat in order to acquire potential benefits such as compensation
paid after eviction or eligibility for public housing.   This group,
however, constitutes only a minority, and is estimated by Sen (1975)
to be only 8 per cent of the total squatter population in Kuala
Lumpur.   Finally, there remain groups among the urban poor,
especially newly arrived migrants, who are unaware of the channels
available to them and who, in the face of the many institutional
barriers that exist and a general alienation from their city
environment, find squatting the only means available to establish
themselves in a city.

5. CONCLUSION

The low income family searching for urban accommodation has several
potential strategies open to it.   The final choice will depend on
their available income, level of building skills, access to
materials, closeness to friends and relations, and familiarity with
the current urban administrative procedures.   The range of potential
housing strategies available to the urban poor are set out in Figure
4.2.   At one extreme is the self-built squatter house (strategy 1)
on government land.   This strategy involves no legal sanction from
relevant authorities (generally no attempt is made to obtain authorisation) and the value of the construction lies in the basic shelter
need it fulfils for the family and not in any realisation of profits.
In almost all respects this form of housing and its mode of construction is marginal to the dominant system of housing production,
though not totally removed from it.   For example, the majority of
self-built squatter housing is constructed of materials purchased
from local sawmills.   At the opposite corner of the matrix there
are housing forms which in all respects are legitimate (i.e. they
satisfy applicable building and planning regulations), but which
are 'traditional' in style of construction and type of materials
used (strategy 5).   This strategy involves a petty capitalist form
of production which by its nature generally precludes any producer-
user form of construction.

Although each strategy may incorporate more than one housing
form it represents a unique combination of the main influencing
factors.   Each factor increases or decreases in significance along
the continuum of strategies.   For example, legality of tenure
increases from strategy 1 to strategy 5.   The use of wage labour
in construction, however, is not significant in strategies 1 and 2
but increases in significance from 3 to 5.   As suggested earlier,
dominant variables are the form of land tenure on the one hand (a
product of the capitalist concept of land ownership) and the degree
of influence of a capitalist or petty capitalist mode of production,
viz. the degree of profit realisation, capital flows and use of wage
labour in the construction process.   Finally, Table 4.7 reticulates
the relationship of the identified housing strategies with method of
construction and form of land tenure.   This tentative model does
not suggest any linear or evolutionary development model of squatter
areas, or other unconventional housing, even though certain development paths are apparent (for example, settlements which are given
temporary land occupation rights can be seen in some cases to improve
in physical quality).   Instead it is of a descriptive nature high-
lighting some of the important structural influences on the unconventional housing subsystem.

Part of the difficulty in discussing the squatter phenomenon
has been the failure by local administrators, planners and researchers
for that matter, to recognise the existence of forms of unconventional housing other than squatting and, therefore, to see squatting
as anything more than illegal occupation of land.   This chapter has
shown that there are different forms of squatting and vernacular
housing and also different methods of producing unconventional
housing.   Thus, there remains no validity in the former unitary
descriptions and explanations of the squatter phenomenon.   Furthermore, a rigidly applied dualistic concept of 'informal' and 'formal'
sectors, while useful as a broad conceptual tool of analyses, is

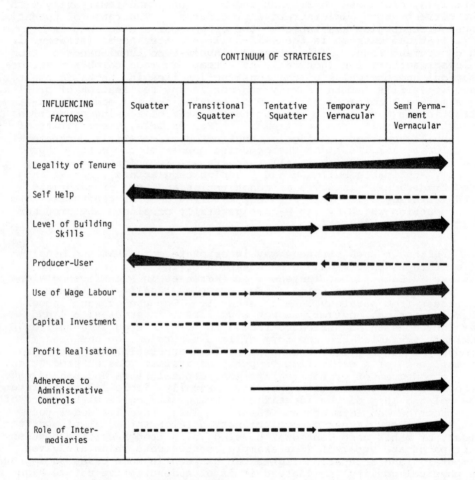

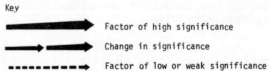

Fig. 4.2: Factors influencing housing strategies.

TABLE 4.7:   LOW INCOME HOUSING STRATEGIES
(as outlined in Fig. 4.2)

Mode of construction	Government land			Private land	
	Illegal	Temporary	Quasi-legal	Illegal	Rent
Self-built	Squatter	Squatter	Tentative squatter	Squatter	Tentative squatter
Contractor	Transitional squatter	Transitional squatter	Temporary vernacular	Transitional squatter	Temporary vernacular
Speculator	Transitional squatter	Temporary vernacular	Semi-permanent vernacular	Transitional squatter	Semi-permanent vernacular

likely to bear little resemblance to reality.   In this regard,
previously labelled 'informal' housing forms exist whose manner of
construction is more closely linked with a capitalist formal sector
than anything else.   Such housing, loosely named vernacular in
this chapter, is not an integral part of the modern conventional
housing system but is part of what Santos (1975a) has called the
'lower circuit' of production.

ACKNOWLEDGEMENTS

The fieldwork on which this chapter is based, was financed by the
Department of Human Geography, Research School of Pacific Studies,
the Australian National University.   I gratefully acknowledge
this assistance.   Terry McGee and David Drakakis-Smith read early
drafts of the chapter and made valuable comments.

REFERENCES

Advisory Council of the   Proceedings, unpublished papers, Kuala
Malayan Union (1946),   Lumpur.

Aiken, S.R. and   'Malaysia's Emerging Conurbation',
Leigh, C.H. (1975),   *Annals of the Association of American
                                 Geographers*, 65, pp. 546-63.

Amin, S. (1974),   *Accumulation on a World Scale: A
                                 Critique of the Theory of Under-
                                 development*, 2 vols, New York.

Burgess, R. (1977),   Informal sector housing? A critique
                                 of the Turner School, paper prepared
                                 for the Institute of British Geographers,
                                 Symposium on The Urban Informal Sector
                                 in the Third World, School of Oriental
                                 and African Studies, University of
                                 London, London.

District and Town Council   *Register of Temporary Buildings*, unpub-
Kota Setar (1976),   lished Council records, Alor Setar.

District and Town Council   *Register of New Buildings*, unpublished
Kota Setar (1977),   Council records, Alor Setar.

Friedmann, J. and   Agropolitan development: towards a new
Douglas, M. (1975),   strategy for regional planning in Asia,
                                 School of Architecture and Urban
                                 Planning, University of California,
                                 Los Angeles.

Friel-Simon, V. and   The squatter as a problem to urban
Khoo Kay Kim (1976),   development: a historical perspective,
                                 paper prepared for Third Convention of
                                 the Malaysian Economic Association,
                                 21-24 August 1976, Penang.

Gerry, C. (1974),   *Petty Traders and the Urban Economy: A
                                 Case Study of Dakar*, World Employment
                                 Programme, Research Working Paper No. 8,
                                 International Labour Office, Geneva.

Government of Malaysia   *West Malaysian Census of Housing*,
Department of Statistics   Government Printer, Kuala Lumpur.
(1972a),

Government of Malaysia   *West Malaysian Census of Housing*,
Department of Statistics   unpublished records, Kuala Lumpur.
(1972b),

Government of Malaysia   Survey of construction industry (1973)
  Department of Statistics   residential construction sector,
  (1976),   unpublished records, Kuala Lumpur.

Hart, K. (1973),   'Informal Income Opportunities and
                             Urban Employment in Ghana', *The Journal
                             of Modern African Studies*, 11,
                             pp. 61-89.

Jackson, J.C. (1974),   'The Structure and Functions of Small
                             Malaysian Towns', *Transactions of the
                             Institute of British Geographers*, 61,
                             pp. 65-80.

Johnstone, M.A. (1975a),   The squatter phenomenon in Southeast
                             Asian cities: some insights into
                             physical, locational and social
                             characteristics, paper prepared for
                             Work-in-Progress Seminar, Department
                             of Human Geography, Research School of
                             Pacific Studies, Australian National
                             University, Canberra.

Johnstone, M.A. (1975b),   *Squatter Settlements in Southeast Asia:
                             An Overview. The Dilemma of Conceptual
                             Approach*, Working papers in Comparative
                             Sociology No. 5, Department of Sociology,
                             University of Auckland, New Zealand.

Johnstone, M.A. (1976),   'Urban Squatters in Southeast and East
                             Asia: A Question of Illegality',
                             Geographica (Malaysia), 11, pp. 30-42.

Johnstone, M.A. (1977),   Urban housing provision in Peninsular
                             Malaysia: a problem of provision?,
                             paper prepared for Work-in-Progress
                             Seminar, Department of Human Geography,
                             Research School of Pacific Studies,
                             Australian National University, Canberra.

Kota Bharu Town Board   *Annual Report*, Kota Bharu.
  (1949),

Kuantan Town Council   Unpublished records, (12a) in File
  (1970),   117/A 'Unauthorised Buildings' (Rumah
                             Rumah Haram), Kuantan.

Kuantan Town Council   Building registers, unpublished files,
  (1970-1976),   Kuantan.

Kuantan Town Council   Register of temporary buildings,
  (1976),   unpublished Council records, Kuantan.

McGee, T.G. (1968),   Malays in Kuala Lumpur: a geographical
                               study in the process of urbanization,
                               unpublished Ph.D. Thesis in Geography,
                               Victoria University, Wellington, New
                               Zealand.

McGee, T.G. (1974),   The persistence of the proto-prolet-
                               ariat: occupational structures and
                               planning for the future of Third World
                               cities, paper prepared for Comparative
                               Urban Studies and Planning Program,
                               School of Architecture and Urban Planning,
                               University of California, Los Angeles.

McTaggart, W.D. (1969),   'Urbanisation in Malaysia...The Small
                               Towns', *Inter Congress Meeting of the
                               Standard Committee on Geography,
                               Pacific Science Association,* 28,
                               pp. 25-31.

Mangin, W. (1967),   'Latin American Squatter Settlements:
                               A Problem and a Solution', *Latin
                               American Research Review,* 2, pp. 65-98.

Ministry of Housing and   Private developers bi-annual reports
  New Villages,   summary cards, departmental records,
                               Government of Malaysia, Kuala Lumpur.

Ng Lee Kiang (1976),   The squatter problem in Chan Sow Lin
                               (with special emphasis on their educa-
                               tion): a case study of squatters in
                               Kuala Lumpur, unpublished B.A.
                               Graduation Exercise, submitted to
                               Faculty of Economics and Administration,
                               University of Malaya, Kuala Lumpur.

Obregon, A.Q. (1974),   'The Marginal Pole of the Economy and
                               Marginalised Labour Force', *Economy and
                               Society,* 3, pp. 393-428.

Pahang Executive Council   Paper No. 51/61 (confidential) State of
  (n.d.),   Pahang, Malaysia, (6) in File DOK 84/49,
                               Kuantan.

Pahang State Government   *Kuantan Urban Development Study,* Final
  (1975),   Report: by M. and R. International
                               (Belgium) in association with AKB and
                               Development Consultants (Malaysia),
                               Perunding Bersatu (P.B.S.), Malaysia,
                               for Government of Malaysia, State of
                               Pahang, and International Bank of Re-
                               construction and Development, Kuantan.

Pirie, P. (1976),   Squatter settlements in Kuala Lumpur,
                             paper prepared for Third Convention of
                             the Malaysian Economic Association,
                             Penang.

Register of Companies   Company Files, Ministry of Commerce
   (1976),   and Industry, Government of Malaysia,
                             Kuala Lumpur.

Santos, M. (1975a),   'Underdevelopment, Growth Poles and
                             Social Justice', *Civilisations*, 25,
                             pp. 18-31.

Santos, M. (1975b),   'The Periphery in the Pole, the Case of
                             Lima, Peru' in H. Rose and G. Gappert
                             (eds), 'The Social Economy of Cities',
                             Urban Affairs Annual Review, IX,
                             pp. 335-56.

Sen, M.K. (1975),   'The Rehousing and Rehabilitation of
                             Squatters and Slum Dwellers: with
                             special reference to Kuala Lumpur,
                             Malaysia' in Tan Soo Hai and Tan Sri
                             Hamzah Sendut (eds), *Aspects of Housing
                             in Malaysia*, Southeast Asia Low Cost
                             Housing Monograph, International
                             Development Research Centre (I.D.R.C.),
                             Ottawa, Canada, pp. 336-78.

Sethuraman, S.V. (1976),   'The Urban Informal Sector: Concept
                             Measurement and Policy', *International
                             Labour Review*, 14, pp. 69-81.

Turner, J.F.C. (1967),   'Barriers and Channels for Housing
                             Development in Modernizing Countries',
                             *Journal of American Institute of
                             Planners*, 33, pp. 167-81.

Turner, J.F.C. (1968),   'Uncontrolled Urban Settlement: Problems
                             and Policies', *International Social
                             Development Review*, 1, pp. 107-22.

United Nations (1973),   'Urban Land Policies and Land Use
                             Control Measures' in United Nations
                             Asia and the Far East, Vol. 11, New
                             York.

Urban Development   Summary of social and economic survey
   Authority (1975),   of squatters in Salak South Area 1975,
                             unpublished records, Kuala Lumpur.

Vernez, G. (1976),   'A Housing Services Policy for Low
                             Income Urban Families in Developing
                             Countries', *Ekistics*, 41, pp. 8-14.

Wegelin, E.A. (1975),   Cost benefit analysis of rehousing
                             squatters in the Klang Valley,
                             Peninsular Malaysia, unpublished
                             report, Urban Development Authority,
                             Kuala Lumpur.

Wehbring, K. (1976),   Squatters in the Federal Territory:
                             analysis and program recommendations,
                             unpublished report to Urban Development
                             Authority by United Nations Housing
                             and Development Advisers, Kuala Lumpur.

World Bank, (1975),   *Housing: Sector Policy Paper*,
                             Washington, D.C.

CHAPTER 5

CIRCULAR MIGRATION AND THE *PONDOK* DWELLING SYSTEM:

A CASE STUDY OF ICE-CREAM TRADERS IN JAKARTA

LEA JELLINEK[*]

1.   INTRODUCTION

Petty traders are important to Jakarta.   Each day many Jakartans
buy drinking water from them because there is no other source of
supply.   The poor, who form the bulk of the city's 6,000,000
people, mostly lack the facilities to store food in the heat and
humidity present throughout the year.   Even more important, much
of the population live on a day-to-day basis and few would have
enough money to buy for more than a day at a time.   So the food
needs of a very large part of Jakarta's inhabitants are obtained
from the mobile traders who operate along the muddy paths and lanes
of the city on virtually every day of the year.   As well as food
and water the traders also sell kerosene, which is the main fuel
used for cooking and lighting, and virtually everything else the
poor are likely to buy.   It naturally requires a vast army of
traders to satisfy the needs of so large a city and this in turn
has an important implication — petty trading is a valuable source
of income in a city where income-earning opportunities are in short
supply.

Thus, petty trading is doubly important to Jakarta.   First,
it supplies essential goods and services, and second, it forms a
major source of employment.   A knowledge of how the petty trader
operates is, therefore, of value both for an understanding of the
lives of Jakarta's masses and in order to formulate reasonable and
responsible policies towards them.

This chapter is concerned with the way petty trading is
organised in Jakarta.   It describes a most unusual, if not unique,
relationship between petty trading in the city, peasants in the
village and a novel communal lodging house which provides far more
than bed and board.

Petty trading in Jakarta is centred around *pondoks*.   These
are dwellings where the petty traders live and from where they
obtain their equipment and raw materials.   But they are not
employees.   Each trader is an independent businessman working for
his own profit.   The *pondok* is managed by a person known as a *tauke*
who may either own the building and equipment or simply run the
pondok on someone else's behalf.   He has to manage his affairs in

---

[*]   Lea Jellinek is a Doctoral Student at the School of Oriental and
African Studies, London University.

a way most Westerners would find impossible.   He or his traders
may not be sufficiently literate to make book-keeping feasible and
pondoks generally run on trust.   Furthermore, his traders come and
go virtually as they please.   They are circular migrants who travel
back and forth between their homes and families in their village and
their *pondoks* in Jakarta.

2.   THE ICE-CREAM *PONDOK* OF IBU MUS

The simplest way to describe the running of a *pondok* is to describe
the operation of a particular example — in this instance the *pondok*
of Ibu Mus.   There was nothing to distinguish Mus' *pondok* from any
other or indeed from any other dwelling in the Jakarta slum (or
kampung) in which it was located.

        The house was made out of bamboo, palm leaves, bits and
pieces of wood and tin, or anything else that could be scavenged.
It measured four by six metres, yet it served as a home and source
of livelihood for fifteen or so inhabitants.

        Life in the Mus household began at 4 a.m. when Ibu Mus and
her husband Pak Manto received the day's delivery of ice.   Mus and
Manto ran an ice-cream *pondok* so ice was an important commodity.
After the ice had been loaded into the cold storage they divided up
the ice-cream ingredients which Ibu Mus had bought at the market
the previous day.   Each trader would receive just enough of the
various ingredients to make the amount of ice-cream he thought that
he could sell.   The skilful trader received a lot of ingredients,
the inexperienced trader somewhat less.   Whilst Mus and Manto sat
on the ground floor weighing out the ingredients, the rest of the
pondok awoke and began to descend the rickety ladder down to the
ground.

        One by one the ice-cream traders collected their allocation
of ice-cream ingredients, mixed them together and poured them into
a pail.   This pail was placed into a larger bucket and chipped ice
mixed with salt was placed around it.   When each trader had his
ingredients and freezing mixture prepared, he sat down with the
bucket containing the pail between his knees and began to spin the
inner pail until the incredients stiffened into ice-cream.   It
was about 7 a.m. when they started rotating their buckets of ice-
cream and they would sit there twisting and turning for the next
three hours or so.

        Ibu Mus turned to her own work after she had finished weighing
out the ice-cream ingredients.   She carefully poured a variety of
herbal medicines that she had prepared the previous evening into
thirteen well washed Johnnie Walker bottles.   Then she changed into
a somewhat more elegant *sarong* and by 6.30 a.m. set out to sell her
herbal medicines.

        Ibu Sajum, Manto's sister-in-law, usually returned from market
at the time Ibu Mus was setting out on her rounds and began to dice
and cook the vast quantity of food she had brought back from market.
Clouds of steam appeared and the sound and smell of hot oil pene-
trated every corner of the little *pondok*.

Plate 5.1

Most of the buildings in this street are *pondoks* and carts available for hire are parked adjacent to them.   *Pondoks* are generally
not found in clusters but are usually located in the back streets
of the *kampungs* where the only access is by narrow, muddy paths.

Plate 5.2

A row of identical carts is the tell-tale sign of a *pondok*.   Such equipment is an essentia[l]
prerequisite for a food trader and is very expensive.   An ice-cream cart for example cost[s]
approximately $A30.   This is a big investment for a trader and a dangerous one since he r[i]
having his cart seized in a government anti-trader campaign.   Most traders prefer to hire
their equipment.   In addition to hiring their cart they often stock it with goods obtaine[d]
on credit and only pay for them at the end of each day's trading.

It was still only 7 a.m. and Trijo and Kemi could perhaps have slept a little longer but by now the *pondok* was almost frantic with activity and they clearly had no prospect of getting any more sleep. The ten ice-cream traders sat in a row mixing their ice-cream. Sajum was busy cooking. Manto occupied himself with all sorts of chores. If there was a spare ice-cream cart he joined the row of ice-cream traders but vacancies did not crop up very often. Even if one of the ice-cream traders was ill there was inevitably someone waiting around for just such an opportunity. Often Manto went to market and returned with an assortment of fresh fruit which he chopped into attractive little pieces and placed some ice fragments on top of them. When they were cold he would take them out on the streets to sell. But even if he did that, Manto still had lots of time on his hands so that on most days he devoted his talents to maintaining the ice-cream carts or carrying out alterations or repairs on the house.

Manto had constructed some concrete drains to channel away the water from the melting ice, which was just as well for the ten ice-cream traders would have destroyed the trampled down earth floor that was found in the rest of the house. Once Manto partitioned off part of the ground floor and rented out the tiny room he had created to a group of hat makers from a village who moved into the *pondok* — a decision aggravating the already severe congestion and overcrowding.

Manto had also built an ice-cream cone-making device. He bought a secondhand mould for the cones and constructed a press with a few scraps of timber. This machine meant that Mus was no longer dependent upon the little cottage industry next door but of course Mus needed someone to operate the cone maker.

Cone-making was allocated to Manto's son-in-law but he was still unable to start for he needed room to dry his sticky cones and the ground floor was still occupied by all the ice-cream carts which had been parked there overnight and by the row of ice-cream traders mixing their ice-cream. Manto's son-in-law simply had to sit and wait his turn and for the moment he could contribute nothing but his conversation.

Trijo and Kemi stood apart from the rest of the household. They were both in their twenties and both bachelors. Unlike the others in the *pondok*, Trijo and Kemi felt no great tie to their village and seldom returned to it. They were the only two members of the *pondok* who were employed on a fixed salary. The others worked for themselves and their earnings varied with their effort and their good fortune. It was just as well that Trijo and Kemi had little desire to visit their village for, unlike the ice-cream sellers, they could not take time off from their work. Trijo worked as a driver and Kemi a waiter. Kemi had in fact tried ice-cream trading but did not find it to his liking. He moved from ice-cream *pondok* to ice-cream *pondok* in the hope of finding his niche but was constantly dissatisfied. Finally, he obtained a job as a waiter through a friend and accepted it in the belief that it would ultimately lead to his employment as a cook. Trijo and Kemi both worked shorter hours and less strenuously than the ice-cream traders but neither earned as much.

At about 10 a.m. the ice-cream was ready.   Each trader tasted
his product and made any final adjustments that he felt were
necessary.   Sometimes he asked his colleagues for their opinions
and at other times he offered a sample to the group of children from
the neighbourhood who invariably congregated when the ice-cream was
nearing completion in the hope that their judgement would be called
upon.   When the product had been approved, the ice-cream bucket
was carefully lifted into a push cart and surrounded by a fresh
combination of salt and ice.   Then, one by one, the traders strode
into the kitchen, stripped and washed themselves.   Ibu Mus was
rather proud of the well that had been built in her kitchen and the
traders knew they were fortunate in being spared not only the cost
but also the walk to and wait at one of the few wells available to
the people of the *kampung*.   After they had washed, the traders
changed into clean singlets and shorts and sat down to the breakfast that Sajum had prepared.

But the breakfast had only been a small part of Sajum's cooking.   She had produced a vast mound of fried savouries and tit-
bits which she now neatly arranged on trays.   Then she too changed
into a traditional village *sarong* and *kebaja**.   She balanced one
tray on her head and rested another on her hips where it was
supported by a sash, and set off to sell her savouries.   Soon
everyone else followed suit.   One by one the ice-cream traders
manoeuvred their carts out of the narrow door of the *pondok* and
Trijo and Kemi went off to work.   By 11 a.m. Manto's son-in-law
was alone in the empty *pondok* and at last had the space he needed
for his ice-cream cone-making.   He cleaned up the mess left by the
ice-cream traders, set up his device and began to work.

Ibu Sajum had a regular clientele.   Most of her customers
worked in a big government office in Jakarta.   They were the
sweepers, messenger boys, guards and tea-makers.   The office Sajum
visited had its own staff cafeteria and traders were not welcome
because they deprived the cafeteria of business.   But Sajum sold
cheaper food cooked in a traditional style and it was much in
demand.

The ice-cream traders too had a regular route.   The traders
from Mus' *pondok* respected one another's territory and did not
steal customers from each other.   But, of course, they had to
compete with the ice-cream sellers from other *pondoks*.   Sajum's
customers were buying their regular meal but the demand for ice-
cream was rather more capricious and varied with the weather and
the taste of the traders' ice-cream.   It required good judgement
and skill to know how much one could cut down on the expensive
ingredients and just how small a serve one could get away with for
a given price.   There was no bargaining for ice-cream.   The people
of the *kampung* knew what the price should be for a particular
quantity.

The traders had invested a lot of money and labour into their
ice-cream.   As it was perishable and could not be refrozen, they

---

* A *sarong* is a piece of cloth, the ends of which have been sewn
together, and a *kebaja* is a women's blouse which reaches below the
waist.

could not afford to return to the *pondok* until their stocks had
been completely sold.   They usually kept to the narrow back streets
of the *kampung*, although the temptation of the major roads was
always there.   There were throngs of people out on the roads and
many of them had rather more to spend than the people who crowded
the back streets of the *kampung*.   But there was a campaign against
mobile traders and those who succumbed to the lure of the major
roads risked losing not just their stalls, but even worse, their
carts and all their equipment.   Confiscation meant disaster for
the petty trader.

As Sajum and the ice-cream traders were beginning their rounds
Ibu Mus' was drawing to an end.   She too followed a constant route
and in most places found regular customers for her herbal medicines
which promised to combat a variety of ills ranging from infertility
to unfaithfulness.   Mus talked to her customers and got to know
something of their difficulties.   She was, after all, dealing with
problems of the body and the soul and not merely satisfying their
appetite.   There was no doubt Mus believed in her medicines.   She
took them herself if she felt unwell and offered them to the members
of her *pondok* if they seemed in need of a tonic.

If any of Mus' wealthier customers mentioned that they had
some unwanted old clothing, Mus offered to relieve them of it and
if by chance others wanted to borrow money or buy some batik, Mus
offered to help them with those needs as well.

By noon Ibu Mus returned home.   She emptied out and thoroughly
washed her thirteen Johnnie Walker bottles and stood them upside
down to dry.   Then she sat down to a meal which Sajum had left for
her.   When she had finished eating Mus set off for market.   She
returned with food for the evening meal which she prepared and
cooked so that a meal would be ready whenever the ice-cream traders
returned.   When that was done she set off for the market again,
this time to buy all the ingredients for the next day's ice-cream
trade that she had been unable to carry on her earlier trip to the
market.   Mus found much to do about the house after the shopping
was over.   She carefully folded and stored away the old clothes
she had collected.   Later she would sell them in her village where
they would fetch a fair price at festive times when the villagers
felt they had to appear in a new, or at least different, set of
clothing.   Mus also collected any left over bread from the ice-
cream traders who offered it to their customers as an alternative
to ice-cream cones.   Mus dried the bread in the sun and stored it
away in glass jars.   This too would fetch a reasonable price in
the village when food was in short supply.   By four in the afternoon Sajum returned from her food-selling and the two women set off
together to collect instalments on the batik Mus had sold on credit
as well as the money she loaned at an interest rate of 30 per cent
per month!

From 6 p.m. onwards the ice-cream traders began to return.
They looked exhausted as they pushed their way through the door of
the *pondok* and parked their empty carts inside.   They had started
work at seven that morning and, if they were lucky enough to have
sold their stocks quickly, would return home after a ten hour day.
If business was slow it might be 9 p.m. or later before they began
to make their way back home.   Each trader unloaded and cleaned his

Plate 5.3

A group of circular migrants in their *pondok*.   The size of *pondoks* varies but they usuall
house between ten and forty people, all of the one sex and mostly from the same or a nearb
village.   The owner-manager or *tauke* often brings his wife and sometimes other family mem
into the *pondok* and they constitute the only females in a predominantly male household.
female *pondoks* are uncommon and usually house prostitutes or cake sellers.

ate 5.4

ving conditions in the *pondok* are invariably spartan. These four traders sleep shoulder
shoulder on boards whilst their clothes and trading equipment are stored around them. One
ader has a make-shift light — a wick suspended in a bottle of kerosene; another lies with
head beside a radio. Such luxuries are not common but all possessions and savings are
t quite openly in the unlockable *pondoks* and seem to be secure.

cart and then silently consumed the meal Ibu Mus had prepared before
climbing up into the attic and going off to sleep. They had neither
the time nor the energy for socialising. The next day's ice would
be delivered in a few hours and their work would begin all over
again.

Life for the poor is seldom easy but it seemed unduly hard
for the ten or so ice-cream traders, squashed literally shoulder to
shoulder in the poorly ventilated attic of Mus' house, amidst the
heat and humidity of Jakarta. At times the space in the attic was
so congested that they had to sit up or take it in turns to sleep.
They worked ten to fourteen hours a day, each day, and in between
had to sleep as best they could. Their sales were never secure.
Ice-cream did not sell well when it rained and at times it rained
torrentially in Jakarta. On the other hand, when it was un-
pleasantly hot and humid, ice-cream was in great demand.

The earnings of the ice-cream traders depended on the amount
of ice-cream they could sell but generally they earned surprisingly
well in comparison with their fellow *kampung* dwellers. Those
employed by the government in unskilled jobs, such as watchmen,
tea-makers and sweepers, had the security of a regular wage and
received a supplement of rice but the ice-cream traders could earn
more than twice the wage of such employees.

Trijo, who was employed as a driver for a small Chinese-owned
business, complained that he worked as long hours as the ice-cream
traders but earned only two-thirds their wage. In fact, the ice-
cream traders earned more than any *kampung* dweller living on a
regular wage. Only other traders, prostitutes or those who stole
or boosted their wages by corruption, could earn as much or more.
Yet there was an obvious paradox: the traders were earning comparatively well but their living conditions were amongst the worst in
the *kampung*.

3.   URBAN-RURAL LINKAGES AMONGST THE ICE-CREAM TRADERS

An explanation of the ice-cream trader's apparent penury in the
face of their relatively high earnings involves going back to the
village, from which they all came, to delve more deeply into their
lives. None of them felt that Jakarta was anything other than a
place to earn money. It was their life in the village that really
mattered.

The ice-cream traders' village was located in Central Java on
dry hilly land that was unsuitable for rice cultivation. They
grew and ate corn but there was not enough to last all the year
round. In times of shortage they made do with cassava which they
also grew. When the cassava ran short, they ate whatever was
available. If the villagers wanted a luxury like rice they had to
buy it and they also needed cooking oil, tea, salt, dried fish,
sugar, matches and other items no matter how modestly they lived.
A small amount of money could be made by the cultivation of cash
crops such as beans and chillies, but apart from this activity there
was no prospect of earning an income in the village. Thus, the

majority of the able bodied males including a son of the wealthiest
family, sought work outside the village.   Some travelled as far as
Sumatra and Kalimantan.   These were mostly bachelors who felt no
strong tie to the village and returned to it infrequently, if at all.
A few left with their families to try and make a life in one of
Java's many cities and towns.   But most left their families to work
their small plots of land in the village whilst they went off to the
city in search of an income.

They became circular migrants and travelled back and forth
between their village homes and their *pondok*.   At any one time up
to a dozen stayed in Mus' *pondok* whilst others lived in one of the
two other Jakarta *pondoks* linked to their village.   Some of the
villagers travelled to *pondoks* located in one or two other big
Javanese cities but curiously, no matter which city they travelled
to or which *pondok* they lived in, all the circular migrants from
Mus' home village worked as either ice-cream or noodle soup traders.
In fact, the diversity of their employment was even more limited
than it might have seemed for ice-cream making and noodle soup
selling required very similar equipment and traders swapped from
one item to another as demand fluctuated.

The circular migrants and the various *taukes* from Mus' village
all knew one another.   Traders sometimes moved from one *pondok* to
another.   The limited amount of socialising that went on in Jakarta
commonly involved visits to one of the two other Jakartan *pondoks*
which contained circular migrants from Mus' village.

Presumably a pioneering villager had originally travelled to
Jakarta and somehow learned the techniques of the ice-cream trade.
If he was able to make any headway in the city he would have felt
obligated to extend his good fortune to his less fortunate relations back in the village.   At first the pioneer would have invited
someone else in to join him.   Then when the two of them were established others would have followed.   Ultimately, as the numbers
increased it would have been necessary to obtain a second dwelling.
No one in Mus' *pondok* could recall its history with any precision,
but the chain of events described above is almost certainly what
happened.   In virtually every village almost all the circular
migrants were engaged in only one or two different forms of trading
even though they travelled to various *pondoks* scattered in all of
the large cities of Java.

Beneficiaries of the *pondok* system

Mus and Manto obviously profited from the running of the
pondok but it would be wrong to see the relationship between them
and the traders as one of exploitation.   They may have earned over
twice as much as the ice-cream traders but they lived as austerely,
worked as hard, and ran several enterprises simultaneously in order
to achieve that income.   Mus, for example, sold herbal medicines,
batik, secondhand clothes and food in the village, and loaned money
in addition to her wholesaling, hiring and catering activities in
the *pondok*.

The relationship was one that really benefited both parties.
The peasant could travel to the city secure in the knowledge that

he had not only somewhere to stay but that he would be provided with
the equipment and knowledge he would need to earn an income.   Even
more important, Mus would furnish him with a legal justification for
staying in the city.   The circular migrants could never qualify for
the residential permits needed to live and work in Jakarta but circumvented this problem by claiming to be the 'guests' of Ibu Mus.

      Thus, Mus' *pondok* gave the potential circular migrant the
certain knowledge that he would have both work and shelter in the
city before he even set out from his village and for this he was
immensely grateful, for neither are easy to find in Jakarta.

      Mus did not charge for the accommodation she provided.   If
there was a vacancy in the *pondok* she was even willing to extend
credit to a new circular migrant to help him make a start as an ice-
cream trader.   What did she expect in return?

      First, it was more or less understood that anyone who stayed
in her *pondok* bought their meals from her.   That was not a very
onerous obligation.   Mus cooked in the traditional village style
with which all the traders were familiar.   Food was more plentiful
in Jakarta so they ate far better than they had in the village and
more cheaply than they could have elsewhere in the city, even though
Mus made a small profit on the meals she sold.

      The second requirement was that the ice-cream traders hired
their carts and bought the ingredients they needed from Ibu Mus.
She bought in bulk and again made a slight profit on her sales.
The ice-cream sellers knew that they could have bought their
ingredients more cheaply direct from the market.   But Mus hired
her carts at charges which seemed standard throughout Jakarta and,
after paying for both ingredients and carts, the traders could
still earn well.   Furthermore, it was more convenient for the
traders to let Ibu Mus buy their supplies.   Going to the market
was tiresome and time consuming and would have reduced the period
they could spend out on the roads selling their wares.

      The relationship between Mus and the villagers was of benefit
to both parties.   Mus was able to secure reliable recruits for her
pondok and that was important to her.   She had to be sure that the
traders would not run off with her carts and that they would repay
the credit she had extended to them.   She could even return to the
village confident that her equipment and the few valuable possessions
she stored in Jakarta would be safe in her absence.   It would have
been against the interests of the circular migrant to act against
the person who made his existence in Jakarta possible.   To do so
could have meant his ostracism from the village because Mus was
able to exercise considerable influence there.

      The circular migrants also benefited from the fact that they
all came from the same village.   If one of them was to return, he
was entrusted with the savings of those who remained, and the
traders knew their hard-earned money would reach their families
back in the village, which was more than one could say of the postal
service!   They trusted one another so completely that they stored
their savings along with their few other possessions in the *pondok*
in little string bags or unlockable suit cases.   The *pondok* may

have been safe from within but it was impossible to secure its
flimsy walls against theft from without, so Mus' household depended
for its protection on the system that was used throughout the *kampung*. The *pondok* was never left unguarded. In fact, Manto had
invited his son-in-law to join him in Jakarta to keep a watch over
the *pondok* whilst everyone was away. His employment at ice-cream
cone-making merely proved convenient because it enabled him to contribute something to the running of the *pondok* whilst fulfilling
his role as guardian of the building and all it contained.

Mus' *pondok* provided the villager with a means of earning an
income that was sufficiently flexible to allow him to return home
to the village whenever the need arose. If a circular migrant
intended to return for some time he arranged for a close relative
to take his place in the *pondok*. If he was only going to be away
from Jakarta for a few days he simply left his cart to Manto who
postponed any repair jobs he may have been planning and took to
selling ice-cream instead of fruit, until the trader returned.

Reasons for returning to the village

The journey home meant a day's train ride and a six hour walk
and the return trip cost the equivalent of a whole week's work in
Jakarta. The traders did not mind leaving the city during the
monsoon season when rain and flooding made not only trading but
even life itself very difficult in the *kampungs*. Those who had
land also returned home to till the soil or help reap its benefits.
At other times they went back to celebrate, to socialise, to tend
the sick and mourn the dead or simply, and understandably enough,
merely to rest. The organisation of the *pondok* was elastic enough
to cope with these comings and goings without difficulty.

Yet life was hard for those who lived in the *pondok*. For much
of the year their families were far away. Whilst they were in the
city their life consisted mainly of work and sleep, with little time
or energy for entertainment. They had no privacy and virtually no
amenities. Mus' *pondok* had its well which gave it an advantage
over most of its neighbours but the household still had to use the
nearest drain as a toilet or queue at one of the few public ones
available. The inhabitants shared the smell of decaying household
rubbish with the rest of the *kampung* but that was an odour that
everyone was used to. None of their neighbours had space to spare
but by the standards of the *kampung* Mus' *pondok* had been intolerably
overcrowded even before Manto rented a part of it to the hat makers.
After that it became almost insufferable but the traders never
voiced a complaint. How did they endure such hardship?

The answer probably lay in the limited expectations they had
of life in Jakarta. They came to the city in search of money and
little else. They never ceased to regard themselves as members of
their village. Some of them owned a small plot of land, and all
had a home and family there. They were seeking money to send back
home and the *pondok* seemed the best place to obtain some. It
equipped them for trading and minimised their living expenses so
that they could save at least half of their earnings to send back
home. They worked hard, spent little and saved all they could. It
was their intention, or perhaps their dream, to retire permanently

Plate 5.5

Although many circular migrants own small plots of land, their holdings are not enough to
sustain them for more than a few months each year.   Male circular migrants return home at
the time of planting and harvesting and leave their wives to tend the fields during the re
of the year.   Sometimes those who remain behind are employed to tend the fields, or even
plough and harvest them.   This is one of the ways in which circular migration helps boost
village incomes.

to their village once they had accumulated enough from their sojourns in the city.

By village standards even the least successful member of Mus' household brought considerable sums of money back home to the village.   But was it worth the effort?   Did that money so improve their life that it justified the hardship and separation such earnings entailed?   Obviously the ice-cream sellers seemed to think so. But if one looked at the way their hard-earned money was spent it soon became clear that their plans to return to the village life, freed from want, were illusory.

Food, clothing and festivities together with the upkeep and improvement of their houses consumed whatever the traders managed to save in the city.   There was not enough left to invest in anything which might have enabled them to escape from their hand to mouth existence.   As long as they could physically cope with the rigours of migratory life they would carry on with their arduous work in the city and occasional visits to the village.   When they could no longer make the journey they would at least have a better home to live in and some pleasant memories to look back upon.   But if the crops should fail perhaps they might ask themselves: 'was it all worthwhile?'

4.   CIRCULAR MIGRATION *PONDOKS* IN JAVA

Ibu Mus' *pondok* was but one of many in Jakarta, and her traders but a few of the many thousands in that city.   Even so, the literature on Jakarta contains virtually no mention of either circular migration or *pondoks*.   There would seem to be two major reasons for this.

First, circular migration has only become prominent in recent years.   There are no figures on its present extent but much indirect evidence to support the contention that circular migration is of recent origin and expanding in scale.

The survey from which the above case study came covered some two hundred circular migrants in late 1975 and early 1976.   Most had been coming to Jakarta for five years or less.   Only a small minority had been migrating for longer than five years and very few for longer than ten years.   Perhaps the circular migrants only persisted in their way of life for a few years and thus gave the misleading impression that the process was of recent origin?   However, this did not seem to be an explanation, for when the circular migrants recalled events in the village they painted a similar picture.   Fifteen years ago there were few circular migrants in their village.   Then gradually the numbers began to increase and continued to do so.   At present there are villages where almost every able-bodied male in the village travels to the city in search of work.   But nearby, there may be villages with only few circular migrants or none at all.

Evidently the process is very erratic.   Hugo (1975) studied the movement of people in fourteen villages of Java and found that

circular migration had become the most prominent pattern of population mobility and was on the increase. Other detailed studies are
lacking, but it does appear that circular migration has only
recently become significant, and this partly explains why it has
not been well described in the literature.

There is a second reason, however, which relates to the
technique of gathering information. The circular migrant has much
cause to be wary of interviewers. He is distrustful of authority
since there is nowhere that petty traders can turn to for justice
in the event of dispute. Their residential status in Jakarta
would not withstand official scrutiny. Residential permits are
only granted to those with stable employment and accommodation, and
few of the circular migrants qualify for them. They invariably
justified their stay by claiming to be the 'guests' of their *tauke*
who owed his permit to the fact that he had been living in Jakarta
long before the regulations were introduced in 1970. The circular
migrants would be known to the local *kampung* official who is meant
to detect the entry of illegal immigrants to Jakarta. But the
local official may well have 'guests' of his own.

Even by 1974 the Jakarta authorities had not admitted to any
circular migrants living in the city. The circular migrant could
go on living and working in peace as long as he stayed out of the
hands of enquiring officials or academics — he did not distinguish
between the two. Under such circumstances formal survey techniques,
especially when they have official backing, are likely to miss the
information they seek. This may be another reason for the paucity
of information on circular migration (Jellinek, 1976, 1977).

Given the lack of data, is it possible to make an estimate of
the number of circular migrants in Jakarta? Hugo (1975) tried to
gain some idea of the numbers involved by looking at all of the
evidence available, most of which is very indirect. He ingeniously
examined transport requirements and discrepancies in the census data
but this did little more than confirm that circular migration was
very widespread.

The total number of traders in Jakarta has been variously
estimated at between 100,000 and 500,000 (McGee, 1975) but there are
no data to suggest what fraction of those people are mobile traders.
However, if only half of all the petty traders in Jakarta are mobile
traders (and casual observation suggests that this is a conservative
estimate) there could well be several hundred thousand circular
migrants working as petty traders in Jakarta. There are circular
migrants in other occupations as well. They form a majority of the
trishaw (*becak*) drivers and there could be as many as 500,000 *becak*
drivers in Jakarta (Soedarno, 1976). So it is clear that the
number of circular migrants in Jakarta is to be measured in hundreds
of thousands. Most of the circular migrants, petty traders and
becak drivers live in *pondoks* and, since there are between ten and
forty people in the *pondoks* there must be thousands of *pondoks* in
the city.

Growing popularity of circular migration

Why should circular migration have become more prominent in recent years?   Is something in the village forcing people to seek work in the city and if so why do they prefer to oscillate to and fro rather than settle permanently there?

Peasants seek work beyond their village when they are dissatisfied with the income they can obtain locally.   Other factors play a part but financial considerations are paramount (Hugo, 1975). This, however, is true of both circular and permanent migrants and there is insufficient evidence to enable us to predict whether a person will migrate and what pattern of migration he will take up. For those who have decided to seek work in the city there are certain features of life there which affect the decision to become circular or permanent migrants.

Jakarta has a number of policies, such as the slum clearance scheme and the anti-trader and anti-*becak* campaigns, whose net effect, irrespective of the motive behind them, is to make life more difficult for the poor.   However, such programs probably do not play much part in the choice between permanent and circular migration.   That choice has already been taken before the migrant has left his village and experienced the difficulties of city life for himself.   Moreover, the poor are essentially indifferent to the law.   They fear the power of authority and suffer many of its excesses, but they are largely ignorant of the fact that the city administration has any responsibility in housing, marketing and employment (Cohen, 1974).   Regulations such as those designed to prevent the inflow of migrants to Jakarta are, therefore, quite ineffective (Soetjipto, 1977).

The poor may remain indifferent to the law but they cannot ignore the harsh realities of Jakarta life.   Income-earning opportunities are difficult to secure without a contact.   Housing is expensive and in short supply.   Considerations like these play a much bigger part in a peasant's decision to migrate than any laws the administration may care to pass.

The potential migrant learns of the city from his fellow villagers.   He will be grateful for a place in a *pondok* if he has no definite prospect of finding a room or a job without joining one. Permanent migrants (who may share accommodation though they never live in communal style *pondoks*) seem to be somewhat wealthier than circular migrants.   If the city does play a part in determining the pattern of migration then it is probably through such mechanisms as the shortage of housing and the difficulty of finding a source of income.   Once there is a link between a village and a *pondok* the extent of the movement between the city and village grows by a process of chain migration.   This surely helps explain why the rate of circular migration appears to be accelerating and why it is almost universal in one village and practically non-existent in another.   The *pondok* facilitates circular migration.   Conditions in the village provide the impetus for migration and the harsh realities of city life may make it easier for the migrants to pool their resources than struggle to survive on their own.

5. THE IMPACT OF THE CIRCULAR MIGRATION-*PONDOK* SYSTEM

The circular migrant-*pondok* network links the village with the city.
This needs to be borne in mind when considering policies which
affect any part of the cycle.   Otherwise such policies may have
repercussions far beyond those intended.   *Becaks*, for example, are
being progressively eliminated from Jakarta.   There must be many
villages which have become largely dependent on the remittances of
Jakartan *becak* drivers and these are going to suffer great hardship
unless some other source of income can be found.   It is quite
probable that the Jakarta administration embarked on its anti-*becak*
campaign in ignorance of the fact that its policy could have a
marked impact on villages many miles beyond its jurisdiction (see
Chapter 9).

     The earnings sent home by the traders are large by village
standards and the presence of even a few circular migrants can have
an impact on an entire village.   Local markets receive a boost.
Jobs are created, for people are needed to till the land of those
who are away and to repair and rebuild their houses (Hugo, 1975).
The remittances are one of the few examples of wealth flowing from
the city to the village — usually it seems to be the city which
gains at the expense of the village.   Yet this money is largely
dissipated on immediate consumption and little, if any, goes
towards schemes which could one day save the migrant the need to
travel to the city in search of an income.   It is perhaps arguable
whether there is a more fruitful way of disposing of such savings
and whether it would be possible to encourage the traders to invest
their savings any differently.   But this does seem to be at least
a potential source of village improvement and one worthy of further
exploration.

     The impact of the circular migrant-*pondok* network on the city
is rather more difficult to define.   Does the increasing number of
migrants mean that they are taking over such activities as mobile
trading and *becak* driving?   If so, what has happened to those whom
they have displaced?   It seems unlikely that former petty traders
have moved into jobs in factories and offices, because such jobs
are not being created in the numbers required.   There is much
uncertainty about the accuracy of statistics on Jakarta but it is
quite clear that the number of people employed in factories is only
a fraction of the number engaged in petty trading and *becak* driving
(Hugo *et al.*, 1977).   Moreover, this number has not altered greatly
over the last few years whilst the number of circular migrants has
probably risen very considerably.

     Thus, it appears unlikely that circular migrants could have
pushed former *becak* drivers and petty traders into factory work for
the jobs have simply not become available.   There is another reason
that makes this possibility unlikely.   People who work in factories
need contacts and bribes to secure their position, and have had more
years of schooling than *becak* drivers and petty traders.   Factory
work is highly sought after and it seems unlikely that anyone could
move from so menial a task as *becak* driving into a greatly prized
position in a factory.

Given these circumstances it is more likely that the circular migrants have not displaced anyone but simply added to their numbers and thus lowered earnings. It does seem, however, that the vast majority of mobile traders and *becak* drivers are circular migrants. By contrast, far fewer circular migrants are to be found selling from fixed stalls which offer a greater return but require more capital for their establishment.

To some extent there is a conflict between employment and economic reform. Technological innovation, however modest, tends to be labour-destroying. One rather primitive ice-cream making machine can produce more ice-cream than all the traders in any *pondok* and as the cost of labour rises, mechanical production will become much cheaper. It is doubtful whether Indonesia's economic salvation will be hastened by importing ice-cream making machines. These would simply throw all the traders in *pondoks*, such as that of Mus, out of work. In fact, it is highly probable that Indonesia could develop economically no matter what happened to Mus' *pondok* though Mus and her traders would be very concerned by changes in the ice-cream trade. The point is a very serious one. Jobs are being destroyed by the introduction of technology in fields such as soft drink and ice-cream making where it is very difficult to detect any gain to the nation. A certain amount of capital is accumulated but this has to be weighed against the very large number of jobs that can be lost through a relatively small but misguided investment.

Becak driving and petty trading will not provide a long-term answer to Indonesia's economic problems but large numbers of people will continue to follow such activities until better options become available (see Chapter 8). To destroy such opportunities without at the same time creating better alternatives, is simply to add to the hardship of those whose lives are already hard enough.

REFERENCES

Cohen, D. (1974),   'The People Who Get in the Way',
                                 Politics, 9, pp. 1-9.

Hugo, G. (1975),   Population mobility in West Java,
                                 unpublished Ph.D. thesis in Demography,
                                 Australian National University,
                                 Canberra.

Hugo, G., Jones, G.W.   *Demographic Dimensions in Indonesian*
  and McDonald, P.F. (1977),   *Development*, Gaja Mada University Press
                                 (in preparation).

Jellinek, L. (1976),   'The Life of a Jakarta Street Trader
                                 Part I', *Working Paper No. 9*, Centre
                                 of Southeast Asian Studies, Monash
                                 University, Melbourne.

Jellinek, L. (1977),   'The Life of a Jakarta Street Trader
                                 Part II', *Working Paper No. 10*, Centre
                                 of Southeast Asian Studies, Monash
                                 University, Melbourne.

McGee, T.G. (1975),   Hawkers in selected Southeast Asian
                                 cities: the comparative research tudy
                                 outline, findings and policy recommenda-
                                 tions, report to be presented at a
                                 Conference sponsored by the International
                                 Development Research Centre, Canada, on
                                 the 'Role of Marginal Distribution
                                 Systems in Development' held in Kuala
                                 Lumpur, Malaysia, 23-26 September 1975.

Soedarno (1976),   'Peasant-Becak Drivers in Jakarta: A
                                 Case Study on Becak Drivers in East
                                 Jakarta; First Report: Period between
                                 15 January and 8 September 1976',
                                 Occasional Paper, Social Science Research
                                 Training Station, Jakarta.

Soetjipto, W. (1977),   Conditions leading to rapid urbanization
                                 in Jakarta and their policy implications,
                                 prepared for ESCAP [Economic and Social
                                 Commission for Asia and the Pacific]
                                 meeting of Experts on Migration and Human
                                 Settlement, 7-13 June, 1977, Bangkok,
                                 Thailand.

CHAPTER 6

INDEPENDENT FOREMEN AND THE CONSTRUCTION

OF FORMAL SECTOR HOUSING IN THE GREATER MANILA AREA

ALAN STRETTON*

1. INTRODUCTION

This chapter examines the role played by independent foremen in the construction of formal sector housing in the Greater Manila Area which includes the City of Manila, Quezon City, Pasay City, Caloocan City, Makati, San Juan, Mandaluyong and Navotas. The foremen, who operate independently of construction firms, obtain their jobs through informal contacts and move from site to site with a regular group of labourers.

In discussing the structure of the building industry in the Greater Manila Area the most striking feature is the coexistence of different markets within the industry. At least four markets can be distinguished: modern, intermediate, conventional and the unenumerated**.

The modern market is that part of the industry concerned with the construction of high-rise buildings and large non-residential buildings; a large non-residential building being defined as one valued at 800,000 pesos or more in 1974 prices***. These projects are supervised by large, mainly locally-owned construction firms employing techniques borrowed from the industrialised countries. The intermediate market includes luxury residential buildings

---

* Dr Alan Stretton is Visiting Fellow, Institute of Applied Social and Economic Research in Papua New Guinea. The research reported in this chapter was undertaken as a Scholar in the Economics Department, Research School of Pacific Studies, The Australian National University, Canberra.

** In United Nations Industrial Development Organisation (1969) Turin argues that the construction industry in less developed economies can be divided into four categories: an international-modern, a national-modern, a national-conventional and a traditional. In the Philippines most large construction firms are locally-owned, so that the international-modern category is an inappropriate name. The national-modern category is roughly equivalent to the intermediate market; the national-conventional category to the conventional market; and the traditional category to the unenumerated market.

*** The exchange rate was $A1 = 8.1 pesos on 21 November 1977.

(costing 400,000 pesos or more) and medium-sized non-residential structures (costing from 400,000 to 800,000 pesos).   These buildings are constructed primarily by the medium-sized firms using techniques requiring some small pieces of equipment, such as concrete mixers, hoists and concrete vibrators.

The conventional market refers to the smaller residential and non-residential buildings (valued at less than 400,000 pesos) which are normally within the scope of the building permit records of the various cities.   Most of these buildings are constructed under the supervision of independent foremen.   The unenumerated market covers the residential and non-residential buildings, often temporary structures, in the low income, slum and squatter areas of the city.   This market was not included in the survey conducted by the author, as a study of the informal sector in Manila is being undertaken by the University of the Philippines and the International Labour Organisation.   This survey includes questions on construction activity, but unfortunately the results were not available at the time of writing.

Whilst such a definition incorporates the predominant type of builder, it is not meant to imply that only one type and size of contractor operates within each market.   It is to be expected that some smaller construction firms will work within the conventional market.   It is also possible that a large non-residential building may be placed in the modern market, not because of complexity (as reflected in cost per square metre), but because of sheer size.   In this case a medium-sized firm might have the technical competence to construct the building, and the problem of obtaining the necessary working capital might be overcome by advances from the owner.   Thus, smaller construction firms might also undertake some work in the modern market.   However, in both the modern and the conventional markets these firms account for only a small portion of the total output.   In the intermediate market, on the other hand, the smaller firm will predominate.   Similarly, independent foremen and large contractors will sometimes operate in the intermediate market.

While this categorisation of the building industry is useful for a number of purposes, it has some limitations.   It gives the impression that there are no links or interactions between the different markets.   As this chapter illustrates, this is definitely not the case.   The independent foremen face a demand for their services determined primarily by conditions in the formal sector. Labourers move freely between the different levels and the large construction firms rely on the smaller builders to train the necessary skilled labour.   Recently there have been encroachments by the large firms into the market traditionally constructed by independent foremen.   However, if these links between the groups are stressed, the four categories illustrate that it is not the dualistic (formal-informal) model which is most applicable in Manila but rather a spectrum within which there is a considerable degree of mobility.

2. RELATIVE SIZE OF THE DIFFERENT MARKETS IN 1974

Official statistics disaggregate private building activity by type
of building (residential, non-residential and additions, alterations
and repairs) but not by size of project.   However, for the year
1974 it was possible to obtain a detailed list of all building permits issued in the Greater Manila Area.   This allowed a division
of private building into the modern, intermediate and conventional
markets.   The value of government building in the Greater Manila
Area is unavailable, but this may not bias the results to any
significant degree as government building represents only a small
part of total building activity (Stretton, 1977a, p. 45).   Table
6.1 shows that in 1974 the modern market accounted for 38 per cent
of the floor area constructed, and 55 per cent of the value of
building activity.   The conventional market, on the other hand,
constructed 50 per cent of the floor area and 34 per cent of the
value.   This is due to the higher cost per square metre of constructing modern market buildings, especially high-rise buildings.
The intermediate market is much smaller than the others with only
11 per cent of the floor area and 10 per cent of the value of the
buildings constructed.

Unfortunately such detailed information was not available for
years prior to 1974.   However, the most significant change in the
structure of the industry since the early 1960s has been the growth
of the modern market, and especially the construction of high-rise
buildings.   This has been associated with the phenomenal development of the Ayala section of Makati into the business and commercial centre of the Philippines.   Combined with this has been a
rapid expansion in the demand for luxury, high-rise residential
units, and the construction of fourteen international standard
hotels to coincide with the World Bank-International Monetary Fund
Conference held in Manila in October 1976.   It is estimated that
the share of high-rise buildings in the industry's output has risen
from approximately 5 per cent in 1960 to 35 per cent in 1974.   Most
of this expansion occurred after 1970.   It appears that in both
relative and absolute terms resources have moved away from the
construction of residential buildings to high-rise buildings.
While the importance of the traditional luxury residential building
may have declined in favour of the high-rise residential unit, it
has been the conventional market which has suffered the largest
fall in output (Stretton, 1977a).

Table 6.2 presents the value of permits issued for residential
buildings in the Greater Manila Area in 1974 by type and cost of
dwelling.   Small residential buildings, which comprised low and
middle income housing, usually of bungalow design and costing less
than 400,000 pesos, accounted for approximately 75 per cent of the
total floor area and 50 per cent of the value of permits issued.
Luxury conventional housing represented 15 per cent and luxury high-
rise dwellings 35 per cent of the value of residential buildings.
The main change in the type of residential building constructed has
been the increase in the volume of luxury high-rise buildings.
This has followed from the introduction and eventual acceptance of
the condominium style of housing.   The condominium concept involves
a development company planning the project, acting as the client to
the contractor and selling individual units of the building to out-
siders.   The purchasers have complete ownership of their own units
and share the common areas with other residents.

TABLE 6.1:   RELATIVE SIZE OF THE MODERN, INTERMEDIATE
AND CONVENTIONAL MARKETS IN GREATER MANILA, 1974

Market	Floor area		Value	
	sq. metres (thous.)	Per cent	Pesos (mill.)	Per cent
Modern[a]	524	38.3	382.4	55.4
Intermediate[b]	156	11.4	72.0	10.4
Conventional[c]	690	50.3	236.0	34.2
Total	1370	100.0	690.4	100.0

a   High-rise and large non-residential buildings.
b   Luxury single-unit dwellings and medium-size non-residential
    buildings.
c   Small residential and non-residential buildings and additions,
    alterations and repairs.

Source: Stretton, 1977a, p. 49.

TABLE 6.2:   BUILDING PERMITS ISSUED FOR RESIDENTIAL
BUILDINGS IN GREATER MANILA, 1974

Building type	Floor area		Value	
	sq. metres (thous.)	Per cent	Pesos (mill.)	Per cent
Luxury, high-rise residential buildings	82.2	16	73.1	35
Luxury, conventional (bungalow) housing	51.4	10	31.3	15
Small residential buildings	380.4	74	104.3	50
Total	514.0	100	208.7	100

Source: Building permits issued in Greater Manila.

A survey of building sites provided information on the type
and size of contractor engaged on the different types of residential building sites. As expected, all of the high-rise dwellings
were built by the larger construction firms. Approximately 80 per
cent of the luxury conventional dwellings were constructed by small
and medium sized firms, while on 20 per cent of the sites the
architect was responsible for the construction under a system
generally referred to as 'by administration'. Under this arrangement the architect not only drew the plans for the building but was
responsible for hiring and supervising a foreman. The architect
also ordered the materials and paid the labourers, billing the
owner every week or month. The larger firms occasionally entered
this market but their share of total output appeared to be quite
small.

Approximately 70 per cent of the small residential buildings
were constructed by independent foremen, working in co-operation
with the owner of the building. A further 10 per cent were built
by independent foremen under the close supervision of the architect.
Small firms accounted for slightly more than 15 per cent of the
market. In the last few years a small number of the larger firms
have entered into the middle income housing market by developing
estates in which they provide the infrastructure and construct most
of the houses. Government sponsored low cost housing has been
constructed either by the National Housing Corporation using prefabricated components, or by large private contractors. However,
these sections represent only a small percentage of the total
market. From the detailed list of building permits issued in 1974,
it was possible to estimate the value of residential buildings
constructed by the large developers. On each occasion they
obtained a large number of permits which were listed in blocks,
each dwelling had the same address, value and floor area. On this
basis it was estimated that dwellings valued at approximately
6,000,000 pesos were constructed by the large developers. This
represented about 5 per cent of the small residential buildings
constructed in 1974. This proportion is likely to be higher in
some towns outside the Greater Manila Area but still part of the
Manila Metropolitan Area.

While the proportion of the market constructed by large
developers is increasing, the independent foremen remain the predominant type of contractor for conventional dwellings. They also
construct most of the non-residential buildings in the conventional
market. In 1974 independent foremen constructed approximately 30
per cent of the value of the industry's output. This share would
have been even higher prior to the shift in the output mix towards
high-rise buildings.

3. SOME CHARACTERISTICS OF INDEPENDENT FOREMEN

Interviews of foremen and building industry labourers conducted in
1975 suggest that most independent foremen began work in the
industry on the building sites in Central and Southern Luzon. They
spent from ten to twenty years acquiring skills by working at the
various trades before reaching the position of foreman. Most
moved to the Greater Manila Area in response to the greater availability of work in the building industry in the metropolis. Very

few migrated to the city as unskilled labourers and entered the
building industry when employment could not be found in the industrial sector, as has been suggested by Turin (1969), Sylos-Labini
(1964) and others. Most foremen and skilled labourers in the
industry adopted a circular migration pattern, leaving their
families in their home town or *barrio*. They returned for short
visits twice a month (see Stretton, 1977a for a full discussion of
the migration patterns adopted by building industry labourers).

Virtually all skills in the industry are acquired through
informal training on the job. No universally accepted criteria
are used to differentiate the various grades of a particular
occupation. A labourer's classification, and hence wage, depends
on the contractor's opinion of the ability of the labourer. Similarly, the move from highly skilled labourer to foreman is not
subject to formally stipulated requirements. Rather, it will
depend on the existing foreman's opinion of the ability of the
individual and the demand for independent foremen. If the level
of activity in the residential building market is high and an
architect or engineer requires more foremen, he will ask his existing foremen if their most skilled labourer is capable of performing
the job. Alternatively, a highly skilled labourer may be asked by
a friend or relative to construct their house. The foreman can
then attempt to establish the contacts necessary to retain his new
position. Initially he may rely on many of the contacts of his
previous foreman.

4.   CONTRACTUAL ARRANGEMENTS

The responsibilities of an independent foreman are similar in scope
to those of a 'labour-only contractor'. He must hire a workforce,
supervise their activities, make technical decisions regarding the
construction of the building, and advise the owner on when to order
materials. However, the foreman does not submit a lump sum tender
at the beginning of the project. Rather, he is paid a wage on a
daily basis. The owner of the building is responsible for purchasing the materials and for paying the labourers. The plans for the
building are drawn by an architect or engineer who may be consulted
on particular technical problems. Under the 'by administration'
system used on the higher cost dwellings, the architect offers a
closer supervision of the foreman's activities. He will usually
visit the site every two or three days.

Under these arrangements the foreman does not require the
financial reserves or the skill in financial management or tendering
that would be necessary under a lump sum contract system. The
daily wage of an independent foreman is equivalent to that received
by a foreman engaged by a small or medium-sized construction firm
(about 20 pesos in 1975) — two or three times that of an unskilled
labourer. Foremen working on large building sites usually receive
slightly more. The independent foreman's wage is primarily a
return for his labour and supervisory skills. He receives little
return for his greater responsibility in organising the labour force
or on technical matters. Foremen employed by firms are closely
supervised by the contractor or the site engineer and play a less

important role in the recruitment of the workforce (Stretton, 1977a, pp. 274-277).

According to the regulations of the Philippine Licensing Board for Contractors, an independent foreman who wishes to become a licensed contractor would require financial assets of 5000 pesos. This is slightly less than the annual income of a foreman fully employed for the year. However, very few independent foremen gave an indication that they wanted to move in this direction.

Independent foremen build with conventional materials (timber, concrete hollow blocks, galvanised iron, tiles, etc.). No pre-fabricated materials or equipment, other than the normal tools of the tradesmen are used. Cement is usually mixed on the ground with spades and carried to the required position in buckets. In addition, independent foremen supervise only one project at a time. As most houses are constructed in four to six months this means that the foremen must search for work two or three times a year. Most jobs are obtained through personal acquaintances or informal contacts maintained with three or four different architects. A person intending to build a house will ask his architect for a reliable builder. The architect will usually suggest one of the foremen he has previously engaged. Alternatively, the owner may approach a relative or friend who has recently hired a foreman and seek his opinion on the quality of the workmanship.

5. THE RELATIONSHIP BETWEEN AN INDEPENDENT FOREMAN AND

HIS LABOURERS

Independent foremen maintain a 'regular' workforce whom they employ on each of their jobs. Most members of this permanent workforce are relatives or old friends of the foreman and usually come from the same *barrio* or district. Its size varies with the foreman, but usually falls within the range of three to fifteen labourers. For sites on which an independent foreman was engaged, the permanent workforce accounted, on the average, for approximately 50 per cent of the total workforce on the site at the time of the interview. Most foremen include unskilled labourers in their permanent group, but they usually account for only 30 to 40 per cent of the total.

Casual labourers are hired in one of two ways. Either the foreman will accept persons who approach the site looking for work, or members of the regular workforce will inform friends in their home town or *barrio* that work is available. These casual workers will include skilled as well as unskilled labourers. Subcontract-ors, for example those involved in electrical or plumbing work, are employed by the owner of the building on the advice of his foreman or architect.

Most unskilled labourers working in the industry in the Greater Manila Area receive the legal minimum wage. Given the surplus labour situation in the Philippines, the small and informal nature of the independent foremen's operations, and the mobility of labour in the building industry, one might have expected independent foremen to pay less than the legal minimum wage. There are a number of countervailing reasons which prevent this from occurring.

First, the foreman does not construct buildings under a contract in which the level of his income is determined by his ability to minimise costs. Instead, the foreman is paid a daily wage to engage a workforce and to supervise their activities. The owner of the building meets all labour costs on a weekly basis. Hence, the foreman has little to gain from employing labour at less than the minimum wage. Second, there is usually a close relationship between the foreman and his regular workforce. They are often related or from the same home town or *barrio* and most have been working together for many years. This represents a relatively stable employment relationship in which the foreman faces both social and cultural pressure to maximise the returns of his labourers. These higher costs are then passed on to the owner of the building.

The owners of the building usually accept the wages stipulated by the foreman, possibly after advice from their architect or engineer. The professional group in the industry would face pressures to observe wage legislation. One might expect an owner to bargain among a number of foremen in an attempt to lower wages and costs. However, the owner's search mechanism when looking for a foreman is fairly limited so that this course of action is rarely adopted.

Short-term employees of a particular foreman may receive less than the legal minimum wage as the cultural and social ties in this relationship are minimal. The practice of a foreman retaining part of the wage for which a labourer had signed is occasionally practised and, in fact, indebtedness among labourers is fairly common. Labourers will normally borrow from the foreman or one of the highly paid skilled labourers. Because of the high interest rates, labourers are often in the position where they are only able to meet the interest payments, and hence remain in debt for quite long periods.

The stability of employment experienced by members of an independent foreman's regular workforce will depend on the ability of the foreman to obtain projects and the variations in the size and composition of the workforce required on each site. Hence not only the level of activity in the industry but also the extent of the foreman's network of contacts will determine the amount of unemployment that the individual labourer will face. When work is not available the labourers who follow a circular migration pattern return to their *barrio*. As they have maintained close contacts by leaving their family in the *barrio*, frequent visits and sending remittances, they are readily accepted back into the village economy. Most labourers wait in the *barrio* until they are informed by their foreman or another of their contacts in the industry that work is again available. Hence, for a labourer committed to employment in the industry, the circular migration pattern provides a means of coping with the instability of employment which he faces. Rather than remain in the city, without income and with a relatively high cost of subsistence, the unemployed labourer returns to his *barrio* where the cost of living is much lower and where there exists the possibility of earning income from activities such as farming or fishing. It is only because of the role of the independent foremen, who remain in the city looking for work and inform their labourers when employment is available, that the labourer is able to return to his *barrio* (Stretton, 1977b).

6. THE CONSTRUCTION OF LOW COST CONVENTIONAL HOUSING

In many countries the provision of low cost housing is usually
associated with government construction.   The Philippines is no
exception and in 1968 the National Housing Corporation was established to erect prefabricated housing units and to mass produce
the standardised component parts.   Until 1974 the National
Housing Corporation made little impact on the housing market.   In
that year it produced an average of 150 units a month, well below
its maximum capacity of 1000 units a month (NEDA, 1975, p. 34).
Since then the Philippines government has released a four year
housing programme which envisages the construction of 250,000 low
and lower-middle income dwelling units between 1974 and 1977.   A
large percentage of the lower-middle income conventional dwellings
will be financed through the Social Security System and the Government Service Insurance System.   These two bodies have traditionally
provided the bulk of the finance for private sector housing.   In
recent years the Government Service Insurance System and Social
Security System have placed greater emphasis on large housing
estates constructed by one large developer.   Orola (1974, p. 66)
states that the Government Service Insurance System is attempting
to achieve its twin aims of maximising the number of housing units
produced and minimising the cost per unit by '...availing itself of
the economies of mass production through mass construction of housing units and...the utilization of housing components prefabricated
by the National Housing Corporation'.

     The form of contract between the developer and the Social
Security System or Government Service Insurance System varies from
case to case, but is usually similar to that described below.   A
sub-division company which plans to develop a parcel of land as a
low cost housing project uses this land as collateral to borrow
approximately 25 per cent of the total cost of the project from the
Government Service Insurance System or Social Security System.
While the property is being developed the financial institution
processes applications from prospective buyers among their members.
As segments of the project are completed the developer receives pro-
rata payment from the Government Service Insurance System or Social
Security System.   The developer repays the loan, which he has used
to purchase equipment and as working capital, at the completion of
the project.

     Until the early 1970s most large housing developers used con-
ventional techniques of construction, although their workforce was
organised in gangs which moved from site to site performing specific
tasks.   Some equipment such as cement mixers and concrete vibrators
were used.   However, since 1972 there has been a noticeable shift
toward the use of prefabricated materials erected with the use of
cranes and other heavy machinery.   Some developers purchase their
prefabricated components from the National Housing Corporation
while others use private suppliers or import the materials.

     Knowledge of prefabricated techniques was available to most
developers well before they adopted this form of construction.   The
National Housing Corporation was established in 1968 and the techniques were reported in most of the local trade journals prior to
the early 1970s.   One of the main reasons for their adoption
appears to have been the fall, since 1972, of the price of capital

relative to labour for those firms able to obtain finance from the
banks and other formal financial institutions.   To the user, the
cost of capital or equipment has two components; the allowance for
depreciation and the cost of financing the purchase of the equipment.   If the contractor obtains a loan in order to purchase
machinery, the cost of finance is the interest payments on that
loan.   While the purchase price of equipment has increased substantially since 1972, the interest rates on the loans from the
Government Service Insurance System and Social Security System have
been, in most years, below the rate of inflation.   Hence, the real
interest rates have been either negative or very low (Stretton,
1977a, pp. 103-109).   Thus, the cost of capital to the large contractor has been below its social opportunity cost, partially
explaining the adoption of labour saving techniques in a labour-
abundant economy.

An alternative to the use of large developers in the construction of low cost conventional housing would be for the Government Service Insurance System and Social Security System to provide
credit to the prospective owner and allow him to engage an independent foreman or small firm.   The same method used to construct
most middle income housing could be used to construct low cost conventional housing.   The government would need to let contracts for
the provision of infrastructure, but there is no reason why the
infrastructure and the houses should be constructed by the same
firm.

7.   A COMPARISON OF THE TWO TECHNIQUES

Employment creation

Paqueo (1973) estimated that direct and indirect labour
accounted for 45 to 49 per cent of the cost of a conventionally built
house.   This compares with 35 per cent in the case of a National
Housing Corporation dwelling.   While the prefabricated techniques
involve greater employment in the production of the materials, this
is not sufficient to offset the much lower workforce required on
the building site.

National Housing Corporation studies have shown that the use
of prefabricated wooden components with conventional concrete hollow
blocks involves an average saving in labour costs of slightly more
than 3 per cent of the total production cost of a unit (Tobias,
1974, p. 192).   This is equivalent to approximately fifty-five
unskilled man days of employment per unit.   If prefabricated concrete panels are used, the fall in employment creation would be
even higher.

The attitude of the large developers to the different techniques of construction is illustrated by the following statement by
Cacho, a former President of the Philippine Contractors Association.
He suggests that there are three alternative methods of constructing
low cost houses:

First, to continue the construction process in building homes in the traditional method using the normal materials available.

Second, to rationalize housing by requiring archictects, designing engineers, and housing developers to come up with housing plans that allow partial prefabrication, modular designs, repetitive and standard parts. The building contractors, in turn, would build houses using modern assembly line techniques that will shorten total completion time with obvious substantial savings.

Third, to start building homes in factories to be transported by trailer-trucks in sections or completed modules and assembled using cranes and other heavy equipment. The plants that build these modules would, in turn, be capital intensive, requiring heavy importation of machinery and using a minimum of manpower. This includes the heavy systems-building and total prefabrication.

The first option would be a step backwards. Although admittedly, it would employ more men and help alleviate the unemployment problem facing us today, it is retrogressive. The third alternative is detrimental to the economy and should not be pursued. It is not applicable to our economy and in the guise of providing a more economical house, our foreign exchange may be wasted unnecessarily...The saying that 'virtue lies in moderation' is a truth that should not escape us. The second option open to us is also suited for developing nations. (Cacho, 1974, pp. 141-142.)

Costs of construction

Cacho (1974, p. 144) argues that '...using prefabricated components, a builder using mass production techniques can come out with a house 20-25 percent cheaper than that produced through the conventional method'. This figure is said to be based on the experience of developers who have used prefabricated techniques. However, Paqueo's study (1973, p. 166) shows that the cost per square metre of floor area was lower for the conventional technique than for the National Housing Corporation constructed dwelling. This suggests that any fall in costs must result from economies of large-scale development, the shorter construction time, or from reducing the floor area of the house. Economies of scale could be achieved by the spreading of overheads, including the costs of design, and by the specialisation of labour.

The fact that large developers are changing from conventional techniques to the use of prefabricated materials, suggests that, to the firm at least, prefabrication is cheaper than conventional methods. However, it does not necessarily follow that the prefabrication technique used by a developer is cheaper than the conventional technique used by an independent foreman.

First, the large developers are given low interest loans from
the Social Security System and Government Service Insurance System,
which lower the costs of the equipment-intensive alternative.   The
opportunity cost of these loans needs to be included in the cost of
the prefabricated unit.   If the house is constructed by an independent foreman, these loans will not be necessary.

Second, the cost of either type of house constructed by a
developer will include profits, overheads, contractors tax, and
costs of equipment.   Most of these expenses will not be present in
projects constructed by independent foremen.   Makanas (1974,
p. 151) has estimated that these factors account for approximately
22 per cent of the total cost of most projects.   On very large
projects they may be less important, but one would still expect
such factors to be a sizeable proportion of total cost.   This
argument suggests that while the prefabricated technique may be
cheaper than the conventional technique constructed by a developer,
it may not be cheaper than the conventional technique constructed
by an independent foreman.

Projects constructed by independent foremen will also face
overheads such as design costs.   However, these could be minimised
if the authorities produced plans for a small number of designs and
these were made available to clients.   If independent foremen were
to specialise in these designs, then their efficiency in constructing low cost housing should improve and further lower the costs of
the conventional techniques.

At this stage it cannot be claimed that the use of independent
foremen in the construction of low cost housing is a preferred
alternative to the use of large developers.   However, it is equally
unclear that the use of prefabricated materials should be encouraged.
Further comparative studies of the costs of the two methods should
be undertaken.   If the conventional technique constructed by
independent foremen is found to be cheaper, then this method would
be preferred on the grounds of lower cost and greater employment
creation.   If the use of prefabricated materials is found to be
less expensive, then the government will need to make a choice
between output and employment creation.

Import content

Virtually all of the materials used in conventionally built
housing are produced domestically, whereas the use of prefabricated
techniques involves importing the materials or expensive machinery
to produce the components locally.   In 1968-69 the National Housing
Corporation imported machinery from West Germany at a cost of
DM64,000,000 (Paqueo, 1973, p. 165)*.   The cranes used in the
installation of the prefabricated components on the site must also
be imported.   Hence, investment in housing constructed by independent foremen may have a higher multiplier effect as the leakages
from the economy will be lower.   It also suggests that the
inflationary effects of a given investment in low cost housing may

---

*   The exchange rate was $A1 = DM2.51 on 21 November 1977.

be lower if conventional techniques are used.   All of the materials
are available locally and bottlenecks are unlikely to develop
following an increase in demand.   With prefabricated techniques
the cost of housing also depends on the balance of payments position
and the availability of foreign reserves to purchase the imported
materials and equipment.   The Philippines has experienced periodic
balance of payments difficulties since 1945.   During such periods
developers would have difficulties in obtaining their imported
materials, machinery and spare parts resulting in a rise in the
cost of construction.   This rise could be substantial in the event
of a foreign exchange crisis forcing a devaluation of the peso.

8.   CONCLUSION

Building contractors in the Greater Manila Area cover a spectrum
ranging from large firms to small independent foremen.   The large
firms are undoubtedly part of the urban formal sector.   The non-
competitive structure of this part of the market, the benefits
resulting from close contacts with government, the size and structure of the firms, and the equipment-intensive techniques of construction are similar to conditions found in other parts of the
formal sector.   The independent foremen, on the other hand, are
small enterprises operating in a strongly competitive market, without any government assistance, and using conventional techniques of
construction which require little or no equipment.   Hence, this
part of the industry is similar to the urban informal sector.
However, the two sections are not operating in isolation from one
another.   Despite their differences there are a number of ways in
which they interact.

First, the independent foremen and their labourers rely on
the urban formal sector for employment.   Buildings constructed by
independent foremen are used by governments, business firms or
their employees.   As conditions influencing demand are fairly
volatile the labourers experience precarious or uncertain employment.   However, the effects on the labourers of demand fluctuations
emanating from the urban formal sector are moderated by the actions
of the independent foremen.   When work is not available the foreman will remain in the city looking for jobs, allowing his
labourers to return to the *barrio* where the cost of living is lower
and there exists a possibility of earning some income from farming
or fishing.   This action also benefits the formal sector because
it allows the labourer to remain committed to employment in the
industry despite any unemployment and uncertainty he may experience.
The client benefits from the higher quality workmanship and lower
costs associated with an experienced, skilled workforce.

Second, the large construction firms rely on independent
foremen and small firms to train the skilled workforce.   Most
labourers obtained their skills while working on the provincial
building sites or for independent foremen in the city.   As the
skills are transferable within the industry and in most years there
exists an excess supply of skilled labourers, the large firms are
under little pressure to conduct their own training programme.

An additional aspect of the relationship between independent
foremen and large firms has recently emerged with attempts by the
large contractors to encroach upon the market for houses traditionally constructed by independent foremen.   The modern firms
have realised that the low cost conventional housing market may be
a profitable venture, providing it is entered on a large scale.
Their moves against the independent foremen have been strengthened
by their close contacts with the government.   This association is
used both to obtain contracts and low interest loans.   The situation
provides an interesting example of the dynamic relationship which
can exist between the formal and informal sectors of the one industry.   There is no brick wall between the two.   Rather, the relationship, including the scope of the different markets, is
extremely flexible, depending on factors such as relative profit-
ability and government policies.

REFERENCES

Cacho, R.P. (1974), 'Housing and the Building Industry', *NEDA Journal of Development*, 1 and 2 (2,3 and 4), pp. 133-49.

Makanas, E.D. (1974), 'Interindustry Analysis of the Housing Construction Industry', *NEDA Journal of Development*, 1 and 2 (2,3 and 4), pp. 150-73.

NEDA (National Economic Development Authority) (1975), *Housing Sector Study*, National Economic and Development Authority, Manila.

Orola, J.P. (1974), 'The Housing Program of the Government Service Insurance System', *NEDA Journal of Development* 1 and 2 (2,3 and 4), pp. 66-81.

Paqueo, V.B. (1973), 'The Employment Impact of Low Cost Housing under Two Alternative Building Techniques', Papers and Proceedings of the Workshop on Manpower and Human Resources, 13-15 October 1972, Los Banos, Laguna, *Philippine Economic Journal*, 12 (1 and 2).

Stretton, A.W. (1977a), The building industry and employment creation in Manila, the Philippines, unpublished Ph.D. thesis in Economics, Australian National University, Canberra.

Stretton, A.W. (1977b), 'Instability of Employment Amongst Building Industry Labourers in Manila' in R. Bromley and C. Gerry (eds), *The Casual Poor in Third World Cities* [forthcoming].

Sylos-Labini, P. (1964), 'Precarious Employment in Sicily', *International Labour Review*, 89(3), pp. 268-85.

Tobias, G.V. (1974), 'Prefabrication of Housing Components in the National Housing Corporation', *NEDA Journal of Development* 1 and 2 (2,3 and 4), pp. 188-96.

Turin, D.A. (1969), 'The Construction Industry', United Nations Industrial Development Organisation, Monograph No. 2, *Industrial Development*, Vienna.

CHAPTER 7

HOUSING TRENDS AND POLICY IMPLICATIONS IN PAPUA NEW GUINEA: FLAUNTING THE FLAG OF ABSTRACTED EMPIRICISM

RICHARD JACKSON[*]

1. INTRODUCTION

This chapter is an exercise in what Slater (1976, pp. 88-93)
scathingly termed 'abstracted empiricism in the service of the
state' for it takes as its starting point a known policy need of
Papua New Guinea, *viz.* the direction in which housing policy and
practice should proceed.   By taking the policy need of a particular
state as its starting point this chapter will often be pragmatic
and parochial.   Yet if, as many other contributors to this monograph suggest, informal solutions are culturally specific and
'appropriate' solutions, then some degree of pragmatism seems not
only inevitable but, within the framework of overall social goals,
essential.

The search for a just and rational solution to the housing
problems of Papua New Guinea appears to be much easier than in many
other Pacific or Southeast Asian countries.   First, because it is
a small country with fewer than three million people and because
its towns are comparatively small — in 1977 the largest, Port
Moresby, had an estimated population of under 120,000 (*Post Courier*,
1 July 1977) — its informal settlements, although extensive, are
nowhere of the same Dickensian squalor as those described elsewhere
in this monograph (see Chapter 4).   Second, because Papua New
Guinea is not yet a poor country.   At present it has one of the
highest per capita international aid grants of any country in the world, being
the recipient of over $A200,000,000 per annum.   Third, because
the very lack of an infrastructural skeleton for the economy does
mean that it is still possible to create new patterns of development.   Admittedly, it is *rather* late to undertake the shaping of a
new economic geography, but it is not yet *too* late, and the problems
are not overwhelming.

2. SOME DIMENSIONS OF THE PRESENT HOUSING PROBLEM

The housing issue is a matter of concern to policy-makers in Papua
New Guinea for several reasons:

(a)   Urban population grew at an annual rate of 17 per cent between 1966 and 1971 — the date of the last national census.   The
next census is not due until 1979, but it is generally agreed that

---

[*]   Dr Richard Jackson is Senior Lecturer, Department of Geography,
University of Papua New Guinea, Port Moresby.

the current rate of urban population growth is between 9 and 12 per
cent per year.   These high rates of growth are partly a result of
the low base figure for urban population in 1966.   They also owe
something to urban boundary changes in the inter-censal period.
Nevertheless, they remain high growth rates involving large numbers
of people.   Between 60 and 70 per cent of this growth is generated
by migration from the rural areas.

(b)   The fastest rates of growth between 1966 and 1971 were for
indigenous females in the urban areas.   During that period their
annual growth rate was over 20 per cent.   This reflected the growing 'familisation' of the urban areas and strongly implied that the
demand for urban family housing was increasing at a faster rate
than that of the urban population as a whole.   Since there were
still 161 males for every 100 females in the towns in 1971, this
trend is likely to continue.

(c)   The National Planning Office (1975) has forecast that by 1986
the urban population will exceed 1,000,000.   Although this figure
may turn out to be a little high, there will undoubtedly be a continued rapid rise in urban population numbers.   Judged by existing
occupancy rates, an increase of the proportions forecast by the
National Planning Office would imply the need for the construction,
on average, of 7000 dwellings for 42,000 persons each year until
1986.

(d)   At present, the total supply of formal housing by all agencies
hovers around the 2000 dwellings per annum mark.   There is no indication that this number can be substantially increased in the near
future.

(e)   At present, more than 60 per cent of the urban population cannot afford the rent of the cheapest housing provided by the National
Housing Commission.   Many of the present formal housing tenants
would not be able to rent their current housing if indirect subsidies were removed.   In the period 1966 to 1971 growth rates for
urban-based population and urban-based employment were roughly
comparable.   Between 1971 and 1977, employment seems to have
increased at an annual rate of not more than 5 per cent, a rate
half, or less, than that of population growth.   Consequently most
people believe that unemployment will rise and the proportion of
persons unable to afford formal housing will increase further.

(f)   Even of those who are supposed to be able to afford the
National Housing Commission housing (those whose average wage is no
less than five times the rental charged), 86 per cent were in
arrears with rental payments in mid 1975.   The arrears totalled
nearly one-fifth of the total rents received by the National Housing
Commission (Ministry of the Interior, 1975).

(g)   By now, it is probable that between 45 and 50 per cent of the
urban population is accommodated in informal housing.   In 1971,
the proportions by town ranged from 27 per cent in Port Moresby to
over 55 per cent in Mount Hagen and Wewak.   In other words,
although the development of other types of informal activities in
Papua New Guinea is very weak, informal housing is the most
important single sector in urban accommodation.

3. THE HISTORICAL SETTING OF THE PRESENT SITUATION

The rationale for the establishment of urban centres in Papua New
Guinea by the colonial authorities was more or less clear — more
in New Guinea, less in Papua.   The New Guinea towns were there to
serve plantation interests, to act as collection points for plantation products destined for export and for the import of equipment
and supplies.   Smaller centres were established in other regions
to ensure that the recruitment of labour for the plantations pro-
ceeded harmoniously and in an orderly fashion.   A few towns, such
as Bulolo, Wau and Maprik, were established as mining centres
(Jackson, 1976).   Whilst the explicit motivation for the foundation of urban centres in Papua was less clearly economic, the growth
or decline of such centres depended, as in New Guinea, upon the
prosperity of that aspect of the colonial economy each centre served.
Such towns did not serve and were not designed to serve indigenous
rural interests; they were distant appendages of the metropolitan
urban hierarchy.

To ensure that these towns developed in a manner suited to
the metropolitan interest, a series of rules and regulations were
established which defined those types of economic activities, those
types of housing, those systems of society which could or could not
be practised or exist in towns.   Although recent attempts to re-
define and reconstruct such laws in order to encourage the emergence
of new urban economic activities, new urban house styles, new urban
living patterns, are necessary and laudable, they will have little
hope of full success as long as the geographic pattern of urbanisation in Papua New Guinea remains as it is.   Such attempts aim to
reform the manner of operation of particular aspects of towns *qua*
towns, rather than as nodes in an overall integrated framework of
development.   Although the attempts to deal with housing problems
in Papua New Guinea have been relatively enlightened and rather
successful, they can also be viewed as inadequate cosmetic attempts
to mask a basically ugly urban structure.

Legislation whose express purpose or indirect result was to
exclude Papua New Guineans from towns, was common in the first
seventy years of colonial occupation (Jackson, 1976).   The most
explicit legislation was the (New Guinea) *Native Administration
Regulations* 1924, section 129, which stated that 'Every native who
remains within any town for a longer period than four days without
employment (proof whereof shall lie with him) shall be guilty of an
offence...'.   In addition, section 74(i) of the (Papuan) *Native
Regulations* 1939, (repealed in 1959) proscribed that 'Any native
who, without lawful or reasonable excuse, is found on any premises
other than those of his employer (if any) within the town of Port
Moresby between the hours of 9 p.m. and 6 a.m. shall be guilty of
an offence...The term 'premises' for the purpose of this regulation
includes all lands, wharves, jetties, houses, buildings of any
description, roads, streets and highways.   The proof of such lawful
or reasonable excuse shall be upon the defendant...'.   Section 51
of the (New Guinea) *Native Labour Ordinance* 1935-9 stated that 'The
Administrator may, by proclamation, direct that...labourers or
servants, other than the labourers or servants or class of labourers
specified in the proclamation, shall not be housed or reside within
the boundaries of any specified town...'.

These three examples must suffice to show the nature of the direct measures used against Papua New Guineans who could aspire to nothing more than the humble status of servants and labourers in the white man's towns.   In addition, a whole web of indirect regulations were enacted governing health, building, zoning, trade and recreation, the chief purpose of which was to deliberately eradicate the slightest trace of anything Papuan or New Guinean from the urban areas.

There were inconsistencies within, and ways around, such legislation.   On the one hand, the Administrator in New Guinea (and his counterpart in Papua) had to use his powers of proclamation to allow for the housing of certain classes of workers — especially house servants — within towns.   With the localisation of some occupations and the growth of industry, the economic necessity of having Papua New Guinean workers housed in towns grew and legislation requiring that employers provide accommodation for such employees was enacted.   But since such accommodation was for employees only, rather than employees *and* their families, the law was satisfied by the provision of barracks for 'single' males only. On the other hand, the web of regulations only applied, or could only be enforced, on public land.   As the legal boundaries of the towns were extended they often included patches of land still under customary tenure which the Administration was unable, for a variety of reasons, to resume.   This was especially true of Port Moresby where pressure of urban growth caused the compact 1898 boundaries to be extended in 1954, incorporating quite large tracts of customary land.   On such land, therefore, the migrants clustered, generally with the consent of the land-holders.

By 1960, urban housing in Papua New Guinea could be categorised into three groups.   First, expatriate housing with associated domestic quarters; second, barracks and hostels which, together with the first category were on government held land within the towns; third, migrant informal settlements located either immediately outside the urban legal boundaries or enclosed within the town on pockets of customary land or, occasionally, on pockets of unused government land.

Ironically, the employer which found it most difficult to fulfil its legal obligations in the provision of employee housing was the Administration itself.   Consequently, large numbers of lower paid government workers had to live in the growing informal settlements.   Urban development began to run well ahead of the legal controls which were supposedly guiding it.   By the mid 1960s, high cost housing was commonly being built without domestic quarters so that servants too began to swell the ranks of the informally housed.   But despite the burgeoning informal housing sector many of the old laws remained in force.   Indeed, they still do.   The most unfortunate of these are the vagrancy laws.

As with other relict laws the enforcement of the vagrancy regulations is erratic.   Technically, it is an offence to be resident in town without employment or legal, and visible, means of support.   In many towns this regulation is very difficult to enforce and the police would probably not try to enforce it were it not for the fact that they believe strongly that most urban crime is committed by the unemployed and that most of the unemployed live

in informal settlements.   Consequently, migrants in informal
settlements within towns and located on government or other alienated land seem to the police to be that sector of the community
largely responsible for crime and against whom the vagrancy laws
may be applied.   Midnight raids are not infrequently made and
result in the arrest of many hundreds of people.   However, despite
the strength of the police belief in their two assumptions, they
are usually unable to support their case.   Local lawyers argue
that a correlation between crime and unemployment is not proven,
whilst many of the recent empirical studies undertaken in such
settlements suggest that there is not necessarily a relationship
between unemployment and shanty residence (National Planning
Office, 1975).

       The overall consequence of housing policy up to the mid 1960s
was the gradual creation of an association between a large number
of low paid, formally employed people and informal, or non-family,
housing.   For a smaller group, the association was between high
income employment and subsidised, formal housing.   The latter
arose through the provision by government of housing at cheap rates
for almost all its employees of European origins; cheap housing
being one of the incentives offered in the recruitment of expatriates
to the public service.   This association has continued despite the
recent extensive localisation of the public service.   Indeed,
localisation has entrenched the association through the growing
strength of the public servants union and through the development
of vested interests amongst the local bureaucracy which are no less
strong than those of the formerly dominant (and still important)
expatriate administrators.   This rapid growth of the public service
associated with localisation was indeed a major reason for the
establishment in 1968 of the Housing Commission, later the National
Housing Commission.

       Thus, the present situation where urban populations are grow-
ing very rapidly, where urban housing demand is growing even faster,
where the ability to pay for National Housing Commission accommodation is restricted to only a minority of the urban population, and
where housing demand greatly exceeds supply, arises out of a
situation in which towns were for long regarded by the colonial
power as being exclusively for white men and (on sufferance) white
women (Inglis, 1974).   The painful adjustment to new realities is
evidenced by the present situation.

4.   THE INFORMAL HOUSING SECTOR

Already the informal housing sector is the largest single provider
of urban accommodation.   The formal sector's inadequacies have many
dimensions.   Not only is there an overall shortage, but there is
not enough of the right sort of housing (Plocki, 1975).   What
housing there is, is concentrated in one or two towns.   At the end
of the 1974/5 financial year, 79 per cent of the National Housing
Commission's houses had been constructed in Port Moresby and 11 per
cent in Lae, leaving only 10 per cent for the remaining towns which
house well over half the total urban population.   Where housing
has been built, the specific locations are often remote from services
and places of employment — the largest single formal housing estate
in Port Moresby, at Gerehu, is at the extreme northern end of the
town, as is the Taraka housing area in Lae.

The response of many urban dwellers to such inadequacies has been straightforward — they build their own homes.   Within limits determined by the cost and availability of building materials, these are of a size and style suited to their families' needs, and are located in as central and accessible a position as the law and its enforcement processes will allow.   Consequently, by the time of the Urban Household Survey at the end of 1973 (Garnaut *et al.*, 1977), one-third of the population of Lae and Port Moresby were living in informal housing.

It was not entirely surprising, therefore, that at the end of 1973 the Papua New Guinea government published its White Paper on informal housing (Ministry of the Interior, 1973).   The most interesting feature of the White Paper was the attitude displayed to informal settlements*.   The public debate in Papua New Guinea on this subject tends, as in other parts of the world, to be highly polarised.   Most of the 'popular' debate as carried forward in the pages of the local press is very much anti informal settlement. Settlers in such areas are generally regarded as constituting the major source of criminals and as being the temporary havens of unemployed transients with little to contribute to a stable urban community.   Such views are those of many Papua New Guineans living in formal housing areas who feel threatened by the informal settlements.   In 1977, when the University of Papua New Guinea proposed to hand over to the National Housing Commission part of its lease for the development of low cost housing, possibly for site and service schemes, it was the senior local officers of the institution who objected to the plan, asking that the supposed social harmony of the present University campus be preserved.

On the other hand, academics, perhaps predictably, have argued quite strongly on behalf of the settlers, their defence being based on the results of a number of individual studies of such settlements (Allen and Jackson, 1975; Forbes and Jackson, 1975; Bryant, 1977).   The general conclusions of this empirical work have been that, on the whole, settlers are responsible for proportionately less crime than the populations of low cost formal housing areas and have high employment rates.   They live in communities which possess a far better balance of sex ratios than the urban areas as a whole and are more likely to live in stable family units than the urban population at large.   In addition, these people tend to stay in urban areas for longer periods than do either the wealthy, but certainly transient, expatriate population or the local bureaucrats whose frequent transfers to other parts of the country ensure that they are less likely to put down firm roots in one place.   Moreover, their houses are in some ways - space, design and comfort - much better than those at the cheaper end of the formal housing spectrum.

The studies of informal settlements which have given rise to these general conclusions have almost all been undertaken in close co-operation with the National Housing Commission, some being commissioned by that organisation.   This close liaison is one

---

* For examples of public attitude see *Post Courier*, 10 February 1975, 27 February 1976, 18 March 1976, 21 June 1977, 4 August 1977 and 16 August 1977.

reason why the Commission has tended to be sympathetic in its
attitude towards the settlements.

The White Paper reflected academic rather than 'popular'
opinions; its relatively progressive policies coming from a well-
informed, enlightened bureaucracy rather than from fearful, lower
and middle classes.   The paper's main conclusions were that existing informal settlements should be recognised as an integral part
of urban development and that they be upgraded and improved through
self-help schemes.   It also recommended that new site and service
areas be laid out, partly for the few who would be displaced by upgrading but primarily to cater for future settlers, and that such
new schemes be planned to fit in with other urban development,
notably with new sources of employment.   Once recognised, improved
and/or provided, such housing areas would be strictly controlled
through a combination of settlement committees and, where necessary,
the strict enforcement of available legislation.   The paper also
advised that restrictions on informal economic activities in such
areas be relaxed.

Services to be provided in the upgrading process were
access roads, shared water reticulation, deep pit latrines,
garbage collection and street lighting.   Such facilities were
only to be provided once a settler had improved his house to regulation standards — a K250 grant and a K250* loan in materials were
available for this.   In practice, such a rule was difficult to
enforce since many of the facilities were communal rather than
individual, whereas the house improvements were largely individual.
Consequently, services have been introduced in many areas where
housing improvement was patchy.   Where possible, the provision of
services was to use the labour of residents who were 'temporarily
unemployed'.   The organisation and control of the settlements and
of the decision-making on the question of who should obtain grants
and loans were to be vested in a settlement committee drawn from
the settlement community.

On the question of the settlement committees the White Paper
outlined the government's views as follows:

A great deal of thought has been given to the means whereby
these committees should be constituted.   There are two
main alternatives.   The first is for the committees to be
formally established under the Local Government Ordinance
as committees of the council.   This method would have the
advantage of giving the committees legal recognition and
of enabling specific powers and responsibilities to be conferred on them.   The second alternative is to leave their
composition completely informal.   A number of such informal
committees already exist, and they have proven to be very
effective where they are recognised and supported by the
authorities working in the settlements.   There is a real
danger that once a committee of this kind is formalised it
is far more difficult to get people to serve on it volun-
tarily without remuneration.   It tends to be regarded as
a level of government and can become over-authoritarian and

* The rate of exchange was $A1 = 0.87K on 21 November 1977.

rigid.   The Government has concluded that the advantages
of formalising these committees are likely to be out-
weighed by these sorts of disadvantages and as a result,
is of the view that settlement committees should be
informal and voluntary...(Ministry of the Interior, 1975,
p. 16).

This important statement contains one of the key questions that has
to be asked of the informal sector — how formal can informal
become?   How can the flexibility and spontaneous success of some
parts of the informal sector be assisted?   Would formal assistance
stultify these characteristics?   To extend McGee's metaphor
(Chapter 1) — the bureaucrats are not having too good a time at
their balls nowadays but they have noticed that ordinary people all
around them have their own scene and it intrigues them.   They want
to learn the new dance but will the bureaucrats, once they believe
they have learnt it give way to the temptation to prohibit its
performance outside the airconditioned ballroom?

5.   THE APPEAL OF THE INFORMAL SECTOR

Policies which aim to encourage the informal sector have certain
attractions to policy makers.   The very wide publicity given by
academics necessarily draws the policy makers' attention to a possible way out of the eternal and seemingly insoluble problems the
formal sector throws up.   A more persuasive reason is that governments need to govern so that they have control over all aspects of
their societies and economies.   Uncontrolled growth of any kind,
social or economic or political, is necessarily a potential threat
to governmental powers.   A third reason is that formal solutions
have, in so many cases, demonstrably failed and failed badly and
expensively; informal solutions attract not merely because they
offer alternatives but because they might be cheaper alternatives.
Inexpensive failures are preferable to costly ones.

        In the Papua New Guinea context all these reasons are evidently
attractive.   In addition, there is the politically important appeal
of doing things in a supposedly independent state in ·a different way
to that followed by the preceding colonial administration.   The
Melanesian Way has, as a political catchword, very considerable
appeal to the new state and its ideologists.   To its proponents the
Melanesian Way is not simply a retrogressive return to the bush
tracks, but is a multi-purpose, multi-laned highway.   It attempts to
weld together cultural values and appropriate technology (in its
widest sense) in politics, in law, in education, in economics, in
religion as well as in such mundane things as housing.   In all
these areas the same basic problem exists: how does one graft the
necessarily rather formal needs of national governance to the local,
and necessarily more informal, approaches to self-reliance?   How
is the informal to be incorporated?   Thus, the question of organising informal housing, raised in the White Paper, has as its basis
the same problem as that of the Village Courts which have been
introduced recently in the attempt to foster traditional ways of
dispute settlement (informal law) within a national system of justice.
Should settlement committees, village court magistrates, informal
literacy teachers and the like be paid?   Can the decisions of such
people be enforced?   If so, will it be by traditional (sorcery) or

formal (jail) methods?   To what extent should culturally specific
practises be regularised to deal with conflicts that emanate from
non-traditional causes; for example, those involved in the planting
of perennial cash crops or those arising between different groups
who previously had no knowledge of each others' ways?   Questions
such as these find their parallels in housing policy: how can
urban communities in which new class structures are already evident
and which are composed of peoples from very different cultural back-
grounds, be satisfactorily organised using 'tradition' social
relationships or building forms?   In short, the current government
attitude in Papua New Guinea is very much inclined to experiment
with new solutions to old problems, many of the solutions to which
come under the heading 'informal'.

        In housing, informal solutions are thus being championed by
the bureaucracy itself, sometimes ambivalently.   It is perhaps
worthwhile at this stage to ask whether the development of the
informal housing sector is paralleled in reality by the development of other informal sector activities.   Until very recently,
the answer to this question was 'no'.   The leading exponents of
informal economic activities have been Jackson, Fitzpatrick and
Blaxter (1976) who have attempted to demonstrate how existing
legislation impedes, oppresses and discriminates against almost
all those forms of small-scale manufacturing, distributive and
service activities which are so characteristic of urban life throughout most of the Third World, but which are so poorly developed in
Papua New Guinea itself.   Jackson, Fitzpatrick and Blaxter argue
that it is colonial legislation which has prevented the development
of informal sector activities and that if such laws were changed
the informal sector would suddenly flourish.   However, the situation
related to housing suggests otherwise.

        This chapter has already shown that legislation of a very con-
siderable degree of severity was set up to regulate urban housing
provision in Papua New Guinea.   Yet this legislation could be
circumvented and eventually became impotent in the face of socio-
spatial reality.   Why then has legislation been apparently successful in blocking the development of other forms of activity?   If
informal housing now provides about half of the total housing stock
in spite of legislation, why has the development of informal manufacturing, distribution and services been so weak?   A small part of
the answer is that such informal activities are only now beginning
to become more important.   Both legal activities, such as the
collection of firewood and bottles, the sale of shells or baskets,
and the making and selling of artefacts, and illegal ones, such as
prostitution, gambling, burglary, theft, and the black-marketing of
beer, appear to be on the increase.   However, few thorough studies
have as yet been undertaken (see May, 1977) and thus no conclusion
as to their extent can be drawn.

        The main part of the answer seems to be that the need to
undertake informal economic activities — from the producers' viewpoint — has not been anywhere near as great as the equivalent
demand for housing.   The demand and the supply sides of the informal

TABLE 7.1: HOUSEHOLD INCOME AND HOUSE TYPE IN PORT MORESBY, 1975

	High cost	Low cost: formal	Low cost: village and settlement	Self-help	Domestic quarters	Average total
Household income per fortnight: (kina)[a]						
from wages	291	138	175	124	102	156
from business activity	2	10	26	23	14	15
from gifts and other sources	18	14	10	7	6	12
Total	311	162	211	154	122	183
Dwelling and land rent per fortnight: (kina)	17	7	–	–	1	5
Average household population, excluding expatriates and visitors (number):						
adults only	3.1	3.2	5.0	3.9	3.3	3.6
Total	5.0	6.5	8.9	7.1	4.8	6.6
Total income less rent per person per year (kina)	1527	624	613	560	662	701
Number in sample	(23)	(71)	(24)	(43)	(15)	(176)

a Monetary figures rounded to the nearest kina.   Dash = less than 0.50 kina.

Source: Papua New Guinea Bureau of Statistics, 1977.

housing equation are both provided from the same source — the
settler, whilst the growth of informal economic activities requires
producers and consumers to be separate entities. The first is
self-reliance, the second is petty market capitalism. Williamson
(1977), after examining the possibilities of defining the informal
sector as a whole concludes:

> The concept of informality whilst often a useful
> semantic peg on which to hang ideas, is not a useful
> one for purposes of analysis. The most important
> difference between people involved in the (formal and
> informal sectors) is simply poverty...These marginal
> economic activities are simply the last resort of the
> poor, and the seemingly low incidence of these activi-
> ties may simply mean that people are not yet poor or
> desperate enough...

Fortunately, there is now available some evidence to support
Williamson's contention that there does not yet exist any sizeable
group of urban dwellers in Papua New Guinea who are desperate
enough to enter the informal sector. Table 7.1 reproduces some of
the results of the Household Expenditure Survey undertaken by the
Bureau of Statistics in Port Moresby in late 1975.   These figures
seem to indicate that the major break in income amongst Papua New
Guineans living in town is between those living in high covenant or
high cost dwellings, and all the rest regardless of whether the
latter are in formal or informal accommodation. Certainly, the
entries under 'business', which can probably all be assigned to
informal income earnings, are largest in the two informal groups of
housing.   They constitute 12.3 per cent of the income of traditional village households and 14.9 per cent of the income of self-
help households, compared with 11.5 per cent for domestic quarter
dwellers, 6.2 percent for those living in low cost formal housing,
and only 0.6 per cent of high income households.   But in no case
does business income form a major source of income.   Overall, the
figures do not indicate abject poverty, and do not point to strong
economic motivation for any group, as a whole, to enter the informal
economic sector, even though 38.1 per cent of the sample was housed
informally.   It seems clear that the housing problems of Papua New
Guinea today are not part of a bigger 'informal' problem.

6.   HOUSING AND THE PATTERN OF URBANISATION

The growth of the informal housing sector in Papua New Guinea is a
response to the inadequacy of housing supply; it is itself a solution to the housing problem rather than a problem of its own.
This is not to say, however, that informal housing can be safely
left to its own devices, left to keep on solving the problems of
those outside the formal housing sphere.   The rapid expansion of
informal housing in the recent past is not yet evidence for the
rapid growth of other informal activities, still less of a growing
desperation amongst an urban proto-proletariat in Papua New Guinea.
Thus, it is not part of an 'informal problem' overall, but *is*
evidence of imbalance of urbanisation in the country as a whole.
Inadequate housing provision is brought about by the rapid urbanisation of Papua New Guinea at nodes which are, in general, poorly
placed to serve national developmental goals.   The housing problem

is a symptom of a more deep-seated malaise in Papua New Guinea,
that of geographically concentrated urbanisation, itself a reflection of the increasingly external orientation of the national
economy.   The real housing problem of Papua New Guinea is the
socio-spatial distribution of housing resources, both within particular cities and between urban centres.   It is in these areas
that policies are needed.

    It is at this point, therefore, that one must refer back to
the rationale behind the establishment of the present urban pattern
which was outlined above.   This rationale, combined with the
historical process of colonial penetration, which reached the
densely settled areas of the highlands last of all, has meant that
Papua New Guinea has inherited a dysfunctional urban system.   In
areas where towns are needed there are often none, whilst many
urban places, including Port Moresby, are extremely poorly located
to serve rural interests.   As a consequence, any attempt to solve
housing problems within the framework of the present urban structure is not only, at best, a cosmetic exercise but is also doomed
to fail as long as the major source areas of urban migrants remain
underurbanised as well as underdeveloped.

    How would a reallocation of resources for urban development
assist the solution of housing problems?   First, one of the major
reasons for the extremely rapid growth in housing demand is the
growing number of females migrating to urban areas and the natural
desire of Papua New Guineans to lead a reasonable family life in
close proximity to urban services.   There is considerable evidence
from villages around Port Moresby, such as Gaire, Tubusureia and
Boera, and around Rabaul, such as the north Gazelle villages, that
Papua New Guineans are prepared to travel twenty miles or more as
daily commuters to work whilst retaining their family ties in the
village.   The break with home and the migration of the wife and
children to join the husband in the urban areas is predominantly a
feature of the long-distance migrants.   Given the locationally
peripheral nature of the urban pattern relative to rural populations, the great majority of migrants in Papua New Guinea are long-
distance migrants; they have no choice but to migrate such distances.
If long-distance migration could be reduced and alternative urban-
based services and employment opportunities made available
the need for family housing in urban areas would be considerably
reduced.   It is notable that migration rates out of East New
Britain and North Solomons areas have always been low, given those
areas' relatively high rate of rural income-earning opportunities
and, just as important, their access to urban services.   Reallocation could thus reduce urbanisation but increase urbanism.

    Second, decentralisation of services or of government, such
as that entailed in the establishment of Provincial Governments,
creates employment.   Third, insofar as reallocation reduces long-
distance migration and encourages the localised spread of urbanism
it reduces some of the oppressive ethnic tensions which are evident
in the towns.   At the same time it encourages a commitment to the
towns as integral parts of the community — something which is
notably absent.   It can do this without splitting up existing local
communities, something which the low cost formal housing schemes of
the National Housing Commission tend to do at present.   Fourth,
reallocation would appear to be one way to break the stranglehold

that foreign interests have on the national economy by realigning
urban functions to serve rural population. The discriminatory
laws of the past can be turned round to discriminate in favour of
the development of the best located towns.   Fifth, rural development cannot take place without the development of urban-type
services.   Whether these are actually located in a physically
defined town is another matter.   Conversely, lack of development
of a rural service centre will impede the development of its
service area.   For example, one of the least developed areas of
Papua New Guinea, the northern portion of Western Province, is
served by the small township of Kiunga which has a population of
1400.   Given the discovery of the large Ok Tedi copper deposits of
the area, several government departments have shown some interest
in establishing representation in Kiunga.   Unfortunately, as no
housing is available for such officers they cannot be posted
there, to the detriment of the rural population (Jackson, 1977).

        What are the chances of a reallocation of urban resources
being achieved?   The efforts since 1975 of the National Housing
Commission to decentralise its activities by establishing offices
in over forty towns by 1979 are themselves encouraging, especially
when this effort is being paralleled by a genuine attempt to divert
resources not only geographically but also socially towards the
provision of site and service schemes as opposed to formal housing
estates.   The political importance of regionalist sentiments in
the country has been given official cognisance by the establishment
of Provincial Governments.   Moreover, the re-elected coalition
government of Papua New Guinea, only two years after Independence
(1975), has established a Ministry of Decentralisation headed by
Fr John Momis whose activities on behalf of his native province,
the North Solomons, have already resulted in considerable devolu-
tion of powers to that area.

        Weighed against structural change is the fact that Port
Moresby now appears to be growing faster than any other urban
centre.   The national government, which is not only the single
largest employer but also the magnet attracting employment in the
private sector, is firmly entrenched in Port Moresby.   In addition,
the new government has publicly announced its intention of giving
priority to urban industrialisation.   If this adheres to previous
policies on industrial location in Papua New Guinea, it will mean
priority to Lae and Port Moresby.   The lack of success of other
Third World countries in restructuring their economic geographies
must also give rise to considerable scepticism on Papua New Guinea's
chances in this field.

                            7.   CONCLUSIONS

The problems of housing in Papua New Guinea can be looked at from
two standpoints: either as a set of individual problems or as a
symptom of the problems of urbanisation as a whole.   Despite the
political emphasis given in this chapter to the need for policies
dealing with the latter, these two areas are closely related.   The
causal link between urbanisation and housing is one which is part
of the substance of the chapter, but the possibility of using housing
as a means of reforming overall urban patterns should not be over-
looked.   Similarly, although isolated housing solutions have been

condemned as 'cosmetic' in view of the need for the restructuring
of the urban skeleton, the emphasis has been somewhat rhetorical
and unrealistic.   Cosmetic policies have their uses, but serve
only to highlight those features of a structure that are themselves
attractive and which function well.   Too often the cosmetic
measures of housing planners in countries like Papua New Guinea are
basically skin lighteners.   However, there do exist methods of
tackling housing problems in isolation from overall urban problems
which can make a useful contribution towards the solution of
housing problems.

Three 'cosmetic' housing problems exist in Papua New Guinea.
First, there is excessive subsidisation of housing for high income
earners.   In 1975, according to the *National Housing Plan Part I*,
there were approximately 10,250 high cost houses in the urban areas
of Papua New Guinea.   If we assume that three-quarters of these
are occupied by persons receiving a rental subsidy and assume that
the average rental subsidy, for expatriates as well as Papua New
Guineans, is somewhat higher than the figure of K27 per fortnight
indicated in the Household Expenditure Survey (Bureau of Statistics,
1977) then 7688 households receive a weekly rent subsidy of between
K15 and K20.   This gives an annual subsidy to high cost housing of
between K6,000,000 and K8,000,000.   That is certainly a problem.
The second problem is that inadequate expenditure on low cost housing means that its supply falls a long way behind demand.   Third,
this demand is increasing at ever faster rates.

The solution to these problems must be to switch funds, which
currently subsidise high cost housing, to low cost, at the same
time transferring funds which are currently concentrated on Port
Moresby to other towns.   Of the high cost housing subsidy estimated
above, 51.9 per cent is expended in the capital.

What prevents the expedition of this simple solution?   First,
entrenched interests; the people expected to organise the transfer
of funding from one aspect of housing to another are themselves
housed in subsidised dwellings.   Even if the switch was made by an
independent body the resulting protests would be loud and long.
The public service could be expected to either come out on a prolonged strike or demand compensatory wage increases or both.   Many
public servants might resign and return to their home areas.   This,
of course, would be one way to solve the housing problem.   Second,
even if the greater part of housing funds were expended on site and
service schemes, is it likely that the spontaneous success achieved
by some 'squatter' settlements could be repeated within a formalised
organisation?   Emphasis on self-help schemes would almost certainly
lead to an even greater degree of ethnic segregation than already
exists in the towns.   Nevertheless, if there is to be segregation
of one sort or another, perhaps ethnic separation is preferable to
socio-economic division.   A third source of difficulty is the
general political opposition in Papua New Guinea to urban expenditure.   The National Housing Commission has estimated that if all
expected housing demands up to 1987 were met by site and service
schemes the cost (K4,000,000 to K6,000,000 per year) would be five
to eight times cheaper than a solution based entirely upon formal
housing provision.   Despite such savings, there exist in Papua New
Guinea lobbies powerful enough to prevent such savings being
instituted on the grounds that even the cheapest urban housing
scheme is too expensive, is against the philosophy of rural

development, or will encourage more migration.   However, the
point is that the rough estimate, given above, of present subsidies
to high income earners' housing exceeds the estimated cost for
housing the whole of the urban population by site and service means.

     With regard to general urbanisation patterns in Papua New
Guinea, solutions are less obvious.   However, given that government is the direct employer of more than 35 per cent of the urban
workforce and probably more, then any decentralisation policy must
examine this source of employment from the outset.   Without a lead
from government it would seem very unlikely that any other employers
would be anxious to bring employment and services to the smaller
towns.   To begin to achieve anything like a real decentralisation,
the provision of housing must itself be transformed.   The history
of housing in the country is full of examples of how policies and
laws can discriminate in favour of one group, one area, one class.
The real lesson to be learned, if the wish to create new patterns
is a truly serious one, is that such discriminatory laws can be
reversed: if the other class, other areas, other groups are to be
favoured then the law and its practitioners, the world's chameleons,
are at the policy-makers' disposal.

REFERENCES

Allen, B.J. and Jackson,   *Boundary Road, Lae, Housing and Family*
R.T. (1975),   *Conditions,* Department of Geography,
                            University of Papua New Guinea, Port
                            Moresby.

Bryant, J.J. (1977),   Access to housing, unpublished M.A.
                            thesis in Geography, University of
                            Papua New Guinea, Port Moresby [in
                            preparation].

Forbes, D.K. and   *A Survey of Nuigo Settlement, Wewak,*
Jackson, R.T. (1975),   Department of Geography, University of
                            Papua New Guinea, Port Moresby.

Garnaut, R., Wright, M.   *Employment, Income and Migration in*
and Curtain, R. (1977),   *Papua New Guinea Towns,* Institute of
                            Applied Social and Economic Research,
                            Port Moresby [forthcoming].

Inglis, A. (1974),   *Not a White Woman Safe: Sexual Anxiety*
                            and Politics in Port Moresby, 1920-1934,
                            Canberra.

Jackson, R. (ed.) (1976),   *Introduction to the Urban Geography of*
                            Papua New Guinea, Occasional Paper 13,
                            University of Papua New Guinea, Port
                            Moresby.

Jackson, R. (1977),   *Kiunga Development Study,* Ministry of
                            Finance, Papua New Guinea, Port Moresby.

Jackson, R., Fitzpatrick,   'The Law and Urbanisation' in R. Jackson
P. and Blaxter, L. (1976), (ed.), *Introduction to the Urban*
                            Geography of Papua New Guinea, Occasional
                            Paper 13, Department of Geography,
                            University of Papua New Guinea, Port
                            Moresby, pp. 71-87.

May, R.J. (1977),   *The Artifact Industry: Maximising*
                            Returns to Producers, Discussion Paper
                            8, The Institute of Applied Social and
                            Economic Research, Port Moresby.

Papua New Guinea Bureau   *Household Expenditure Survey, Port*
of Statistics (1977),   *Moresby: Preliminary Bulletin,* Govern-
                            ment Printer, Port Moresby.

Papua New Guinea Ministry   *Self-Help Housing Settlements for Urban*
of Interior (1973),   *Areas,* Government Printer, Port Moresby.

Papua New Guinea Ministry   *National Housing Plan Part I*, Govern-
  of Interior (1975),   ment Printer, Port Moresby.

Papua New Guinea National   *Population, Urbanisation and Employment,
  Planning Office (1975),   1971-1981*, Manpower Planning Unit,
                             Discussion Paper No. 1, Port Moresby.

Plocki, Z. (1975),   *Towards a Melanesian Style in Archi-
                             tecture*, Occasional Paper 3, Institute
                             of Papua New Guinea Studies, Port
                             Moresby.

Slater, D. (1976),   'Anglo-Saxon Geography and the Study of
                             Underdevelopment', *Antipode*, 8(3),
                             pp. 88-93.

Williamson, P.G. (1977),   Is There an Urban Informal Sector or
                             Just Poverty?, *Yagl Ambu* [forthcoming].

PART III

TRANSPORT: OVERVIEW

PETER J. RIMMER[*]

Transport's pivotal role in moving people and goods in Southeast
Asia and the Pacific has resulted in individual countries devoting
10 per cent to 20 per cent (and even more) of their Gross Domestic
Product (GDP) per annum to the transport sector (World Bank, 1972).
As the *Southeast Asian Regional Transport Survey* (Little, 1972)
demonstrates this investment is earmarked for improving international shipping facilities to handle container ships; strengthen-
ing internal transport networks through the development of national
highway systems, the upgrading of railroads and the initiation of
urban expressways; expanding intercontinental airports; and revamp-
ing administrative arrangements.   This proposed investment reflects
the priorities afforded shipments of overseas exports, tourists and
urban congestion.   Despite these besetting transport problems and
priorities Peter Rimmer (Chapter 8) and Dean Forbes (Chapter 9) deal
with trishaws, Howard Dick (Chapter 10) examines junks and *prahus*
and Harold Brookfield (Chapter 11) considers auxiliary schooners in
the Caribbean and their negligible role in the Pacific.   As transport planners in Southeast Asia and the Pacific may be puzzled by
the emphasis on the spontaneous, non-hierarchical, labour-intensive
traditional sector, there is a need to justify these particular
studies.

Three major reasons are given for justifying expatriate
transport studies in Southeast Asia and the Pacific:

(a)   the aims of existing transport policies (and the direct or
        indirect involvement of developed countries) are considered
        to be inimical to the short or long-term interests of Third
        World countries;

(b)   there are options for improvement that are not being pursued;

(c)   the research has lessons for developed countries.

Inimical policies

Encouraged by developed country purveyors of advanced transport technology, governments in Southeast Asia and the Pacific have
perceived their role as stimulating the development of the modern
transport sector — a policy that implies not only the spread of
'modern' technology but also the spread of rational bureaucratic

---

* Dr P.J. Rimmer is Senior Fellow, Department of Human Geography,
Research School of Pacific Studies, The Australian National
University, Canberra.

organisation.   This policy is pursued by active discrimination in
favour of the foreign and state-owned corporate enterprise through
the granting of monopoly status, the provision of infrastructure,
and through low (or negative) interest rates and tax concessions.
The 'traditional' sector is neglected and largely unregulated except
when it comes into conflict with the heavily regulated 'modern'
sector.   Where conflicts have occurred restraints have been imposed
on the former, such as limiting the number of trishaws as in Penang;
restricting their area of operation, as in Jakarta; and by neglect-
ing to provide adequate infrastructure, as in the case of *prahus* in
Indonesia.

        All four transport chapters suggest that the modernisation
policy is, in varying degrees, incompatible with the short and long-
term interests of the different study areas.   Rational bureaucratic
organisations, whether operating transport or marketing systems, are
invariably inappropriate when matched against the realities of the
social and cultural environment in both Southeast Asia and the
Pacific.   Conversely, enterprises operating trishaws, *prahus* and
auxiliary schooners are relatively efficient and give a high level
of service (no public subsidy is required — or available).   Despite
their apparent fragility these enterprises are most resilient in
the face of severe constraints.   Governments would do well to
abandon their modernisation policy, which involves the motorisation
of unmechanised units, and remove discrimination from these unincorporated enterprises.   Indeed, these chapters will have succeeded
if they give trishaws, *prahus* and junks visibility and respectability by removing the stigma of a poor man's technology from them and
encourage policy-makers to make fuller use of their potential (not
only as movers of goods and people but as possible suppliers of
jobs, manpower training and skills).

        In making this policy switch it must be remembered that
governments cannot consider transport in a vacuum because of its
reciprocal relationships with other activities.   As Forbes highlights in Chapter 9 any precipitate reduction in the number of
trishaws in Ujung Pandang would have serious repercussions on urban-
rural interdependence.   The need to ensure that rural areas have an
equitable share of trade between town and country is highlighted by
Brookfield in Chapter 11 which focuses on the key role of small
schooners in facilitating small-scale trading in the Caribbean and
on the fact that the marine informal sector in the Pacific has
almost perished.

        These observations can be distilled into a fresh set of guide-
lines which Third World countries may offer advisors and manufacturers from developed countries.

(a)   Do not force us to import expensive capital equipment,
       replacement parts and high powered techniques;

(b)   do not give us energy-inefficient 'solutions';

(c)   do not give us transport systems that will worsen our
       countries as places to live and work in;

(d)   do give us jobs as well as mobility;

(e)   do not forget existing transport systems and non-corporate
        organisations and practices — build on them;

(f)   remember we cannot afford your Paris Metros, your San
        Francisco BARTS, your Tokyo Mono Rails, nor even your loss-
        making public bus systems*.

Options

        There are alternatives to state-owned corporate enterprises.
However, these are masked in our binary view of the world reflected
in technological and organisational dichotomies.   There is scope
for 'intermediate' non-corporate enterprises operating both modern
and intermediate technologies as noted by Dick in Chapter 10.
Brookfield also draws attention to the need for 'intermediate
marketing organisations' in Fiji.   Opportunities for the leasing
of units operated by corporate enterprises by non-corporate enterprises was not canvassed in the transport set of chapters but it is
a proposition worth considering.   Indeed, there is a need to focus
more attention on the role and institutional framework of non-
corporate organisations operating trucks, jeepneys, *bemos* in Indonesia, *silors* in Thailand, barges and minibuses; they offer a
fruitful topic for investigation.

        There is also scope for resolving transport problems by non-
transport solutions through, for example, changing the timing of
activities in space and over time.   Rimmer recognises in Chapter 8 the
possibility of trade-offs between transport and land use in Penang.
However, these opportunities are not discussed fully in the monograph because the set of transport chapters are supply-oriented.
As there is no chapter on transport demand we cannot highlight
variations in the availability of transport to different income
groups.   Although low income groups have major food, housing and
job problems all income groups have linkage problems.   An emphasis
on connecting shelter and jobs via the transport system would have
exposed interdependencies between transport and the other problem
areas — food distribution and shelter.   This suggests that we
need to look beyond transport (which is not a reasonable social
objective in its own right) to the more fundamental objective of
mobility and, ultimately, to the matter of *access* in society.

        As Britton (1977, p. 33) emphasises:

        The basic social objective is *exchange* and *interaction*,
        which can be attained through either *moving the person
        or the message* (i.e. there would be both telecom and
        transport options).   In the "vocabulary" of the planner
        this has been interpreted largely as [the] technical
        challenge of providing *adequate transit*.   However, we
        are now beginning to think in terms of the broader objec-
        tive of *mobility*, although the real problem ultimately
        boils down to the much more fundamental problem of
        improved access.

---

* Paraphrased from an address by Enrico Macchia, Acting President,
Organisation for Economic Co-operation and Development (OECD)
Development Centre to the First International Para Transit Workshop
held at Abbaye de Royaumont Asnières-sur-Oise, France, 30 June 1977.

Since *access* is the ultimate objective the methods of transport discussed in this monograph have much to commend them.

Lessons for developed countries

The organisation and operation of informal transport enterprises in Southeast Asia and the Pacific have important lessons for
developed countries as illustrated by reference to urban public
transport.   Davis (1977) reports a shift in developed countries
from complicated capital-intensive transport networks, typified by
underground and surface railways, towards flexible, more labour-
intensive smaller vehicles exemplified by buses, trucks and taxis.
This process has been continued in public transport by para-transit
schemes such as dial-a-ride, demand responsive bus systems, shared
taxis and van pooling.   Many of these schemes have been implemented
with little knowledge of the rich variety of para-transit systems in
Southeast Asia.   Unfortunately, few of these versatile and responsive transport enterprises involving some type of vehicle sharing,
collective taxi or route deviation minibus have been documented.

There is little published information on non-corporate enterprises operating urban passenger services in Southeast Asia and the
Pacific apart from Textor's (1961) examination of the now defunct
pedicab operations in Bangkok, Grava's (1972) investigation of
jeepneys in Manila, Critchfield's (1970) excellent study of a
Jakarta trishaw rider and sundry notes on low cost transport in
Southeast Asia and elsewhere as instanced by Cottee (1975), and
Jacobs and Fouracre (1976).   While these studies are not without
considerable merit they provide inadequate bases for planning
similar operations in developed countries.   It is hoped that the
studies in this volume will not only help fill this gap but will
also emphasise the importance of considering both land *and* sea
transport.

Investigations of informal transport enterprises in Southeast
Asia and the Pacific should also deepen our conceptual frameworks
and sharpen our methodological tools for re-examining transport
systems in developed countries in a new light.   Unlike Southeast
Asia and the Pacific many of the mistakes in transport investment
in developed countries can be camouflaged by capital expenditure on
alternatives.

REFERENCES

Britton, F.E.K. (1977),   *Para Transit in the Developing World: Neglected Options for Mobility and Employment; Volume I: Workshop Proceedings and Program Recommendations from the First International Para Transit Workshop held at Asnieres-sur-Oise, France, 30 June - 2 July 1977*, Development Centre, OECD, Paris.

Cottee, R. (1975),   'The'll be one along in a minute': Madrid's 'Middle-class' Microbuses Are Making the Old Saying Come True', *Commercial Motor* (page numbers not available).

Critchfield, R. (1970),   *Hello Mister Where Are You Going: The Story of Husen a Javanese Betjak Driver*, Alicia Patterson Fund, New York.

Davis, F.W. (1977),   *Regulatory Barriers to Innovation and the Knoxville Experience*, University of Tennessee Transportation Center TC-003, Knoxville.

Grava, S. (1972),   'The Jeepneys of Manila', *Traffic Quarterly*, 26, pp. 465-83.

Jacobs, G.D. and   'Intermediate Forms of Urban Public
 Fouracre, P. (1976),   Transport in Developing Countries', *Traffic Engineering and Control*, March, pp. 98-100.

Little, Inc. A.D. *et al.*   *Southeast Asian Regional Transport
 (1972),   Survey Book One*, Asian Development Bank, Singapore.

Textor, R.B. (1961),   *From Peasant to Pedicab Driver: A Social Study of Northeastern Thai Farmers Who Periodically Migrated to Bangkok and Became Pedicab Riders*, Yale University Southeast Asian Studies, New Haven.

World Bank (1972),   *Transportation Sector Working Paper*, Washington, D.C.

CHAPTER 8

THE FUTURE OF TRISHAW ENTERPRISES IN PENANG

PETER J. RIMMER[*]

...some...authorities are considering or have
already implemented plans to restrict or
eliminate the use of the trishaws, motor-
trishaws, 'jeepnies', and pirate taxis from
certain areas of the urban centres...In
Singapore, pirate taxis are now illegal and
have been frequently and effectively prosecuted
by police.   In Jakarta the *becak* or trishaws
are now prohibited from certain sections of the
central area.   In Manila, there are pressures
to restrict the operation of 'jeepnies'...

William Lim, *Equity and Urban Environment in
the Third World*, Singapore, 1975, pp. 130-1.

1.   INTRODUCTION

This study examines the future of the trishaw industry within
Penang (the city of Georgetown), Malaysia's second largest city
with a population of 326,000 in 1970.   It is prompted by the rapid
structural change occurring in the transport sector of the primate
cities of the Association of South-East Asian Nations (ASEAN) —
Bangkok, Jakarta, Kuala Lumpur, Manila and Singapore.   These changes
involve the encroachment of *formal* transport enterprises on the
informal transport sector.   As there is a strong tendency to pass
down changes in transport organisation from primate cities to
secondary centres, the key issue in Penang is what will happen to
informal transport activities such as trishaws and their labour
market if structural changes are precipitated by the encroachment
of formal transport enterprises.

Before proceeding with the study of the trishaw industry in
Penang there is a need to distinguish between formal and informal
transport activities.   If this terminology is defined more
precisely in terms of *corporate* and *non-corporate* enterprises it is
possible to identify the process occurring within Southeast Asian
cities and illustrate its nature by reference to the traffic
situation in a particular area of Penang.   This allows an assessment of the reasons given for wanting to ban trishaw activities in
Penang.   However, the nature of the trishaw industry has to be
considered prior to any alternative transport policies being adopted.

---

[*] Dr Peter J. Rimmer is Senior Fellow, Department of Human Geography,
Research School of Pacific Studies, The Australian National University, Canberra.

2.   CORPORATE AND NON-CORPORATE ENTERPRISES

The informal public transport sector, following International Labour Office (1972) criteria, can be characterised by its relative ease of entry for new enterprises, heavy reliance on indigenous resources, family ownership, small-scale operation, unregulated and competitive markets, labour-intensive and adapted technology, and skills acquired outside the formal education system.   In contrast, the formal public transport sector is distinguished by a converse set of attributes.   Thus, entry by new enterprises is difficult, there is a heavy dependence on foreign resources, bureaucratic organisation, large-scale operations, protected markets, capital-intensive and often imported technology and workers with formally acquired skills which are often expatriate.

     This distinction between informal and formal transport enterprises is in many cases self-evident but where there is overlap Sethuraman (1976) suggests a list of criteria for identifying the former.   An enterprise may be included in the informal public transport sector if it satisfies *one* or more of the following conditions:

(a) it employs ten persons or less (including part-time and casual workers);

(b) it operates on an illegal basis, contrary to government regulations;

(c) members of the household of the head of the enterprise work in it;

(d) it does not observe fixed hours of operation;

(e) it does not depend on formal financial institutions for its credit needs;

(f) almost all those working in it have fewer than six years of formal schooling;

(g) it does not use any mechanical power.

     When these conditions are matched against urban transport enterprises in Southeast Asia they are of varying relevance in allocating them to the informal and formal sectors.   While family connections are recognised as a prime attribute the employment condition needs refinement to distinguish between not only large and small transport enterprises but also those of medium size. Similarly, the distinction between mechanical and non-mechanical power would have to be expanded to identify not only modern and traditional vehicles but also intermediate vehicles which may be an adaptation of imported technology.   In addition, the illegality condition is inapplicable because every enterprise, formal or informal, is liable to confiscation through an alteration in national laws.   Apart from the lack of collateral by some small firms the relationship between scale of enterprise and access to institutional credit is probably overplayed in a situation where personal trust is a prime determinant.   Variable hours of operation and educational requirements are even weaker indicators because formal transport enterprises have flexible hours and varying literacy requirements.   These conditions are also more distinctive of occupational rather than enterprise characteristics.   However, the

problem with Sethuraman's attempt to put the distinction between
formal and informal transport enterprises on a more satisfactory
basis is the artificiality of dualism when matched against the complexity of the real world.

        In these circumstances it seems more apposite to avoid the
implicit connotations of the formal-informal dichotomy and distinguish between *corporate* (state or foreign-owned) transport enterprises and *non-corporate* transport enterprises which range from
individual and family units barely recognisable as firms to
registered limited liability units.   This distinction also over-
comes the problems of discussing organisation and technology.
Modern, intermediate or traditional technologies can be operated by
either corporate or non-corporate enterprises (see Chapter 10).
However, the real value of the corporate-non-corporate distinction
is that it supplies a springboard for focusing on the *process*
affecting passenger transport services in Southeast Asian cities.

3.   THE INCORPORATION PROCESS

Incorporation occurs through the penetration of the corporate public
transport sector into areas previously the exclusive sphere of non-
corporate enterprises.   Although centrally-administered and
publicly-funded corporate transport enterprises have experienced
severe fiscal problems in Western cities the incorporation process
is gathering momentum in ASEAN's primate cities.   This process is
occurring even though non-corporate enterprises are efficient movers
of people and receive no direct government grant.

        Figure 8.1A reflects what happens when a corporate enterprise
operating stage buses expands by increasing the number of units
operated.   The action diminishes the sphere of influence of 'non-
corporate organisation 2' also operating stage buses.   A chain
reaction occurs as 'non-corporate organisation 2' invades the exclusive sphere of influence of 'non-corporate organisation 1' operating
taxis or trishaws to compensate for losses.

        The anticipated impact of a second corporate enterprise opera-
ting minibuses is shown in Figure 8.1B to affect both existing
corporate and non-corporate enterprises.   The sphere of influence
of 'corporate organisation 3' operating stage buses is restricted
and 'non-corporate organisation 2' operating stage buses is further
downgraded in function.   Another chain reaction occurs as the
latter enterprise encroaches on 'non-corporate organisation 1' operating taxis or trishaws.

        Incorporation along these lines is currently occurring in the
primate cities of Southeast Asia and is closely monitored by transport planners.   However, the extension of corporate public enterprises within smaller urban areas is undertaken without much
detailed consideration.   Indeed, this study is prompted by the
prospect that the smaller Malaysian cities, such as Penang, may
receive minibus enterprises following their successful introduction
in Kuala Lumpur where they provide unscheduled services on fixed

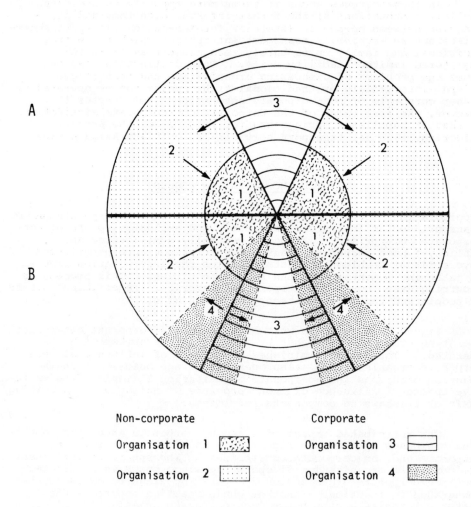

Fig. 8.1:   Schematic representation of the incorporation process.
            (A) The expansion of corporate organisation 3 creates a
            chain reaction that impacts on non-corporate organisa-
            tion 2 which, in turn, affects non-corporate organisation
            1.   (B) The intrusion of corporate organisation 4 impacts
            on corporate organisation 3 and non-corporate organisa-
            tion 2; non-corporate organisation 2, in turn, affects
            non-corporate organisation 1.

routes*.   However, the nature of their impact is difficult to
assess without an examination of the city's transport enterprises
and modes.

    As there is no scope for such a detailed analysis within this
chapter attention is focused on traffic at Magazine Circus which,
in many respects, offers a microcosm of the problems besetting
Penang's transport system.   A range of options for combatting
congestion at Magazine Circus is identified.   The most promising
option appears to be the elimination of slower vehicles such as
trishaws from the traffic mix — a strategy that would leave Penang
with the usual set of private vehicles, public buses and taxis that
serve Western urban areas.   However, a deeper understanding of the
transport task performed by the unmapped and little explored trishaw
operations prompts caution against action to restrict or prohibit
them before their future role is considered.

4.   MAGAZINE CIRCUS

Three children travelling by trishaw to their respective Malay,
Tamil and Chinese primary schools are delayed at Magazine Circus,
shown in Figure 8.2.   The hold-up at 1 p.m. is caused by pedestrians, other trishaws, handcarts, bicycles, trade tricycles, motor-
cycles, lorries, school minibuses and private cars edging their way
in a poorly disciplined manner around the Circus to exit by their
chosen route.   As this delay is likely to be only two minutes the
congestion at Magazine Circus is surpassed in its intensity by other
traffic situations occurring in ASEAN's primate cities.   However,
as all roads leading to and from Magazine Circus are near capacity
and the area bounded by Maxwell Road, Magazine Road and Penang Road
is being redeveloped as a shopping-office-bus terminal complex, the
Penang situation is sufficiently analogous to illustrate the dilemma
facing the expatriate and Western-trained indigenous transport
planners — what policies to adopt to overcome the congestion
problem facing the secondary cities of Southeast Asia?

    The congestion illustrated by the delay to school children at
Magazine Circus could be tackled in several different ways:

(a) capital could be expended on building a bridge, street widening
    and improvements to road intersections;

(b) more and higher quality modern types of public transport could
    be supplied by introducing more comfortable, airconditioned and
    limited stop stage buses as outlined by Arup (1973), increasing
    the number of school buses with the right to carry other
    passengers outside school hours, and amalgamating private and
    public bus companies;

---

* Penang already has minibuses operating school and factory services.   Indeed, the minibus concept is not new to Penang as between
1925 and 1941 there were 'hired' buses operating with a motor car
or light van chassis fitted with a body that could accommodate between seven and sixteen passengers.

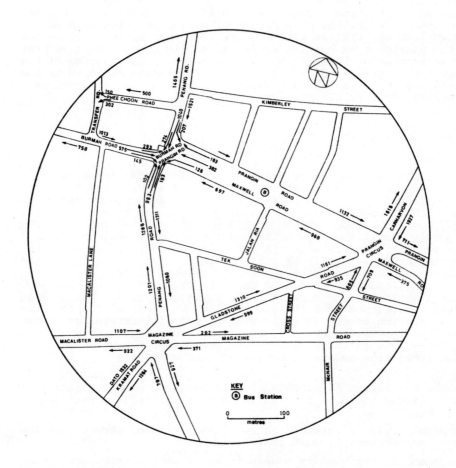

Source: Arup, 1975.

Fig. 8.2:   Average daily traffic count in the central area of
            Penang zoned for redevelopment, 1975.

(c) demand-related policies could be introduced which involve the staggering of school hours, carpooling to bring, for example, the number of occupants in private cars on school trips beyond the 2.38 persons achieved in 1975 (Arup, 1975), and establishing reserved lanes for buses;

(d) private motor cars could be restrained in congested areas through a policy of area licensing, increased parking fees and park and ride services;

(e) the nature of activities could be changed, for example, by zoning the intake of schoolchildren so that they attend the nearest school as traffic volumes decrease by between 21 per cent and 41 per cent at Magazine Circus during school holidays (Arup, 1975).

Some of the options proffered in this instance may be inappropriate to Penang. For example, zoning the area of a school's intake would not be feasible in a multi-racial society, and staggering school hours would also be difficult as schools already operate two shifts (7 a.m. - 12.30 p.m. and 1 p.m. - 6.30 p.m.). Traffic restraint based on the Singapore model also would be too elaborate for Penang.

However, the overriding danger in Penang, as in other secondary Southeast Asian cities, is that the authorities will attempt to resolve urban traffic problems through 'the primate city method' of urban redevelopment and road widening. Invariably, this method is coupled with the restriction or prohibition of the slower transport modes such as trishaws because no attempt has been made to segregate them from other forms of traffic (Kota Bharu is one exception).

A reduction in the number of trishaw enterprises can be achieved in several ways:

(a) regulation can be used to set an upper limit on the number of trishaws;

(b) restrictions can be applied to circumscribe the activities of trishaws over space and time;

(c) the trishaw can be eliminated completely.

Bangkok prohibited the trishaw from operating within the metropolitan area in 1961. Within Kuala Lumpur trishaw operations have been confined to specific streets in the city's central area whereas in Jakarta they are excluded from the central city area for much of the day. In contrast, Penang has been content to set an upper limit on the number of trishaws.

On 29.11.69 Council decided that no new trisha licences be issued but transfers be allowed among trisha riders registered on or before 26.8.69. Riders registered after this date are not to be issued with trisha licences. Thus the policy of unlimited licensing of public trishas has been discontinued (Lembaga Pengurus Kerajaan Tempatan Pulau Pinang, 1974, p. 2).

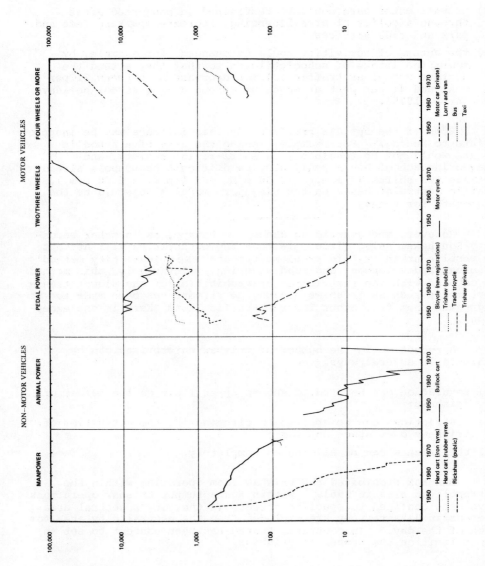

Fig. 8.3: Changes in vehicle numbers within Penang between 1946 and 1976.

As Figure 8.3 shows the impact of restrictive regulation has
resulted in a slight decline in trishaw numbers from their post-war
peak in 1969.   Such a trend is in sharp contrast to the varying
performance of new bicycle registrations and the marked increase in
the number of motor cycles, lorries and vans, taxis, buses, and
private cars (which have yet to reach a saturation point).   The
gradual erosion of trishaw numbers in Penang is too prolonged for
some interest groups and there is pressure for eliminating trishaws.
Arguments for undertaking such precipitate action are identified and
evaluated.

5.   BANNING TRISHAWS

Trishaws in Penang perform an important public transport (and goods
carrying) role in linking the main points of traffic generation and
attraction shown in Figure 8.4.   While stage buses provide long
distance scheduled services on fixed routes, school and factory
buses offer scheduled services on variable routes and minibuses
promise unscheduled services on fixed routes, taxis and trishaws
supply unscheduled personal transport services on variable routes.
Taxis concentrate on long distance trips and trishaws on short
distance trips within the urban area, particularly in the inner
city.   Trishaws possess many of the qualities desired by transport
planners — low energy requirements, non-polluting and ease of
access to the ultimate destination.   However, their operations are
under threat of further restriction and elimination.

This threat stems from the nature and type of operations.
Trishaws obstruct the smooth flow of motor traffic because of low
cruising speeds (10-15 kph) and low acceleration rates from a
standing start at an intersection.   The pedallers allegedly possess
hazardous driving habits and are reputedly accident-prone posing a
threat to passengers and other vehicles.   Passengers are also too
dependent on the personal whim and financial inducement of the
pedaller.   In addition, pedallers are accused of providing an
inadequate public service as they avoid low density areas and poor
neighbourhoods, and concentrate services at night on the local
shopping and entertainment area shown on Figure 8.5.

Such arguments have to be given varying weights.   There is
little doubt that the removal of slower vehicles from the traffic
mix would boost the practical capacity of traffic lanes from 750 pcu
(passenger car units) per hour to 1000 pcu per hour (Arup, 1975).
However, there is no evidence that trishaw pedallers monopolise bad
driving habits.   The menace they once posed to motor vehicles in
Penang has been lessened by the institution of one-way streets
because trishaws can operate in both directions without disrupting
traffic.   While poor lighting on trishaws does present a traffic
hazard at night there is little statistical evidence to suggest
that they are more accident-prone than other vehicles*.   The absence

---

* Royal Malaysian Police (1976, p. 18) indicate that trishaw riders
comprised 1.1 per cent of total casualties in 1973 and 1974.   As
these figures are not related to kilometres travelled comparisons
between modes cannot be made.

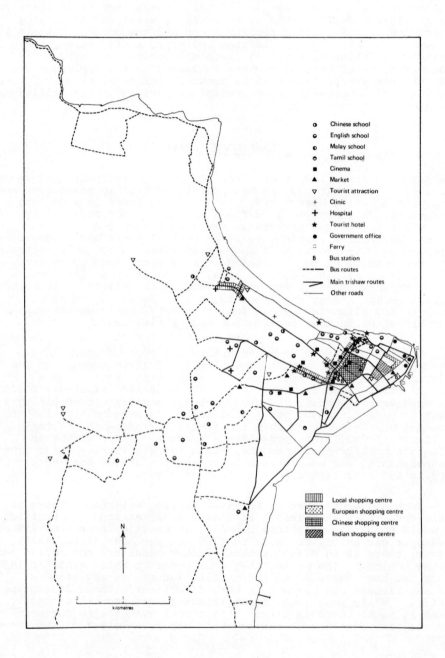

Fig. 8.4: Main points of traffic generation and attraction in
           Penang between 6 a.m. and 6 p.m., October 1976.

of effective lighting is essentially a matter of ensuring that existing regulations are enforced. These regulations also extend, in
theory, to fares, but in practice rates are negotiated and differ
according to such variables as weather, demand and the prospect of
a return fare (taxis operate in a similar fashion). While potential users may feel aggrieved by these practices, trishaws do
provide a service beyond the limits of the stage bus network. However, as they are demand-responsive they cannot be expected to
provide a total coverage of the urban area during day and night
(Figs 8.4 and 8.5).

These reasons are unlikely to persuade local government to
abandon its passive attitude towards trishaw operations in Penang.
Hence, proponents for abandoning trishaws claim that they pose
social and transport problems. Trishaw enterprises supposedly
induce overurbanisation by encouraging rural migration to the city.
Pedallers, because of their inflated numbers, are allegedly prone
to exploitation by unscrupulous owners, while their absence of
permanent workplace (and, sometimes, residence) makes them difficult to control by licensing. Trishaw pedallers are also held to
constitute a security problem because they provide the opportunity
for self-serving enterprise such as drug pushing or petty theft.
In addition, the pedalling of trishaws is also perceived as a
humiliating activity because it involves exploitation of man by man.

Again, such reasons carry varying weights. A random survey
in Penang covering 112 trishaw pedallers, indicates that two-thirds
of them were born within the city and do not correspond to the
rural migrant stereotype. Although it would be difficult to
claim that there is a universal bond of paternalism between owner
and pedallers, exploitation is largely confined to hiring defective
vehicles — on the other hand, the besetting problem of the owner
seems to be how to obtain the daily hire from the pedaller. The
licensing of riders does create a bureaucratic problem but it is
essentially a matter of local government enforcement. While
trishaw pedallers provide a convenient scapegoat for various social
ills, such as drug pushing and petty theft, there is no guarantee
that the various practices will disappear with the elimination of
trishaw enterprises. In countering these arguments for prohibiting
trishaws, there is no desire to condemn a man to the hard life of
trishaw pedalling with its precarious income but there is no alternative employment in Penang which will absorb an aging and relatively unskilled workforce.

This catalogue of arguments for eliminating the trishaw should
not be overemphasised. Lim (1975, p. 130) states that the real
reason for demanding their prohibition is that they create an image
of underdevelopment. While trishaws are perceived by the urban
élite as a poor man's technology they do possess many desirable
service features. It is important that these be given visibility
and respectability so that policy-makers are encouraged to make full
use of their potential. Before considering how this can be done it
is necessary to examine trishaw enterprises in terms of their
capacity for raising incomes and promoting employment.

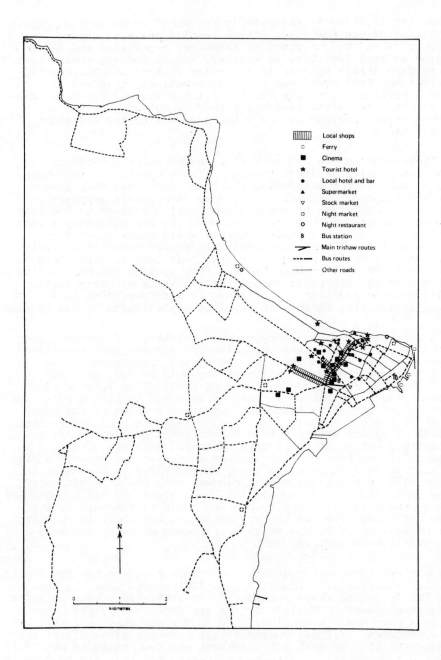

Fig. 8.5: Main points of traffic generation and attraction in
           Penang between 6 p.m. and 12 midnight (2 a.m. Sundays
           and public holidays), October 1976.

6. TRISHAW ENTERPRISES

A survey of trishaw enterprises in Penang was made during October
1976 in order to identify the factors that restrict employment
potential and earnings of participants in the non-corporate transport sector.   The enterprise is broadly defined to:

> include any economic unit engaged in the production of
> ... [transport] services — whether it employs only one
> person (the proprietor) or more; whether or not it uses
> fixed capital; whether or not it has a fixed location
> for business (Sethuraman, 1976, p. 76).

Thus, a trisha-pedaller is treated as constituting an individual
enterprise although he hires no employees, owns little capital and
has no fixed business location.

Information derived from the survey can be grouped into
Sethuraman's (1976) three categories:

(a)   *the enterprise and its linkages with the economy* — location,
main and subsidiary activities, history, legal constraints,
vehicle ownership and operating characteristics including
sources of labour, capital and materials;

(b)   *head of enterprise* — sex, age, native language, formal
education and training, father's occupation, business
associates and attitudes to local government policies and
possibility of alternative location, occupation or activities;

(c)   *household of head of enterprise* — degree to which other
members of household work in the enterprise, participate in
the workforce, contribute to household income or are unemployed.

According to the registers of the local council (Lembaga
Pengurus Kerajaan Tempatan Pulau Pinang) there were 583 enterprises
operating 2445 trishaws in October 1976.   Of these enterprises 539
were operated by owner-pedallers — 536 were owner-pedalled and
three were officially allowed to hire their vehicles to other
pedallers.   The remaining 1906 trishaws belong to forty-four
multiple owners of which the largest five enterprises held 42 per
cent of the total trishaw fleet and the top ten over 53 per cent.
However, the balance has shifted in favour of the single owners as
the effect of the regulation instituted by the local council in
1969 is to transfer ownership from multiple to single owners — a
move fostered by a reduction in the Public Trisha Licence fee
applicable to single owner drivers from $M30 to $M18* from 1
January 1970 (Lembaga Pengurus Kerajaan Tempatan Pulau Pinang, 1974).
Thus, as there are marked differences in the basic conditions,
structure and conduct of multiple and single owner enterprises they
are considered separately.

---

*   The exchange rate was approximately $A1 = $M2.70 on 21 November
1977.

Multiple owners

As ownership cannot be transferred from one member of the family to another, interest in examining the multiple-owned enterprise is centred on their capacity to move out into other activities. Hence, much effort was devoted to locating and defining the nature of the multiple-owned trishaw enterprises before discussing their conduct.

When the survey of the structure of multiple owner enterprises commenced there were difficulties in reconciling registered fleets and trishaws listed by the owner until it was realised that the largest fleet held by the Trishaw Riders Association included vehicles belonging to multiple owners. If these trishaws are transferred to the multiple owners the number of enterprises is increased to 610. Among the revised number of seventy-one multiple owners the Trishaw Riders Association remains as the leading owner in terms of numbers but the shares of the five largest owners is reduced to 30 per cent and the top ten to almost 42 per cent. A further revision is necessary because a further twenty-seven trishaws registered by the Trishaw Riders Association belonged to four existing multiple owners and the remaining 264 to single owners. If these are redistributed the largest five enterprises have 22 per cent and the top ten over 33 per cent of the total fleet.

These figures are still a misleading guide to the number and spatial concentration of enterprises because ownership is fragmented among families which are effectively working as a single enterprise. This problem can be countered, to some extent, by grouping the trishaw fleets of owners with the same address. As Table 8.1 shows the number of multiple owners is reduced to fifty-five and the share of the first five enterprises is increased to almost 25 per cent of the total fleet and the top ten to over 37 per cent.

This revision does not accommodate multiple owners located at different addresses who combine to operate a single enterprise, although there is evidence that such connections exist. In addition, fourteen multiple owners gave accommodation addresses at which there were no visible signs of a trishaw business being conducted.

Apart from eight multiple owners who could not be located the remaining thirty-three owners had some visible connection with the trishaw business. Ten enterprises operated from premises devoted to business uses other than transport, such as a coffee shop and a secondhand business, which presumably offered some alternative income to trishaw ownership. Three other enterprises were reputed to perform brokerage services in providing registration plates for new and refurbished vehicles.

Trishaws were subsidiary to other activities in seven of these enterprises. Five enterprises hired trishaws as an adjunct to their bicycle repair business, one enterprise was primarily devoted to manufacturing trishaws and trade tricycles, while another concentrated on manufacturing ancillary equipment such as hoods. The remaining thirteen enterprises were primarily hirers

TABLE 8.1:   DISTRIBUTION OF TRISHAW OWNERSHIP
PENANG, OCTOBER 1976

Number of vehicles	Registered ownership in local council records	Redistribution of multiple owners in Trishaw Riders Association	Redistribution of remaining vehicles in Trishaw Riders Association	Amalgamation of multiple owners with identical addresses
1	539	539	830	830
2- 5	9	23	20	15
6- 10	4	10	9	8
11- 15	6	7	7	6
16- 20	4	7	6	4
21- 25	1	2	3	2
26- 30	3	4	4	3
31- 35	1	1	1	2
36- 40	4	4	4	0
41- 45	1	1	1	1
46- 50	1	1	1	2
51-100	7	8	8	10
101-250	2	2	2	2
251-500	0	1	0	0
Over 500	1	0	0	0
Total	583	610	896	885

of trishaws.   These enterprises had capacity for repairing trishaws
(including welding); some also manufactured ancillary equipment and
had proven capacity for manufacturing trishaws as and when required.
It is this hard core of specialist trishaw enterprises that will
presumably have the greatest difficulty in shifting to other activities.

As with all others, these specialist enterprises, with the
exception of a sole Malay owner, were established by overseas
migrants and their immediate families with little business experience,
education or capital.   A close examination indicated that they were
experiencing some difficulties.   In October 1976 approximately one-
quarter of their fleet was in dock awaiting hire or undergoing
repair.   Such statistics should not cause undue surprise because
these stocks are an essential feature of any hiring business.   An
analysis of local council records shows that there were 1727
registered trishaw pedallers in October 1976 with an average age of
48 years (mode 49 years).   Even with an allowance of 200 pedallers
yet to be registered demand fell short of the number of trishaws
for hire.

No enterprise reported buying a new trishaw between 1974 and
1976.   A new trishaw costs between $M650 and $M750 and has an
anticipated working life of ten years.   An owner would expect to
recover this outlay within two years on receipt of a premium daily
rental of $M1.20 — the average rates were $M0.80 per day or $M24
per month.   However, owners only received 70 per cent of their

expected rental as pedallers default on payments.   As there was no
prospect of raising hire charges without losing the trishaw pedaller
to another owner and with repair costs rising, these owners were
experiencing dwindling returns.   They could, to some extent,
cushion the impact of falling returns by either requesting deferral
of their licensing fee or withdrawing some trishaws from operation
to avoid paying the licensing fee — a practice that would not
deprive them of the operating licence.

Apart from one owner who had moved into taxis there was little
attempt to shift into other activities such as motor cycles and
school buses.   The operators claimed that credit was only available at high interest rates and under strict conditions.   It was
not surprising, therefore, that the one-third of tricycle manufac-
turer's output devoted to trishaws is for owner-pedallers.   As
total production appeared to be only thirty vehicles per year trishaw
production was unlikely to provide much of an incubator for the
development of technical skills.

Owner-pedallers

The prime interest in examining owner-pedallers is to dis-
cover the extent to which their personal incomes are raised by
ownership.   Thus, the emphasis is on isolating a group of owner-
pedallers to match against hired pedallers.

Such an exercise poses the problem of how to draw a sample
from an estimated 1000 pedallers hiring vehicles from multiple
owners, together with the 830 owner-pedallers comprising 539 single
owners operating on their own account and 264 single owners managed
by the Trishaw Riders Association.   There is little point in trying
to trace pedallers to addresses given in local council records
because they are not only extremely mobile but may also sleep in
their trishaw.   The dilemma was resolved by studying 112 trishaw
pedallers interviewed in the course of trying to trace 516 randomly
selected trishas — a 20 per cent sample of the licence plate
numbers allocated to trishaws in Penang.

Of the 112 trishaw pedallers interviewed twenty-one owned
their own vehicles and ninety-one hired them.   When these ownership patterns were compared with local council records there were
some surprises.   Five of the pedallers claiming to be single owners
had vehicles registered in the names of multiple owners.   Nine
vehicles in the survey registered as belonging to single owners
were pedalled by hirers.   Such results highlight the problems of
drawing sample populations within the non-corporate sector.

Bearing this cautionary note in mind the information on owners
and hirers is compared in terms of Sethuraman's (1976) three
categories (Table 8.2).

1.   *Enterprise and its linkages with the economy*

Owners had a marginally higher target income than hirers.
Most of them bought their trishaw through savings but others
borrowed, used their pension or lottery winnings.   On average

TABLE 8.2:   CHARACTERISTICS OF SAMPLE GROUP OF OWNER-

PEDALLERS AND HIRERS, OCTOBER 1976

		Owners (n=21)	Hirers (n=91)
Enterprise			
1.	Average daily target income ($M)	6.1	5.8
2.	Principal source of capital for buying trishaw (per cent)		
	savings	38.1	-
	borrowed	19.1	-
	pension	14.3	-
	lottery	14.3	-
	not available	14.3	-
3.	Average riding experience (years)	14.8	10.6
4.	Permanent stand (per cent)		
	with	38.1	24.2
	without	61.9	75.8
5.	Contract (per cent)		
	with	38.1	16.5
	without	61.9	83.5
6.	Full-time pedaller (per cent)		
	full-time	95.2	94.5
	part-time	4.8	5.5
7.	Main market (per cent)		
	outside rider	19.1	64.8
	school	38.1	8.8
	other	42.8	26.4
Personal characteristics			
1.	Language group (per cent)		
	Chinese	66.7	30.8
	Indian	23.8	30.8
	Malay	9.5	38.4
2.	Average age (years)	48.6	40.3
3.	Birthplace (per cent)		
	Penang	76.2	70.3
	elsewhere	23.8	29.7
4.	Residence (years)		
	Penang	46.3	30.7
5.	Education (average number of years at school)	2.7	4.0
6.	Marital status (per cent)		
	married	85.7	72.5
	not married	14.3	27.5
7.	Language (per cent)		
	English speaking	19.1	26.4
	non-English speaking	80.9	73.6
8.	Motor driving licence (per cent)		
	with	9.5	9.9
	without	90.5	90.1
9.	Aspirations (per cent)		
	own trishaw	-	19.8
	other business	-	80.2
10.	Main reason for becoming pedaller (per cent)		
	contract finished	28.6	24.2
	low wages	9.5	19.5
	no other work	33.3	32.1
	other	28.6	24.2
11.	Main reason for not moving out of pedalling (per cent)		
	no opportunities	33.3	50.0
	too old	23.9	3.4
	other	42.8	46.6
12.	Last job (per cent)		
	agricultural worker	9.5	0.0
	urban labourer	38.1	27.5
	factory worker	14.3	22.0
	unemployed	4.8	27.5
	other	33.3	23.1
13.	Father's occupation (per cent)		
	agricultural worker	4.8	13.3
	urban labourer	14.3	17.3
	factory worker	19.1	12.0
	other	61.8	57.4
Household characteristics			
1.	Average number of dependants	4.6	3.5

the owners had been riding longer.   More of the owners had
permanent stands and fixed contracts especially to carry
schoolchildren.   The majority of hirers were 'outside riders'
who travelled around the city looking for custom rather than
remain at one of the regular stands shown in Figure 8.6.

2.   *Personal characteristics*

Chinese speakers predominated among owners whereas the three
major language groups were more evenly represented among
hirers.   The owners were on average older than the hirers.
Most were Penang-born having spent most of their life in the
city.   In contrast, the hirers had spent longer at school,
and relatively more could speak English.   One-fifth of the
hirers had aspirations of becoming an owner-pedaller.   Both
types of pedaller moved into trishaw riding because of either
the termination of contracts or unemployment — low wages in
existing occupations was a reason specifically attracting the
hirers.   The pedallers did not move out due to the lack of
alternative employment opportunities.   In particular, many
of the owners considered themselves too old for another
occupation.   However, there was no marked variation between
owners and hirers in their father's occupational status.

3.   *Family characteristics*

There was little difference between owners and hirers in the
number of dependants.   The owners and hirers were unanimous
in not wanting their sons to become trishaw riders because
they considered the life to be too hard.

These comparisons are suggestive rather than definitive.
However, the emphasis on the variables that determine a trishaw
pedaller's income — characteristics of the enterprise on which his
income depends, personal characteristics and family characteristics
— may indicate how the income of trishaw riders might be improved
thus increasing their access to food and shelter.   Before pursuing
this goal it is important to consider the trishaw's role in the
light of possible developments in transport policy.

                7.   MODERNISATION FOR MODERNISATION'S SAKE

The questions we should now ask are:- Should [this mode]
of transportation be eliminated? in what other ways
will the...working population travel to work, the housewives to market, and the children to schools?   [Is this]
mode of transportation in any way obstructing the process
of urban development?   Are there alternative employment
opportunities for...trishaw riders?   What are the basic
reasons for the increasing chaos of the central area?
(Lim, 1975, p. 131).

Trishaws in Penang have many desirable features.   While trishaws
may not provide Grava's (1976) seedbeds for the acquisition of
technical and entrepreneurial skills they do provide personalised,
demand responsive, high frequency and highly accessible transport

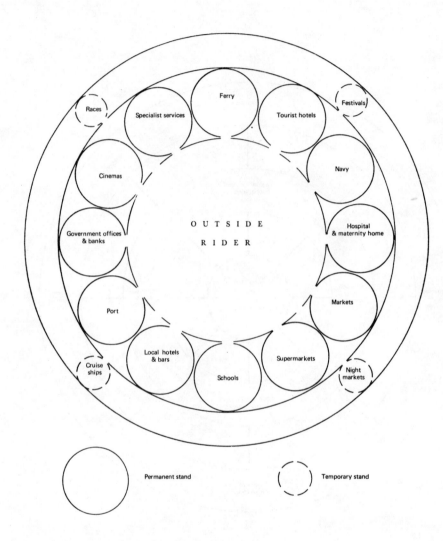

Fig. 8.6: Permanent and temporary stands used by trishaw pedallers in Penang, October 1976. 'Outside rider' is the term given to a pedaller who travels round the city looking for custom.

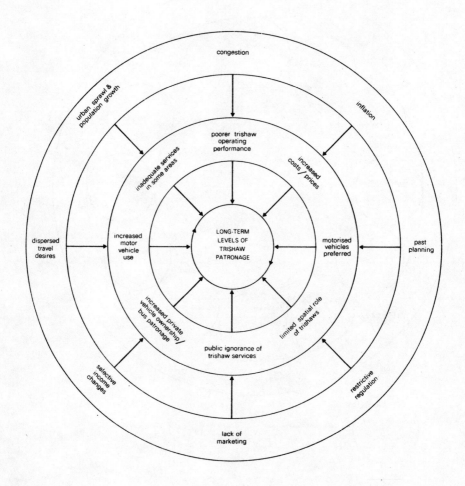

Fig. 8.7: Factors impinging on long-term trishaw patronage,
           October 1976 (adapted from Commonwealth Bureau of
           Roads, 1976, p. 102).

services closely attuned to local needs.   Besides being labour
absorptive in situations of chronic unemployment and underemployment these non-corporate enterprises have the added advantage of
flexibility as to route, destination and time of journey — a
feature that proponents of para transit services, such as dial-a-
ride, demand-responsive buses, shared taxis, bus pooling and self-
drive taxis, hope to emulate in Western cities.   Although they
offer an alternative to the private car and corporate public
transport, their future is clouded.

As indicated in Figure 8.7, it is expected that the long-term
patronage of trishaws will be threatened by external forces.   These
include increases in average income and its reflection in the
growth of car ownership; the decentralisation of population, jobs
and services; restrictive regulations; lack of marketing; and
inflation.   There may also be a decreasing demand for trishaws
because one's status in Southeast Asia is perceived very much by
one's mode of travel.   However, if there is a concern with what
Wilson (1972) terms 'accessibility provision' rather than congestion *per se*, there is still a role for the trishaw because it is
closely tailored to the prevailing land use in the inner city.

Any attempt at modernisation through restricting or eliminating
trishaws would not only deprive workers, housewives, schoolchildren
and the sick of a valuable transport service but would have serious
repercussions on the industry's employment potential.   The trishaw
industry's capacity to survive will be tested further if minibuses
are introduced or private non-corporate bus enterprises are incorporated.   The latter threat may not be so immediate because
corporate and non-corporate stage bus enterprises work under
different labour laws.   However, if incorporation or the introduction of minibuses did occur the trishaw industry may come under
pressure at a time when it has been weakened by deconcentration of
ownership.   This process is occurring through the policy of encouraging owner-pedallers at the expense of multiple owner enterprises.   Unless the future of the trishaw industry is guaranteed,
such a policy may merely be a means of transferring obsolete equipment to those least able to afford it and, irrespective of its good
intentions, will not provide the desired springboard for generating
new enterprises.

If an expansion of job opportunities accommodates the trishaw
workforce, it is important that the rich variety of intermediate
modes, such as auto-trishaws and jeepneys are examined.   These
alternatives may be more suited to the accessibility needs of
particular income groups than minibuses and stage buses.   It may
also be important that such activities are organised on non-
corporate lines to maintain employment, thus promoting a more
equitable distribution of income and a more efficient allocation
of resources.   Such enterprises could range from individuals and
partnerships to limited liability companies.   In particular, there
may be scope for the medium-size transport enterprises and intermediate technologies which have been consistently neglected by
decision-makers in the past.

ACKNOWLEDGEMENTS

The help received from the Lembaga Pengurus Kerajaan Tempatan Pulau
Pinang (especially Thomas Gan), the Trishaw Riders Association,
trishaw owners and trishaw pedallers is gratefully acknowledged.
In particular, the quality of field assistance provided by Nathan
Zainal is very much appreciated.   The help received from Kamal
Salih, Michael Pangiras, and Suat Choo of the Universiti Sains
Malaysia is also recognised.

REFERENCES

Arup Ove and Partners   *City of Georgetown, Penang — West*
    (1973),   *Malaysia: Traffic Study Part One*,
                               London.

Arup Ove and Partners   *City of Georgetown, Penang — West*
    (1975),   *Malaysia: Traffic Study Part Two:*
                               Summary and Findings, London.

Commonwealth Bureau of   *An Approach to Developing Transport*
    Roads (1976),   *Improvement Proposals*, Occasional
                               Paper No. 2, Melbourne.

Grava, S. (1976),   Extracts from locally generated trans-
                               portation modes of the developing world
                               (or: how to get the most mobility for
                               little money and who gains from it all),
                               paper prepared for First International
                               Para Transit Workshop, Development Centre,
                               Organisation for Economic Cooperation
                               and Development, held at Asnières-sur-
                               Oise, France 30 June-July 1977.

International Labour   *Employment, Incomes and Equality: A*
    Office (1972),   *Strategy for Increasing Productive*
                               Employment in Kenya, Geneva.

Lembaga Pengurus Kerajaan   *Annual Report of Jabatan Kanderaan for*
    Pulau Pinang (1974),   *the year* 1974.

Lim, W. (1975),   *Equity and Urban Environment in the*
                               Third World With Special Reference to
                               ASEAN Countries and Singapore,
                               Singapore.

Royal Malaysian Police   *Statistical Report on Road Accidents in*
  (1976),   *Peninsular Malaysia 1974*, Government
                            Printer, Kuala Lumpur.

Sethuraman, S.V. (1976),   'The Urban Informal Sector: Concept,
                            Measurement and Policy', *International
                            Labour Review*, Vol. 114(1), pp. 69-81.

Wilson, A.G. (1972),   *Minutes of Evidence*, Expenditure
                            Committee on Urban Transport Planning,
                            H.M.S.O., London, pp. 250-58.

CHAPTER 9

URBAN-RURAL INTERDEPENDENCE:

THE TRISHAW RIDERS OF UJUNG PANDANG

DEAN FORBES*

'I own some land in my village in Jeneponto. After the
harvest in the village I came to the city to earn money
riding a trishaw. I stay in my uncle's house so I do
not have to pay for housing. My wife stays in the
village. When its the rainy season I return to the
village to work the land. The harvest this year was
very poor'.

'Many trishaw riders return to the village to plant the
rice and return later to harvest it. Sometimes they send
money back instead, which is used to employ people to
harvest the rice. Each year the number of trishaw riders
increase, as more and more need money to supplement their
produce from the village. Now we have irrigation in the
village, but I don't know whether this will help the
trishaw riders'.

Two Ujung Pandang trishaw riders (October 1976).

1. INTRODUCTION

Trishaw riders dominate the streets of Ujung Pandang. Over 17,500
of them are crammed into a city that is no more than about ten
square kilometres in area. By sheer numbers of people employed,
the trishaw industry is the most important part of the informal
sector in Ujung Pandang. This chapter concentrates on three
aspects of the trishaw industry**. First, it describes the
organisational structure of the trishaw system, pointing out that
essentially it is an efficient small-scale transport operation which

---

*   Dean Forbes is Tutor, Department of Geography, Monash University,
Clayton, Victoria.

** This paper is drawn from a Ph.D. dissertation currently in
preparation. It is titled 'Development and the Informal Sector: A
study of small scale businessmen in transport and food distribution
in Ujung Pandang, Indonesia'. Field work was carried out in Indonesia in October-November 1975 and February-December 1976.   It was
funded by the Centre of Southeast Asian Studies, and the Department
of Geography, Monash University. By examining informal sector
operators in manufacturing (preparing and selling icecream),
distribution (fish and fruit and vegetable sellers) and services
(trishaw riders), the dissertation attempts to assess the potential
contribution of the informal sector in the development of Indonesia.

is of great use to its predominantly middle-class patrons, and a
profitable investment for those non-owner riders who purchase trishaws.   Second, it examines, as indicated in the above quotations,
urban-rural interdependence showing how trishaw riders are a source
of cash and goods for the rural areas, and the trishaw industry an
outlet for the seasonal over-supply of labour.   This is an important aspect of the lives of trishaw riders in Ujung Pandang and a
phenomenon which has received very little attention in the literature.   Indeed, McGee (1976, p. 19) has highlighted that the interaction between the proto-proletariat and the rural informal sector
is one of the least analysed aspects of the urban informal sector.
Friedmann and Wulff (1976, p. 17) also indicate that little is
known about the flow of cash from urban migrants to their home
areas, primarily because it is only amenable to micro-analysis.
Finally, some of the conceptual and planning implications of the
argument are assessed which draw particular attention to the growing
dilemma about how the informal sector best fits into a strategy of
urban development.

2.   THE TRISHAWS OF UJUNG PANDANG

Ujung Pandang is the principal city of the province of South
Sulawesi and with a population of 434,766 in 1971 is one of the
largest cities of the Indonesian archipelago outside of Java.
According to 1971 Census data the city workforce was 107,694 (Biro
Pusat Statistik, 1974, p. 160).   It was estimated there were over
17,500 trishaws operating in Ujung Pandang in 1975 so that trishaw
riders comprise about 15 per cent of the employed city population.
In addition to the 15,590 registered trishaws, officials estimate
that another 2,000 unregistered trishaws operate on the periphery
of the city or at night (see Table 9.1).

TABLE 9.1:   NUMBER OF REGISTERED TRISHAWS

Registration	1973	1974	1975
Total trishaws	12,498	13,684	15,590
Trishaw owners	6,509	6,817	7,790
Trishaws per owner	1.9	2.0	2.0

Source: Dinas Pendapatan, Daerah Kotamadya Ujung Pandang.

     In general the trishaw system provides an indispensable trans-
port service to the urban population, although because of the cost
structure, it is patronised by the middle income groups rather than
by the urban poor.   Trishaws can be engaged at any point in the
city and the passenger taken to almost any other point at a cost
usually not in excess of Rp45 per kilometre*.   Prices are arrived

---

*   The exchange rate in 1975 was $A1.00 = Rp510.

at either by bargaining or through monthly contracts; they can vary
significantly.   The prices are maintained by a combination of the
reluctance of many of the status conscious middle-class to bargain
for a low fare and the apparent lack of competition among trishaw
riders.   A rigid etiquette operates among trishaw riders when
soliciting customers.   A rider may be available to take passengers
but must not solicit a customer until trishaw riders with prior
claims to the customer relinquish their claims.   As this often
involves the customer moving to another group of vacant trishaws
the ploy is often successful.   When trishaw riders do compete it
often leads to violence.   Flare-ups in the continuing trishaw
'war' in Ujung Pandang are often attributed to indiscriminate
competitive behaviour among riders.

It is not uncommon for trishaw riders to be regularly in the
employ of a particular family and to act as chauffeur, child-minder,
guardian or escort.   They are in great demand in ferrying children
to and from school and conveying unescorted women to and from
markets or to the houses of relatives.   In these situations the
trishaw rider is often under monthly contract, both employer and
trishaw rider referring to one another as *langganan* (lit. working
clubmembers).

Trishaws also play an important part in providing services
which enable various informal sector businesses to survive.   They
are especially important in moving the produce of small traders
from the markets to the site of their stalls and in moving informal
sector manufactured goods such as light furniture.   Without these
relatively low cost services (relative to, for example, motorised
transport) the small businesses of the informal sector could face
much higher costs (Jellinek, 1976).

The modal daily income of a sample of 111 Ujung Pandang trishaw riders was Rp300-RP399, and only 12 per cent earned more than
Rp600 per day (Table 9.2).   Ten per cent earned less than Rp200 on
the day preceding the interview.   There is some seasonal variation
in income caused by price fluctuations.   For instance, it is more
expensive to rent a trishaw during *bulan puasa*, the Muslim fasting
month, when trishaw riders who are obeying the fast suffer considerable discomfort, and demand from fasting patrons for trishaw
services increases.   Similarly, during the monsoon rains which
assault Ujung Pandang between December and March, demand for trishaws
and prices, increases accordingly.   During these periods trishaw
riders' incomes increase marginally.   If trishaw riders are unable
to work due to ill-health or family obligations, or if the trishaw
is confiscated by the authorities, they are still expected to keep
up rental payments while the vehicle is their responsibility.   Over
a period of time these factors reduce trishaw riders' incomes
accordingly.   To earn their daily income most riders work from
dawn until 2.30 p.m., then like most of the rest of the population
sleep during the heat of the afternoon.   They resume work around
6.00 p.m. and many do not finish until midnight when the last of
the evening entertainment closes.   Very seldom do trishaw riders
work less than a twelve hour day.   Although they have a well earned
reputation as the *enfants terribles* of the city it can be misleading, for, as a group, their income is very small, their livelihood
is insecure, and their work is long and arduous.

TABLE 9.2:   NET DAILY INCOME OF TRISHAW RIDERS

Rupiah per day	Number	Per cent
Less than 200	10	9
200 - 299	17	15
300 - 399	34	31
400 - 499	8	7
500 - 599	13	12
More than 600	13	12
No reply	16	14
Total	111	100

Most trishaw riders rent their vehicles from the owner who is
called their *punggawa** (cf. Chapter 5).   Some are owner-riders (18
per cent) or they are buying their trishaws on instalment from a
punggawa (6 per cent) (Table 9.3).   There were 7790 registered
trishaw owners in Ujung Pandang in 1975, an average of 2.0 trishaws
per owner.   Riders who are in the process of purchasing trishaws
pay Rp250 per day, Rp50 of which is taken for rental and Rp200 for
repayment.   One respondent whose case did not seem atypical, will
eventually pay Rp182,500 for his trishaw over a period of twenty-
four months.   The cost of a new trishaw to a cash customer is
Rp65,000.   Rental prices for trishaws are dependent upon condition.
Payment of between Rp200 and Rp250 per day is not uncommon for a
trishaw in good condition, while an older trishaw fetches between
Rp100 and Rp125 per day.   No matter whether the rider is renting
or buying a trishaw, his payment to the *punggawa* is very large.
Although *punggawa* are responsible for major repairs to the trishaw
the profits made by the *punggawa*, the controller of capital, are
extremely high by comparison with the income of the trishaw rider.

In most cases the rider and *punggawa* maintain a straightforward business relationship.   Trishaw riders are introduced to
punggawa by mutual acquaintances who are then expected to ensure
the regular payment of rent and the safety of the trishaw.   The
punggawa usually has little contact with his riders other than in
the collection of money.   He collects rent daily and if it is not
forthcoming terminates the agreement.   There is a high degree of
mobility among trishaw riders, who often have no allegiance to
particular *punggawa* and change *punggawa* at will.   Generally the
punggawa has no interest in the trishaw business other than a
regular return on his investment.   *Punggawa* are often from the
wealthy middle-classes, especially middle ranking army officers,
schoolteachers and Chinese shop-owners.   This pattern is unlike

---

* The term *punggawa* is used throughout South Sulawesi to refer to
the person with the most capital in an economic relationship.   The
trishaw owner is referred to as a *punggawa* by the people who rent
his trishaw.   If that *punggawa* were involved, in turn, with another
person with more capital and organisational control, he in turn
would refer to him as a *punggawa*.

other components of the informal sector.   For instance there is a
close and lasting link between small-scale ice-cream manufacturers
and sellers and their *punggawa*.   They are usually all from the
same village, may be related and may live together (see Chapter 5).
The *punggawa* controls the business through his extensive knowledge
and experience, his capital finances the business and the worker
develops a dependency upon the *punggawa* for cash and other assistance.   This type of organisation is rare among trishaw riders,
probably because the business requires less specialist knowledge
and training than in other parts of the informal sector.

TABLE 9.3:   MEANS OF ACQUIRING A TRISHAW

Means	Number	Per cent
Rented	82	74
Owner/rider	20	18
Buying on instalment	7	6
Borrowed	2	2
Total	111	100

3.   URBAN-RURAL INTERDEPENDENCE

Over 86 per cent of South Sulawesi's population in the 1971 Census
lived in the rural areas.   But the rural areas, like many parts of
Indonesia, are losing population as people drift towards the towns.
Many of these people are able to find employment only in the informal sector and it is here that the trishaw industry is very
important.   Eighty-seven per cent of trishaw riders who were interviewed in Ujung Pandang were migrants who were born in the rural
areas of South Sulawesi.   Sixty-seven per cent were Makassars from
the contiguous southern *kabupaten* of Jeneponto, Takalar and Gowa
(Table 9.4, Fig. 9.1).   Most trishaw riders were peasant rice

TABLE 9.4:   BIRTHPLACE OF TRISHAW RIDERS

Birthplace	Number	Per cent
Jeneponto	45	41
Takalar	20	18
Gowa	9	8
Other Sulawesi	21	19
Other Indonesia	1	1
Sub-total migrants	97	87
Ujung Pandang	14	13
Grand total	111	100

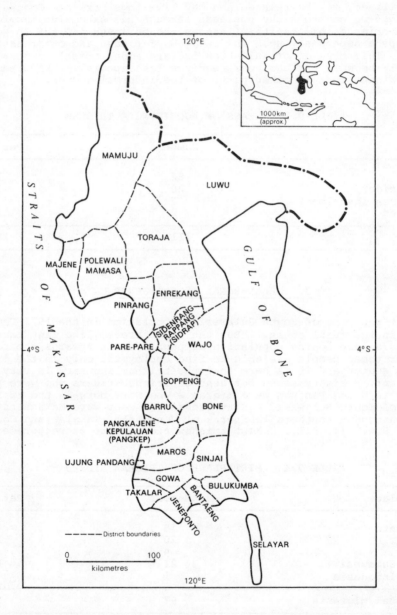

Fig. 9.1: South Sulawesi showing *Kabupaten* and *Kotamadya*.

farmers before leaving the village, and many still are peasant rice
farmers during the season.   Their reasons for moving to the city
were primarily economic.   Seventy-three per cent claimed economic
hardship in the rural areas, contrasted with the potential of a
cash income in the city, prompted their movement (Table 9.5). Often
respondents indicated that it was the poor seasons when the rains
were inadequate to produce a good harvest which induced their search
for a supplementary income.   They owned small parcels of land which
often did not produce sufficient food for the entire year.   Even
during good seasons the land was inadequate to produce a surplus
large enough to provide cash, and if the season was poor then hunger
would follow.   Many gave the impression that life in the village
hovered uneasily around the subsistence level.   Even if employment
was difficult to find in the city at least it offered the prospect
of a cash income.   Only seven respondents were in employment six
months before going to Ujung Pandang and only three of these were
in wage employment.   There were other non-economic reasons for
moving to Ujung Pandang.   Seven respondents were brought to the
city by their parents whilst four moved to the city to take advantage of the schools and health services provided there.   Furthermore, the rebellion which was led by the Bugis guerilla Kahar
Muzakar caused considerable disruption in the rural areas.   Between
1950 and 1965 the guerillas held large parts of the rural areas of
the province.   Five respondents said they came to the city because
the guerillas' conflict with the army endangered their security and
disrupted their lives (Harvey, 1974 provides an excellent detailed
study of this period).

TABLE 9.5:   REASONS FOR MOVING TO UJUNG PANDANG

Reasons	Number	Per cent
Economic problems	71	73
Non-decision maker	7	7
Security problems	5	5
Services (school, doctor)	4	4
Other	10	10
Total	97	99[a]

a   Does not equal 100 per cent because of rounding.

    The period which respondents have lived in Ujung Pandang is
shown in Table 9.6.   They arrived over a broad time period, 10 per
cent having been in the city for less than a year and 12 per cent
more than twenty years.   Fifty-seven per cent had lived in the
city for less than ten years.   This is also a partial reflection
of data collection problems in that the sampling areas were all in
the southern part of the city and thus tended to have a higher
Makassar content than the northern parts of the city where more
Bugis live.   Despite this bias, the data do, in fact, reflect
patterns of migration in South Sulawesi.   Bugis migrants have
often moved to Sumatra and resumed farming activities in the relatively empty lands of Jambi province rather than move to Ujung Pandang (see Lineton, 1975 for analysis of out-migration from Wajo).
The Makassars, on the other hand, frequently moved to Ujung Pandang

and into employment in the informal sector.   The southern Makassar
kabupaten are particularly suited to the development and maintenance of close ties with the city.   They are relatively close to
the city, road access is good and mini-bus services are frequent
and cheap.   It costs Rp600 from the furthest *kabupaten*, Jeneponto,
to Ujung Pandang, compared to over Rp1000 from Bugis *kabupaten* like
Wajo and Soppeng.   Most importantly the Makassar *kabupaten* are
extremely poor because they are in very dry areas which receive
less rain than other provinces.   Irrigation projects have been
recently commenced in Gowa and Jeneponto so it will be interesting
to note the effect this development will have upon movement to
Ujung Pandang.

TABLE 9.6:   LENGTH OF TIME LIVED IN UJUNG PANDANG

Years	Number	Per cent
Less than 1	10	10
1 - 4	26	27
5 - 9	19	20
10 - 15	11	11
16 - 20	12	12
More than 20	12	12
No reply	7	7
Total	97	99[a]

a   Does not equal 100 per cent because of rounding.

        Apart from initial patterns of migration there is consider-
able secondary movement in the form of seasonal migration and the
flow of goods and money.   Only 15 per cent of migrants did not
make a return trip to their village twelve months prior to their
interview.   Sixty-three per cent made at least one trip back to
their village, and 50 per cent more than two trips (Table 9.7).
However, it would be incorrect to interpret this information just
as 'urban' trishaw riders making frequent pilgrimages back to their
villages.   It is not unusual for 'rural' people to come into the
city for short periods.   The case of one trishaw rider is of
particular interest in this regard.   He usually lives in a village
in Takalar where he grows rice and is also the village barber.   His
customers pay for his services in kind, usually with rice, and so
although his services are in demand, and he receives fair payment,
it is not in cash.   When his instruments became old and ineffective
he decided to come to Ujung Pandang to earn some money.   This he
did by renting and riding a trishaw.   When interviewed, he had
been working for a month and thought that at the end of another
month he would have enough money to return home.   Some rural people
come on primarily social visits to their relations and then find
they do not have enough money to return to their village.   This
problem is solved by a one or two week period riding a trishaw.

        To make a precise distinction between urban and rural people
would contradict the argument, but is is important to note whether
trishaw riders are primarily urban-based with rural connections or

rural-based with urban connections.   Trishaw riders were asked
whether they were married, and if they were, where did their spouses
live.   Fifty-eight were married and thirty-six spouses were living
with their husbands in the city whilst twenty-two were living in the
village.   Imperfect though this answer is, it does indicate that a
substantial portion of the trishaw riders was most likely rural-
based. Under Muslim law it is possible to have more than one wife,
and it is also possible for husbands and wives to live apart, or
alternatively wives can move about with their husbands.   Despite
these limitations it is stressed that movement between the city and
rural areas is widespread among trishaw riders; it occurs frequently
and it is in both directions.   It is from village to city and from
city to village, and it involves both urban-based and rural-based
people.

TABLE 9.7:   FREQUENCY OF RETURN TO VILLAGE DURING
PREVIOUS TWELVE MONTHS

Times	Number	Per cent
None	15	15
Once	13	13
2 - 4	21	22
5 - 12	18	19
More than 12	9	9
No reply	21	22
Total	97	100

Perhaps the most important component of urban-rural interdependence is the seasonal flow.   Sixty per cent of trishaw riders
said they returned to their villages at the time of rice planting
and 68 per cent said they returned for the rice harvest (Table 9.8).
They returned to work on their own land or else to work as contract
labourers on other villagers' land.   Their payment was in the form
of a share in the harvest which they could give to family who lived
in the village or else bring back to Ujung Pandang.   One trishaw
rider replied that he had only a little land in his village which
is in the rice bowl *kabupaten* of Wajo.   The land is cultivated by
his brother-in-law and the two families share the harvest. He often
returns to Wajo to assist in the harvest.   However, he had decided
not to return during the particular season in which he was interviewed because of some problems with his trishaw in Ujung Pandang.

TABLE 9.8:   TRISHAW RIDERS WHO RETURN TO THE VILLAGE FOR
PLANTING OR HARVESTING RICE

| | Planting | | Harvesting | |
	Number	Per cent	Number	Per cent
Return	58	60	66	68
Do not return	29	30	22	23
No reply	10	10	9	9
Total	97	100	97	100

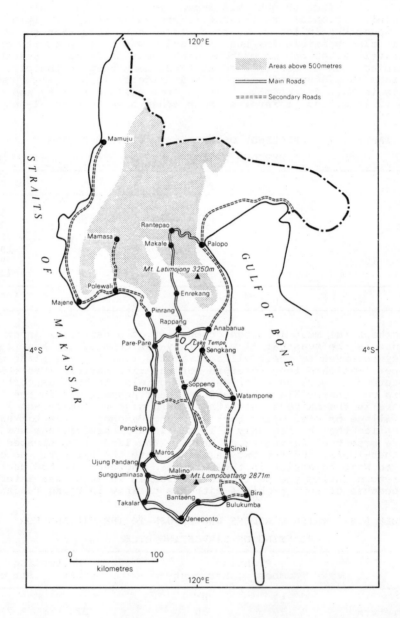

Fig. 9.2: South Sulawesi showing roads, main towns and
           relief.

Another trishaw rider from Takalar has a small plot of land in the
village.   He regularly returns to tend and harvest the rice and
gives the crop to his mother, sister and eldest son, all of whom
live in the village.   He survives on his income from riding a
trishaw and a part-time job as a messenger in a school.   Twenty-
five trishaw riders, most of whom attended both the planting and
the harvest, returned to the city with rice from their villages.
Thirteen brought back less than thirty litres of rice or about a
month's supply for a small family.   Twelve brought back more than
thirty litres of rice, and five of these brought back enough rice
for the whole of the year.   Many did not bring back rice from the
village because their wives and families in the village needed the
food.   They purchased prepared food from roadside stalls in Ujung
Pandang and were entirely dependent upon their cash income.   Others
argued that rice was as expensive in the village as in the town,
and that there was no sense in trying to purchase rice in the
village unless one actually had a surplus.

       There is something of a seasonal balance in the patterns of
interdependence between South Sulawesi and Ujung Pandang.   South
Sulawesi is a peninsula which receives two monsoons annually, the
south-west monsoon striking the west coast between December and
March and the south-east monsoon striking the east coast between
May and July (Fig. 9.2).   The two peak periods of labour demand in
growing rice are the planting time which is at the beginning of the
monsoon and the harvest which is after the monsoon.   As these two
peak periods occur at different times on different sides of the
peninsula, the flows to and from the villages ensure that the city
has a reasonably regular supply of labour.   Just as the workers
from Jeneponto in the south-west are returning to their villages
for the rice planting during October, so the workers from the
eastern *kabupaten* like Bone will be returning to the city having
completed their harvest.

       There is also significant movement of cash and goods between
urban and rural areas.   Gifts, for instance, are obligatory if one
moves from city to village and create an important if unquantifiable
flow.   Of more importance are cash flows.   Very few trishaw
riders indicated they accepted money from people in the village,
but one third said they had sent money to the village during the
preceding twelve months.   Usually it was sent monthly and in lots
of Rp500 or Rp1000.   The average remittance was Rp10,000 per year.
The principal recipients of money were parents and wives, though
occasionally other family members such as uncles and brothers
received money.   Often money sent from the city is used to pay
labourers to farm trishaw riders' rice fields.   Without an extended
period of field work in the rural areas, it is difficult to assess
the importance of this flow of cash.   Studies in Java indicate
that remittances from informal sector operators in Jakarta are
crucial to the maintenance of village agriculture (see Critchfield,
1970, p. 4).   Among the Toraja from the mountainous northern *kabupaten* of South Sulawesi the accumulation of cash in urban areas,
primarily in informal sector shoe manufacturing and repairs, plays
an important part in maintaining and providing mobility in the
rural agricultural sector (see Crystal, 1974, p. 133; Forbes, 1976,
pp. 8-9).   The Toraja maintain strong ties between homeland and
city and money sent back from the city is used for four main purposes in Toraja land.   Rice fields are purchased, buffalo and pig
holdings built up, new wooden houses are constructed and money is

set aside for ceremonial use.   An average remittance of only
Rp10,000 per annum among trishaw riders in Ujung Pandang suggests
that their cash remittances are probably not a major force in agriculture as among the Toraja.   How important this cash is to maintaining levels of living in Makassar villages requires further
investigation.

       The patterns of urban-rural interdependence occur because of,
and are facilitated by, basic similarities in the system of production used by rural peasants and urban trishaw riders.   As trishaw
riders and rural peasants are often the same people, similarity is
hardly surprising.   According to the Franklin-McGee capitalist-
socialist-peasant models of production they share a 'peasant system
of production' (see Franklin, 1965, pp. 145-66 and 1969, pp. 98-102;
McGee, 1973, pp. 135-42).   The informal sector, which seems closely
related to the peasant system of production concept, is defined as
that portion of the urban economy,

       '...characterized by an almost complete absence of
       bureaucratic organization, by a prolific use of low
       skilled indigenous labour, by reliance on local re-
       sources, expertise and markets, by its small-scale and
       by minimizing overhead costs' (Overseas Development
       Group, 1973, p. 23).

       The principal characteristic of the peasant system of produc-
tion is the labour input.   Thus, 'in the peasant economy the individual entrepreneur is committed to the utilisation of his total
labour supply - that of his family, who may and often do find
alternative or additional sources of employment ' (Franklin, 1965,
p. 148).   However, in the capitalist system of production 'labour
becomes a commodity to be hired and dismissed by the enterprise
according to changes in the scale of organisation, degree of mech-
anisation, the level of market demand for products' (Franklin, 1965,
p. 148).

       It is not intended to review the concept of the peasant system
of production in detail save to note that peasant rice farmers in
South Sulawesi, and trishaw riders in Ujung Pandang, both have total
labour commitments to their work and therefore satisfy this most
important criteria.   However, it is important to describe some
additional characteristics which peasant rice farmers and trishaw
riders share, and which in turn create interdependence.

       Perhaps the most important characteristic is that both urban
and rural peasant systems of production create a large group of
poor people.   In these systems the return to labour is far less
than the return to land (in the village) or capital (in the city).
Rural peasants are very often living in poverty and when this
poverty is exaggerated by poor seasons then their most realistic
option is to migrate to the town and search for employment.   The
trishaw system of Ujung Pandang is the most easily obtainable income
earning opportunity for most Makassar migrants.   But the trishaw
rider's income in the city is also very low and subject to considerable variation and fluctuation.   It provides only a marginal life-
style and as there are no readily available welfare services in
Indonesian cities (save for the family network) it is very difficult

to support a wife and family on such a meagre income.   Many trishaw riders remain dependent upon their farms in the village to produce a small quantity of rice each year, which is then consumed by the trishaw rider's family in the village or is brought back to the city for the use of the trishaw rider himself.   This also means he must return to the village at the crucial times of the year, at the planting and harvesting of the rice, unless he can afford to send money to pay labourers to work his fields.   Circular migration initially grows out of the inadequacy of the economic return from the urban and rural systems of production.   The solution which the trishaw riders have adopted in an attempt to alleviate their poverty, is to become circular migrants who combine the economic advantages of the rural areas such as rice production, with the cash income available in the city.

Urban-rural interdependence is, however, not just a result of the economic aspects of the systems of production.   The migration of male heads of households means families are very often split, grandparents and children living in the village and husbands and wives in the town, a situation which promotes regular visits and exchanges. Trishaw riders in Ujung Pandang also become disenchanted with city living and their poor accommodation, particularly if they sleep in their trishaws in the streets, and return to the rural areas for a rest.   Furthermore, the annual pilgrimage home to celebrate Ramadhan, the feasting at the end of the Muslim fasting month, and various other village celebrations, also reinforces the close social connections between urban and rural areas.   Of course, the flow is not always from city to village.   Villagers often travel to the city to visit relatives or else to break the boredom of village life. The trishaws provide an easy means of earning cash when this happens and thus facilitate the movement.

Urban-rural interdependence is a rational response by poor people to the realities of their environment.   It would probably not occur if migrants were involved in wage employment.   That is, in terms of the Franklin-McGee typology, if they were part of the capitalist system of production.   On the other hand three important characteristics of the peasant system of production of the urban informal sector and the peasant rural economy, as they operate in South Sulawesi, facilitate these patterns of interaction.   First, unlike many parts of the informal sector, entrance into both economies is relatively easy.   Trishaw riders are usually from rural areas and able, in most cases, to return to the village and work in the fields without encountering major problems, especially during the harvesting when labour is in demand.   Entrance into the trishaw business is similarly relatively easy compared to, for instance, recruitment into wage employment.   Most trishaw *punggawa* recruit their riders through personal acquaintance with a third party, and there are always plenty of acquaintances available to assist rice farmers who wish short-term work with a trishaw.   Chain migration is also a frequent occurrence.   The sponsor of migration, usually a relation living in the city, provides the intending migrant with information, accommodation and food, and arranges a trishaw for rental.   Urban-rural interaction, then, is facilitated by the ease of entry into the urban and rural sectors.   Second, the labour requirements of both sectors are flexible and able to cope with an increase in labour.   Unlike the wage employment sector, where workers are either needed or not needed and hired or fired accordingly, the urban informal and peasant rice sectors

accommodate an increase or decrease in numbers by a sharing of the
work load and a sharing of the profit.   Both sectors are highly
labour-intensive and are dependent upon this flexible labour input.

     The third factor which facilitates interaction is the
seasonal balance in the demand for labour in the rural areas.   By
virtue of the peninsula receiving two monsoon rains, most of the
east coast rice crop is tended and planted at different times of
the year to the west coast, and so the movement of trishaw riders
back to one side of the peninsula corresponds to the movement of
peasant farmers from the other side back to the city.   This pattern
effectively means there is seldom a build-up of excess labour in
the city or a corresponding scarcity of labour in the village.
Consequently the city is able to support a far larger group of
trishaw riders each year than would be the case if labour movement
occurred only during a single season.   Papanek (1975, p. 17) makes
mention of a similar seasonal balance in Java.   Certainly in South
Sulawesi the seasonal balance is a very important factor which
facilitates the pattern of urban-rural interdependence.

                         4.   CONCLUSIONS

Extensive rural-urban migration has always been seen as one of the
most important characteristics of contemporary Indonesia, and a
number of studies, such as Temple (1975, pp. 76-81), have sought to
analyse this phenomenon.   But while rural-urban migration is one
of the most spectacular manifestations of population movement it is
only, in many cases, the tip of the iceberg.   It is important to
view rural-urban migration as the beginning of an on-going process
of movement and interaction which continues to link the urban
migrant in an important two-way connection with his rural birthplace.   It follows from this that the push-pull arrangement of
factors, which have generally been used to explain rural-urban
migration, are inadequate to explain a pattern of urban-rural interdependence.   The overall socio-economic context is a far better
framework for analysis.   Movement in South Sulawesi is a response
to an economic system, a mode of production, which also facilitates
the very pattern which it causes.   Peasants are normally regarded
as rural farmers, but in South Sulawesi they often have a spell in
money earning activity in the city, so quite literally an accurate
description of many trishaw riders is of peasants in the city.
This also tells us something about the city and its relationship
with its hinterland.   Capital flow is not only from the rural
areas to the urban areas.   While the pattern of interdependence can
hardly balance the city's parasitic dependence on the hinterland, it
does, at least highlight the circularity of that flow.   As Friedmann and Wulff (1976, p. 16) note in regard to city-hinterland relationships '...urban development is and has been financed, at least
in its initial stages, by the mobilization of a surplus from agricultural producers'.

     There are planning implications which follow from this analysis.
The strategy adopted in many Indonesian cities is to try and
eliminate the trishaw industry in the city, or at least reduce
their numbers by reducing the area where trishaws can operate. Ali
Sadikin has attempted this in Jakarta with questionable success.

It is also the policy which the administration, led by the police, is trying to implement in Ujung Pandang. They argue that 17,500 is far too many trishaws for Ujung Pandang. Trishaws by virtue of sheer numbers are the main cause of traffic accidents, and the trishaw system is a convenient refuge for undesirables. It is planned to reduce their number to 13,500 in 1977 and still further in subsequent years (*Pedoman Rakyat*, 14 April 1976). There are other more subtle ways of restricting trishaw numbers. Trishaw riders are continually hounded with licence checks and vehicle registration checks. Police are zealous in their efforts to ensure that trishaws do not use a few designated main roads, and similarly zealous in restricting them to the small side-paths of streets which invariably contain extensive corrugations and a crowded traffic of pedestrians. Each infringement costs the rider dearly. It is not certain that the policy will actually have the desired effect of reducing the number of trishaws in the city, but if it did, the impact on the city and its hinterland could be severe. A reduction and gradual phasing out of trishaws from Ujung Pandang will initially create unemployment, or, more likely, a crowding of ex-trishaw riders into other informal sector occupations such as food retailing. This is surely not what the urban planners had in mind. It will not induce riders to return to the rural areas, as Ali Sadikin argued in *Wet Earth and Warm People**, because poverty is an almost inevitable part of life in the village for these people. If a miracle of foreign investment provided alternative formalised employment opportunities in Ujung Pandang, this would change patterns of interdependence because of the latter's reliance on fixed employment schedules. Labour could be prevented from its seasonal flow causing labour shortages in the village at planting and harvest. Wives and dependent children who would normally stay in the village may be forced to move to the town to be with men unable to make regular visits back to the village, and the intra-provincial transport business would probably be adversely affected by a marked drop-off in travel. However, it is most unlikely trishaw riders will find wage employment, either in the government or in industry, and it is also most unlikely they will return to the villages. Their only alternative will be to find other informal sector employment in Ujung Pandang, probably in retailing fresh or prepared foods.

An alternative approach to urban planning, and one that is increasing in favour, is to try and develop the informal sector in the hope that it will eventually lead to the creation of viable small businesses. (This type of support is discussed in more detail by McGee (1975) in a study for the International Development Research Centre; McGee, 1976, pp. 20-23 and Forbes, 1976, p. 11.) A programme of this nature could be commenced in Ujung Pandang initially by reducing the pressures upon trishaw riders such as over zealous control, and secondly by providing active encouragement to trishaw riders by providing services such as cheap loans which would allow riders to purchase their own vehicles. In the short-term the effect of such action would be to marginally upgrade the incomes of trishaw riders, and hence marginally upgrade the lives of the urban poor by virtue of the transfer of resources through urban-rural interdependence.

---

* A documentary film produced by the National Film Board of Canada.

In the long run, however, such action would only serve to highlight
an important dilemma of urban development.   Assistance to the
urban informal sector will ultimately serve to legitimise the
socio-economic structures which were responsible for the pattern of
urban-rural interdependence in the first place.   The cause of this
process was poverty, and though poverty may be alleviated it is not
eliminated by patterns of interaction because if one accepts
Thorner's (1962, p. 206) definitions, '...in peasant economies the
peasant as a group is subject to and exists to be exploited by
others'.   Rather than simply assist in the marginal upgrading of
the income of the trishaw riders, it would be more useful to examine
the causes of poverty in the rural areas and the causes of poverty
in the urban informal sector.   It is clear that in the short-term,
however, the trishaw riders, the urban middle-classes and the rural
poor stand to gain by maintaining the trishaw industry of Ujung
Pandang as it is.

ACKNOWLEDGEMENTS

I am most grateful to Professor M.I. Logan, Dr G. Dixon, Dr K.B.
O'Connor, Mr G.R.R. Swinton and Ms J.M. Williams for their advice
and assistance in the preparation of this paper.   However, I
remain responsible for any inadequacies.

REFERENCES

Biro Pusat Statistik (1974),   *Sensus Penduduk 1971, Sulawesi Selatan*, Series E No. 23, Maret, Jakarta.

Critchfield, R. (1970),   *Hello Mister Where are You Going: The Story of Husen, a Javanese Betjak Driver*, The Alicia Patterson Fund, New York.

Crystal, E. (1974),   'Cooking Pot Politics: A Toraja Village Study', *Indonesia*, 18, pp. 119-52.

Forbes, D.K. (1976),   Development: a view from the street, unpublished working paper, Sulawesi Regional Development Survey, Ujung Pandang.

Franklin, S.H. (1965),   'Systems of Production, Systems of Appropriation', *Pacific Viewpoint*, 6(2), pp. 145-66.

Franklin, H. (1969),   'The Worker Peasant in Europe', reprinted in Shanin, T. (ed) (1971), *Peasants and Peasant Societies*, pp. 98-102, Penguin Education, Middlesex.

Friedmann, J. and Wulff, R. (1976),   *The Urban Transition*, London.

Harvey, B.S. (1974),   Tradition, Islam and rebellion: South Sulawesi 1950-1965, unpublished Ph.D. thesis in Government at Cornell University, Ithaca.

International Development Research Centre (1975),   *Hawkers and Vendors in Asian Cities*, Ottawa, Canada.

Jellinek, L. (1976),   'The Life of a Jakarta Street Trader Part I', *Working Paper No. 9*, Centre of Southeast Asian Studies, Monash University.

Lineton, J. (1975),   'Pasompe Ugi: Bugis Migrants and Wanderers', *Archipel*, 10, pp. 173-204.

McGee, T.G. (1973),   'Peasants in the Cities: A Paradox, A
                                   Paradox, A Most Ingenious Paradox',
                                   Human Organization, 32(2), pp. 135-42.

McGee, T.G. (1975),   Hawkers in selected Southeast Asian
                                   cities: the comparative research study
                                   outline, findings and policy recommenda-
                                   tions, Report presented to the Confer-
                                   ence on Hawkers and Vendors and the
                                   Development of Asian Cities, sponsored
                                   jointly by City Hall, Kuala Lumpur and
                                   the International Development Research
                                   Centre of Canada, Kuala Lumpur.

McGee, T.G. (1976),   'The Persistence of the Proto-
                                   proletariat: Occupational Structures and
                                   Planning of the Future of Third World
                                   Cities', *Progress in Geography*, 9,
                                   pp. 1-38.

Overseas Development   *A Report on Development Strategies for
 Group (ODG) (1973),   Papua New Guinea*, International Bank
                                   for Reconstruction and Development,
                                   Washington.

Papanek, G. (1975),   'The Poor of Jakarta', *Economic Devel-
                                   opment and Cultural Change*, 24(1),
                                   pp. 1-28.

Temple, G. (1975),   'Migration to Jakarta', *Bulletin of
                                   Indonesia Economic Studies*, XI(1),
                                   pp. 76-81.

Thorner, D. (1962),   'Peasant Economy as a Category in
                                   Economic History', reprinted in Shanin,
                                   T. (ed.),(1971), *Peasants and Peasant
                                   Societies*, pp. 202-18, Middlesex.

CHAPTER 10

INDONESIAN PRAHUS AND CHINESE JUNKS:
SOME ISSUES OF DEFINITION AND POLICY
IN INFORMAL SECTOR STUDIES

H.W. DICK*

1. INTRODUCTION

Understanding of economic dualism has been enhanced in the 1970s by use of the terms *formal/informal*, rather than *modern/traditional* as formerly, because it has directed attention to factors besides technology.   As yet, however, rigorous definition of the formal and informal sectors is still lacking:

> Since the term 'informal sector' was first used...it has
> gained considerable currency in the literature on devel-
> opment policy in general and employment policy in
> particular.   Despite, or perhaps because of, the growing
> interest in the subject...a good deal of confusion has
> arisen as to what the expression really means.   Not
> surprisingly, therefore, the policy prescriptions differ.
> (Sethuraman, 1976, p. 69).

The task of definition must therefore precede discussion of policy.

International Labour Office (1972, p. 6) in the employment mission report on Kenya made the first careful attempt to define the informal sector with a listing of seven distinguishing characteristics:

(a) ease of entry;
(b) reliance on indigenous resources;
(c) family ownership of enterprises;
(d) small scale of operations;
(e) labour-intensive and adapted technology;
(f) skills acquired outside the formal school system;
(g) unregulated and competitive markets.

Like subsequent more comprehensive lists of characteristics such as McGee (1973, p. 138), these are a useful but ill-assorted bunch.   Analysis is facilitated if they are grouped into three sets:

---

* Dr H.W. Dick is Lecturer, Department of Economics, University of Newcastle, Newcastle, New South Wales.

  (i) technology: small-scale (d), labour-intensive and adapted
      technology (e);

 (ii) market structure and behaviour: ease of entry (a), unreg-
      ulated and competitive markets (g);

(iii) access to resources: reliance on indigenous resources (b),
      family ownership (c), and skills acquired outside the
      formal school system (f).

    Technology and market structure and behaviour have been
fairly well studied but access to resources is only superficially
understood.   It should involve more than whether resources are
foreign or domestic, whether ownership is family-based or impersonal,
and whether skills are acquired 'on-the-job' or in the school
system.   It is perhaps best understood as *organisation*, embracing
both the external connections by which resources are acquired and
the internal management by which resources are directed.   These
three sets of characteristics obviously need not produce the same
definitions of the informal sector.   Whether the emphasis is placed
upon technology, market structure and behaviour, or organisation
must depend upon the purpose for which a definition is required.

    Whatever the criterion, a neat formal/informal sector
dichotomy is probably impossible.   This has been recognised in the
case of technology with acceptance of the category of *intermediate*
as well as modern and traditional technology.   It has yet to be
recognised in the case of organisation.   Dichotomies such as
modern/traditional, bazaar-centred/firm-centred (Geertz),
capitalist/peasant (McGee) and upper circuit/lower circuit (Santos)
mask the importance of intermediate forms of organisation.   Yet,
between the large corporations which are obviously in the formal
sector and the hawkers, petty traders, and small scale manufacturers and transport operators which are obviously in the informal
sector, there lie both intermediate technologies and intermediate
organisational forms.   If the organisation of the formal sector is
described as 'corporate' and that of the informal sector as
'unincorporated' (see Rimmer, 1976), then the intermediate
organisational form may be described as non-corporate.   Its
origins can be traced back to premodern commerce and manufacture
before scientific machine technology and the large scale 'rational
bureaucratic' corporation.

    Part 2 of this chapter attempts to identify the main features
of the non-corporate form of organisation as it applies to prahu
shipping in Indonesia and junk shipping in China.   In particular,
the means are examined by which this form of organisation copes
with the basic commercial problems of scarce capital and high risk,
managerial diseconomies of size, imperfect knowledge, and organisational loyalty.   Part 3 considers some policy implications in the
Indonesian context with specific attention to discrimination in
government policy, competition from intermediate types of shipping,
and the possible reasons for the lack of official interest in prahu
shipping except to promote motorisation.

2. ORGANISATION OF PRAHU AND JUNK SHIPPING

Introduction

The dominance of junk shipping in the water transport of pre-war China is seldom appreciated. Ou Pao-san estimated that as a percentage of net value added in the shipping industry in 1933, junk shipping (the traditional sector) contributed 86 per cent and steam shipping (the modern sector) only 14 per cent (Hou, 1965, p. 166). Koizumi (1972, p. 5) estimated that before 1937 there were about 500,000 junks in the whole of China with a gross tonnage of 5,000,000 tons (of which three-fifths were in the lower Yangtse region) compared with about 1,000,000 gross tons for steamers in Chinese waters including those under foreign flags. In 1940, after the outbreak of the Sino-Japanese War, it was estimated that there remained between 220,000 and 300,000 junks with a gross tonnage of at least 2,000,000 tons (Koizumi, 1972, p. 5). Half of these were in Central China where it was further estimated that of the 10,000,000 tons of goods transported per annum, 85 per cent was carried by junk, 8 per cent by steamers, 5 per cent by trains and 2 per cent by other means (Koizumi, 1975, p. 6).

The shares of prahu and modern shipping in the interisland shipping of Indonesia in the 1970s are virtually the converse of the situation in pre-war China. The estimated 10,000 prahus of 100,000 gross tons constituted little more than a fifth of total non-tanker interisland tonnage (Dick, 1977, p. 49). In terms of non-oil cargo flows, the Long Term Fleet Development Team (1973, p. 17) estimated that for the period 1974-79 prahus would carry only 10 per cent or about 1,000,000 tons per annum and small scale (local) motor shipping 18 per cent. Perhaps half of the tonnage of cargo carried by prahu would be accounted for by timber which in 1972 was estimated as 400,000 tons (Dick, 1975a, p. 93). Other important prahu cargoes are copra, basic foodstuffs, fertiliser, construction materials, consumer goods, and petroleum products (Dick, 1975a, pp. 97-102).

Scarce capital and high risks

The high opportunity cost of capital and the high risks of investment in sail shipping both encourage individuals to commit to any venture the smallest amount of capital consistent with high short-term profits. One of the most common ways of doing this is through partnerships (*kung-ssu*: Chinese, *kongsi*: Indonesian). Their importance and mode of operation in the case of junk shipping in North China is indicated by Nakamura (1972, pp. 25-9):

> In common with most other small businesses in China,
> operation by individuals is rare and the great majority
> of shipping broker firms in north China, perhaps as many
> as ninety-nine percent, are operated by partnerships with
> joint capital. Most partnerships consist of ten to
> thirty people....
>
> Such partnerships are formed among people who are related
> or old friends. Most of them have capital but lack
> business experience. Some have commercial talent but

> don't wish to have the responsibility of running their
> own business.   In most cases the manager...comes from
> among their number, though sometimes he is an employee
> ....Often the shareholder/manager is the originator of
> the whole undertaking and he persuades the other share-
> holders to put up capital.   He bears full responsibility
> for the growth or decline of the undertaking....The
> partners have no say in the running of the firm....
>
> The particular advantages of this type of partnership
> are that it combines fragmentary amounts of individual
> capital and allows a large amount of business to be
> done on the basis of a small amount of capital.   The
> emphasis on personal and kinship relations in Chinese
> commerce is an additional safeguard against malpractice.

The particular type of partnership referred to was one of unlimited
liability in proportion to the amount of shareholding.   Nakamura
(1972, p. 29) observes that there has been a tendency for these
partnerships to become joint-stock corporations with limited
liability; although he argues that this reflects a decline in
public trust, it is evident in Indonesia that the modern joint-
stock form is easily adapted to the non-corporate form of organisation and has obvious advantages for partnerships wishing to increase
their scale of operations.   Although Nakamura was writing of
shipping brokers, according to Kosaka and Nakamura (1972, p. 54) a
similar situation applied to junk ownership in North China:

> Often what appears to be individual ownership disguises
> a partnership.   It is common for a group of partners
> united by ties of common origin to select one of their
> number to act as owner and captain.   Occasionally
> investors also spread their capital in several junks.
> This is particularly true around the coast of Shantung
> where the dangers of loss at sea are great.

This passage makes clear the relationship between spreading of
capital and the riskiness of investment.

Prahu shipping in Indonesia also displays similar forms of
ownership although these are difficult to document because, as in
China, individual ownership often disguises joint ownership with
sleeping partners.   How partnerships arise can be seen most clearly
in the case of a captain trying to accumulate sufficient capital to
purchase his own prahu (see Dick, 1975a, pp. 104-5).   Rather than
wait a long time until he can accumulate sufficient funds on his
own account, and given that he has no access to institutional
sources of finance, he would typically approach relatives, the
owner(s) of the prahu on which he is serving, and the forwarding
agents with which he deals to form a partnership in which he would
be the active partner.   Even if he eventually accumulates
sufficient funds to buy out his sleeping partners, the risks of
having all his capital in one prahu make it attractive to invest in
a second syndicate in which he would probably hold a larger share
to acquire a second prahu, for which another captain, probably a
minor partner, would be found.   When he has as many prahus as he
can actively manage, he could invest in other partnerships as a
sleeping partner.   The main choices are to invest in trade ─

for example in the timber being carried by his own prahus — or in village land as security for his old age. Some owners spend on a pilgrimage to Mecca or on education for their children. Invariably however, the pattern of investment or consumption is a traditional one (see also Dick, 1975b, pp. 92-3).

Managerial diseconomies of size

There are marked diseconomies in the ownership and management of more than one prahu or junk. With only one vessel, the individual owner or active member of a partnership can serve also as captain. Beyond this number, other captains must be appointed and there emerges a problem of control which is only partly overcome if the captains are also partners and have some personal connections with the main owner. Dick (1975a, pp. 102-3) describes the difficulties faced by prahu owners as follows:

> The eternal problem for the prahu owner who is not a captain is to ensure that he receives his due share of the earnings. Although he usually appoints a close relative as captain, this is not an adequate safeguard, nor is the 10 to 20 percent bonus which the captain is paid out of the owner's share of the earnings. Away from the *kampong* or the port in which the owner resides, the captain is a quite independent manager...Given this degree of independence and the aspiration of most captains to build their own prahus, there is a great temptation to under-report the prahu's earnings to the owner...The outcome is a complex game of double bluff, a perpetual battle of wits and nerves...The owner must draw upon family loyalty, the incentive of the bonus payment, information obtained from agents, other prahu owners and harbour masters and sometimes even use 'bully-boys' or 'thugs' to ensure that he is cheated as little as possible.

For these reasons, there is general agreement that about five prahus is as many as one owner can manage; fleets of as many as ten prahus have been known but insofar as they survived only for short periods of time they have been exceptions proving the rule.

A number of ways are found for coping with these diseconomies of size. First and most obvious, both in Indonesia and in China ownership and management of only one or two vessels is common. Thus Kosaka and Nakamura (1972, p. 54) maintain that in North China 'the characteristic form of ownership is for the individual to own and operate one junk...Ownership of several junks by one man is rare, because of the need for freedom in junk movement which makes supervision difficult.' (This is not inconsistent with joint ownership of junks.) Similarly, according to Koizumi (1972, p. 7) 'in individual enterprises the owner is usually also the captain'. And, in the case of Central China, Nagasaka (1972, p. 74) observes that 'the great majority of owner operators in Soochow were also captains working on their junks with the crew'. Second, owners may charter junks, mainly to transport companies; the advantage of this is that the owners obtain a fixed income per period and need no longer keep a close check upon the earnings of the junk, limiting their management only to manning and maintenance.

Chartering is apparently unknown, however, in Indonesia. The third
strategy, also unknown in Indonesia, is for the owner/manager of
more than a few junks to hire a man known as a 'gang boss' to whom
he delegates managerial responsibility for a number of junks.
According to Koizumi (1972, pp. 7-8):

> Where there are a large number of junks, the manager
> may hire a 'gang boss'...to control one junk or a group
> of junks, and delegate some of his responsibility to
> the latter...Generally both the 'gang boss' and the
> captains are hired on the basis of family relationships
> ...The 'gang boss' is responsible to the owner for every-
> thing.   Since he hires and fires the crew, and controls
> the sailing, mooring and collection of cargoes, the
> amount of profit also depends entirely on him.

This arrangement permitted some partnerships to own ten or more
medium and large junks and operate them under unified control
(Koizumi, 1972, p. 7).   It suggests that there is, with organisational modifications, unexploited potential for concentration of
capital in prahu owning and operating in Indonesia.

Imperfect knowledge

     The barrier of imperfect knowledge between captains as
suppliers of shipping services and traders as consumers is overcome
by intermediaries known in China as shipping brokers and in
Indonesia as forwarding agents.   Koizumi (1972, p. 15) explains
their importance to junk captains:

> It is virtually impossible for a junk operator to
> dispense with the services of brokers.   Continuously
> on the move and with no fixed offices like a steamship
> company, he would be unable without them to obtain
> cargoes for transport.   Because most of his time is
> spent sailing, he does not know the market situation.
> His profit depends on a quick turnaround...

Traders are similarly dependent upon them:

> All traders and travelling merchants who want to hire junks
> for the transport of goods must go through the hands of a
> shipping broker.   Their ignorance of shipping practice
> and navigation routes, their inability to fill a junk
> completely and the problem of ensuring the timely movement
> of goods, all combine to make it inconvenient and un-
> profitable for them to hire a junk independently (Koizumi,
> 1972, p. 15).

Besides canvassing cargoes and guaranteeing captains to traders,
brokers and forwarding agents would organise coolies for stevedoring, provide warehousing facilities, and arrange internal customs
clearance and the payment of indirect taxes.   These services would
be rendered in return for a commission either upon the value of
goods (if the captain buys for sale at his destination) or upon the
value of freight (if cargo is carried on consignment).

In China, there was much evidence by the 1930s that the once powerful shipping brokers were being displaced by transport companies. Using mainly chartered junks, these carried goods on their own account instead of acting merely as intermediaries. Koizumi (1972, p. 11) observed that:

> Modern-style transport operators have recently been
> established in Central China and the shipping brokers
> are gradually losing their former status.   However,
> this development is limited to small areas in the
> environs of modern cities.

Hayashi (1972, p. 35) suggests that the decline of the brokers in Central China could be related to the 'strong modernizing influences' emanating from Shanghai and to the competition from modern transport in the form of steamships and railways.   The development of transport companies, better able to cope with such forces, seems to have been stimulated by the formation of the Japan Forwarding Company and the Inland River Steamship Company after the Japanese invasion of 1937.   Many transport companies operated under contract to the Japan Forwarding Company while most of their chartered junks were towed as barges by vessels of the Inland River Steamship Company (Hayashi, 1972, p. 37).   Thus, most large-scale, long distance transport was handled by the transport companies and the Inland River Steamship Company leaving only small-scale, short distance transport to the brokers (Hayashi, 1972, p. 36).   Growth in the number of transport companies was facilitated by the fact that unlike brokers, who required official licences, they had merely to register (Hayashi, 1972, p. 35).

Although the transport companies were a modern development, they retained 'old forms of management'.   This was reflected in their heavy reliance upon chartered junks, which Hayashi (1972, p. 36) attributed to three factors:

> First, handling junks requires technical skill and
> involves problems of supervision and management.   It
> is easier to form a contract with the captain...
> Second, the purchase of junks requires the investment
> of an appreciable amount of capital which would be
> foolish for a company with limited capital.   Finally,
> short-term junk chartering is cheap and helps profits.

In other words, the transport companies continued to act like the brokers they replaced in trying to limit their commitment of fixed capital and their managerial responsibilities while maximising short-term profits.

In Indonesia, it is only of recent years that forwarding agents have emerged into prominence.   References in the 1920s to large prahus carrying a supercargo and to runners hired by Chinese firms in Makassar to meet incoming prahus and bargain for their custom, both suggest that if intermediaries existed, their role could hardly have been well-developed (Dick, 1975a, p. 82).   In 1935, however, the co-operative Roepelin (*Roekoen Pelajaran Indonesia*: Indonesian Shipping Association) was founded in Surabaya to act as a broker between captains and traders and to provide

credit and insurance (Dick, 1975a, p. 78).   Although Roepelin
virtually collapsed in 1938 when the founder was arrested on charges
of smuggling, it seems to have served as a model for the establishment of a large number of one-man unincorporated forwarding firms,
especially in Surabaya, Makassar, Banjarmasin and Jakarta.   After
the Japanese seized Indonesia in March 1942, they set about trying
to organise prahu shipping along lines similar to that which they
had applied to junk shipping in China after 1937.   All prahus
larger than five gross tons were required to be licensed and those
larger than ten tons to be brought under the control of bureaux in
Jakarta, Surabaya, and Makassar (Dick, 1975a, p. 79).   No information is available as to the impact of these measures which, in any
case, were undermined by the collapse of private interisland trade
as the war wore on.   They lapsed with the Surrender.   No new
major developments then occurred until 1964 when, as the outcome of
a meeting of prahu owners and operators organised on the instigation
of the Minister of Communications, there was formed the first
industry association; this *OPS Pelajaran Rakjat* was in 1971 reorg-
anised as Pepelra (*Persatuan Pengusaha Pelayaran Rakyat*: Association of Prahu Shipping Firms)(Dick, 1975a, p. 81).   In the same
year, Government Regulation No. 5/1964 was introduced requiring all
cargo-handling to be carried out by licensed shipping firms.
Although this was directed at reorganising the formal sector of the
shipping industry, it was applied also to prahu shipping.   The
hitherto one-man forwarding firms, therefore, had to incorporate
and acquire at least two prahus to qualify for a licence as a
shipping firm (Dick, 1975a, pp. 81-2).   The licensed firms,
organised in Pepelra, have since become the focus of prahu shipping
in all main ports except Banjarmasin where, because prahus can load
a full cargo of timber from one sawmill, business is still carried
on directly between captain and trader with the licensed forwarding
agent arranging only official formalities.

    The emergence of the forwarding agent transformed the prahu
shipping industry.   First, whereas before the Second World War
prahus, like junks before the era of transport companies, usually
traded in the goods which they carried; since then it has become
the norm for all but small prahus to carry goods on consignment,
earning profits only from freight charges*.   This trend has both
caused a substantial increase in prahu size — the largest prahus
pre-war were small by present standards — and further enhanced the
importance of the forwarding agent in accumulating full cargoes to
ensure fast port turnaround; the captain can no longer afford the
time to canvass cargoes himself.   Second, specialisation by route,
inward and outward cargo, and sometimes even type of cargo have

----

* Kosaka and Nakamura (1972, p. 53) show that the most characteristic form of junk operation in North China is for the captain of
the junk to carry his own goods for sale.   Even when he is
transporting for others, any excess cargo space is used to carry
goods purchased in commercial harbours for sale along the route.
Local products from the hinterland are then bought for sale on
return.   They also observe that in North China 'earning a living
solely by transporting for others is very rare except where
special circumstances are found'(see Dick, 1975a for the situation
in Indonesia).

permitted forwarding agents to provide almost regular liner services
between main ports; this has enabled prahus to compete with motorships in frequency of sailings as well as in care of cargo, facilities for handling claims, credit terms and even insurance. Therefore, although the forwarding agents neither own or charter any
significant number of prahus on their own account, it is probably
reasonable to equate their role with that of the transport companies
in China rather than with the brokers; bills of lading are drawn up
on behalf of the forwarding agent and not the prahu itself, which
is in the position of a contractor. Third, the focus of the
industry has shifted away from the prahu owners, still living mainly
in rural areas, having no incorporated status and seldom owning
more than two or three vessels, to the urban-based forwarding
agents, who have also come through their dominance of Pepelra to
speak with the government on behalf of the industry. The Indonesian prahu industry is thereby much more cohesive than in China
where, although there were associations of junk operators, these
were centred upon individual brokers (Koizumi, 1972, p. 12).

Organisational loyalty

    Low productivity and corruption are problems faced by any
organisation but are particularly intractable in Asian countries
where loyalty to impersonal organisations is as yet little developed.   Social values have been described as 'particularistic'
rather than 'universalistic' (Feuerwerker, 1958, p. 23).   While
these values undermine the rational bureaucratic form of corporate
organisation of the formal sector, the non-corporate form of
organisation is able to use them to achieve organisational loyalty
from the highest managers to the lowest employees.   Thus, in the
case of a partnership, the manager is invariably well-known to at
least one of the main partners if not a partner himself.   He in
turn chooses captains either related or well-known to him and they
appoint their crew on the same basis:

        When hiring crew members, junk captains initially took
        people from among their family and this was particularly
        true of small junks and those operating less successfully.
        However, the larger the junk and the more successful the
        business, the larger the number of crew members hired
        from outside the immediate family (Kosaka and Nakamura,
        1972, p. 63).

A similar situation applied in Indonesia (Dick, 1975b, pp. 93-4).
Hayashi (1972, p. 47) shows that shipping brokers also relied upon
personal connections in hiring employees:

        Most of the employees of a company are employed through
        recommendation and the majority are relations or acquaint-
        ances of the manager.   Major posts are usually held by
        shareholders who do not need a guarantor.

He further explains how the system of recommendation works:

        Most people employed by brokers are recommended by well-
        known captains or friends, and the recommender also stands
        as guarantor.   The guarantor is bound to pay compensation
        for any financial losses caused by the employee (Hayashi,
        (1972, p. 38).

All managers and employees are thereby organised in a hierarchical
network of personal relationships ensuring responsibility and
loyalty to the owner or owners.

Corruption within a commercial firm can best be understood as
profit-sharing by default.   In the non-corporate form of organisation regularised profit-sharing in proportions related to the
opportunities for corruption is relied upon both to reduce the
incentive for corruption and to promote high productivity.   In the
case of the managers and employees of shipping brokers, profit
shares were supplementary to basic salaries and wages (Nakamura,
1972, pp. 31-3).   In the case of junk captains and crew, however,
remuneration was entirely from profit shares:

> Profit is reckoned as the money remaining after food
> expenses for the crew have been subtracted from total
> income.   The profit is divided between the owner and
> the crew in a ratio which varies in different areas but
> is usually around seventy percent for the owner and
> thirty percent for the crew in southern Shantung, and
> fifty percent each in northeastern Shantung.   The method
> of division among the crew depends on status and skills...
> (Kosaka and Nakamura, 1972, p. 56).

Crew earnings could be supplemented by tips, especially for handling
cargo as coolies (Teshima and Arai, 1972, p. 66), and by petty
trading:

> Most of the crews supplemented their income by doing some
> independent trading on their own behalf using free cargo
> space, by trading on behalf of others, or by pilfering.
> When trading they profited from the local variations in
> prices.   Transporting rice to Shanghai and cigarettes
> back to Soochow could, for example, double one's capital
> after three round trips.   (Teshima and Arai, 1972, p. 67).

Similar systems of profit-sharing operate in the case of Indonesian
prahus, the precise systems varying between ethnic groups and
regions (Dick, 1975b, p. 88).   Petty trading also seems to be a
supplementary source of income, although its importance is difficult to document.   One difference in the Indonesian case is that
the crew receive equal shares but the captain receives in addition
a bonus of 10 to 20 per cent of the owner's share.   Whatever the
system, profit-sharing constitutes a monetary incentive to work
and personal relationships ensure organisational loyalty.

Conclusion

The non-corporate organisation of prahu and junk shipping
appears to be an efficient means of coping with the main commercial
problems in a way appropriate to the economic and social environment.   Scarce capital and high risk are tackled by consolidation
of small amounts of capital in partnerships with one member active
as manager; this combines the advantages of concentration of capital
on the one hand with fragmentation of individuals' capital on the
other.   Managerial diseconomies of size are minimised by keeping
firms small and relying upon direct personal management.   Imperfect

knowledge is dealt with by the use of intermediaries between
captains and traders in the form of brokers or forwarding agents.
Finally, organisational loyalty is maintained both by establishment
of a hierarchical network of personal relationships based upon kin-
ship and common geographic or ethnic origins and by implementation
of profit-sharing systems of remuneration with shares in proportion
to the degree of responsibility and the opportunities for corruption.

In two important respects, the organisation of prahu shipping
may be atypical of 'traditional' enterprise generally. First, the
geographic dispersion of shipping operations necessitates the
separation of ownership of fixed capital from control of its use in
production; managerial authority is vested in the captain and
usually delegated by him to an intermediary. The situation is
little different, however, in the case of production in fixed locations such as textile weaving or handicraft manufacture if, under
some putting-out system, ownership of fixed and working capital is
in the hands of intermediaries or wholesalers. Second, shipping
probably involves a larger investment in fixed capital than most
other kinds of 'traditional' enterprise and trade in particular.
Nevertheless, it is precisely the capacity of the non-corporate
form of organisation to handle fairly substantial investment in
fixed capital that has permitted it to extend into small and medium-
scale mechanised production, including even steel-hulled motor
vessels. Organisational forms have evolved to meet the requirements of new technologies, it is true, but not to the extent of
becoming transformed into the modern corporate form of organisation
(see Dick, 1977, especially Chapter 7). For this reason, a
definition of the informal sector based upon organisation would be
much wider than one based upon technology.

The non-corporate form of organisation has survived precisely
because of its adaptability and its appropriateness to the economic
and social environment. Demonstration of this has been provided
by ill-informed attempts to introduce more modern forms, as the
Japanese attempted to do in the case of junk shipping after 1937:

> ...the operation of junks, the operation of partnerships,
> the method of hiring based on family or personal relation-
> ships, and the method of proportional distribution of
> profits, all have a 'feudal' character and are part of an
> undeveloped environment. Proof of how deeply rooted this
> system is is provided by the failure of the Water Transport
> Section of the North China Transport Company Ltd...to
> reform it after 1937. The company bought up large
> numbers of junks but was unable to operate them with
> modern methods. Because of the difficulty of supervising
> so many junks from a shore-based office, the lack of care
> and maintenance on the part of the crew, and the increase
> in desertion and pilfering, the enterprise was found to be
> uneconomical and inefficient. (Koizumi, 1972, p. 8.)

The condemnation of the non-corporate form of organisation as
'feudal' sits uneasily alongside the failure of modern reforms. As
long as the economic and social environment remains essentially unchanged, governments would be better advised to try to use non-
corporate organisation than to supplant it.

3.   POLICY IMPLICATIONS

Does prahu shipping play a larger or smaller role in Indonesian
interisland shipping as a result of government policies?   Compared
with formal sector shipping, prahu shipping is virtually unregulated.   Prahus must be measured and registered in order to obtain
an annually renewable pass and must receive clearance from both
customs and the harbour master before leaving port (Dick, 1975b,
pp. 101-2).   Prahu owners themselves, however, are not licensed
unless engaged in stevedoring.   Under Government Regulation
No. 2/1969 (as under No. 5/1964 which it revoked) firms engaged in
stevedoring must own at least two prahus (to qualify as a shipping
company) and be licensed.   Prahu freight rates are entirely
unregulated (although there is some nominal regulation of stevedoring rates) and there are no controls over nor assistance for investment.   Government policy has a direct impact, however, in its provision of, or failure to provide, port infrastructure and an indirect
impact through the several forms of investment assistance to the
formal sector.

The neglect of infrastructure in the prahu ports penalises
prahu shipping by increasing cargo-handling costs and slowing turnaround time in port.   In the 1960s, when there was general
deterioration of port facilities, prahu shipping probably suffered
less than formal sector shipping through being far less dependent
upon specialist facilities.   With the rehabilitation and new
investment in port facilities in the 1970s seldom benefiting the
prahu ports, the stage now seems to have been reached where there
might be higher marginal benefits from small investments in facilities in the prahu ports than from similar investments in the main
ports.   Dick (1975a, pp. 87-8) has documented some of the cases of
serious neglect of infrastructure in prahu ports.   Even in Sunda
Kelapa where the government of Jakarta has spent considerable sums
upon improvements, the quay length remains quite inadequate for the
number of prahus needing to unload timber cargoes, necessitating
queuing and long waiting times outside the port.   In addition, the
shallow draught caused by silting of the river has imposed size
restrictions on the building of new prahus with loss of significant
economies of scale (Dick, 1975b, pp. 99-100).

More serious discrimination against prahu shipping occurs in
the many forms of assistance which reduce the cost of capital to
the formal sector (see Dick, 1977, Chapter 11).   First, while
prahu owners are quite unable to obtain long-term loans from
government banks, formal sector firms have access to funds at 15
per cent per annum; as the rate of inflation has been higher than
15 per cent for most of the 1970s, this has involved providing
formal sector firms with capital at negative real rates of interest.
Although prahu owners could probably obtain loans from private
sector banks at rates of 3 per cent per month (more than 40 per
cent per annum), these rates are too high to be attractive for anything other than very short-term borrowing.   Second, indigenous
(*pribumi*) formal sector firms have also benefited from World Bank
rehabilitation loans made available after 1973 at interest rates of
9¼ per cent per annum and, since 1974, have been able to acquire
ships on hire purchase from the National Commercial Fleet Development Corporation at a rate of interest of 10 per cent per annum.
The only special form of assistance available to prahu owners is

small business credits at 12 per cent per annum.   However, not
only is there stiff competition for the limited funds from all
sectors of small business but, also, prahu owners are apparently
eligible only if borrowing for motorisation, which in many trades
is not yet economic.   Third, under the Domestic Investment Law,
formal sector firms undertaking substantial new investment are
eligible for significant tax concessions including tax holidays,
accelerated depreciation allowances, and exemptions from import
duties.   Prahu owners are eligible for none of these concessions.
Thus on all three grounds it seems reasonable to say that prahu
shipping is facing subsidised competition from the formal sector.

When the full range of government regulatory policies
vis-a-vis the formal sector are taken into account, however, the
implicit subsidy to the formal sector (or implicit tax upon the
prahu sector) appears much smaller.   Dick (1977) has argued that
the net effect of government policy is probably to reduce the
efficiency of formal sector shipping through the weakening of
competitive pressures; new entrants are discouraged by licensing
policy while existing inefficient firms are those benefiting most
from investment subsidies.   Therefore, although prahu shipping is
penalised by neglect of infrastructure and disqualification from
investment assistance, these are at least partially offset by the
advantages of being virtually unregulated.

Evidence that on balance prahu shipping may not be greatly
disadvantaged *vis-a-vis* the formal sector is the fact that its main
competition comes not from the formal sector but from *lokal* shipping
— small-scale wooden and steel hulled motorships of between 35 and
175 gross tons — which is also virtually unregulated.   The main
regulatory requirement is that a *lokal* shipping firm, like a prahu
shipping firm engaged in stevedoring, must own at least two ships
with a minimum combined gross tonnage of 175 tons in order to
obtain a licence.   *Lokal* shipping is eligible for none of the
forms of investment assistance available to the formal sector.   The
two main advantages conferred upon *lokal* shipping by government
policy are better access to state bank credit and use of the better
facilities in the small ship ports which are shared with prahus.
Neither advantage would seem to be crucial.   It is probably far
more important that *lokal* shipowners, being mostly Chinese, and
formerly traders, have good access to capital within the predominantly Chinese business community while prahu owners, who are
entirely indigenous (*pribumi*) Indonesian, are forced to rely almost
entirely upon their own resources.

Lokal shipping is even more difficult than prahu shipping to
fit into the formal/informal sector dichotomy.   In terms of
technology, it extends from intermediate technology in the case of
wooden-hulled motor vessels to modern technology in the case of
steel-hulled motor vessels.   In terms of organisation there is
also considerable variation depending to some extent on the size of
the firm.   When firms are small there tends to be more reliance
upon joint ownership; and vessels in excess of the minimum of two
required to be owned under the terms of a *lokal* licence are often
just managed on behalf of the numerous unlicensed owners.   As
accumulated profits are reinvested, the number of vessels under
direct ownership displace those formerly managed and the active
members of the firm displace former sleeping partners.   A growing
firm thereby relies relatively less and less on management and

more on capital.   From being little more than a management agent
at one extreme, a firm may eventually acquire ships larger than 175
gross tons and in effect graduate to the formal sector.   Even so,
elements of the non-corporate form of organisation are liable to
remain in the reliance upon personal ties in management and upon at
least quasi profit-sharing systems of remuneration to generate
organisational loyalty.   Thus, in practice there is a continuum of
organisational forms and where the line is drawn between formal and
informal sectors can be quite arbitrary.

    If this analysis is correct, then in the Indonesian inter-
island shipping industry at least, the competition faced by the
informal sector (prahu shipping) arises less from the existence of
a formal sector as such than from the upward mobility of successful
informal sector firms adopting more modern technologies and accumulating capital.   In other words, competition is not merely a
reflection of the conflict between two pre-existing modes of
production but is generated from within the informal sector in the
process of development.   It is important to note, however, that
this has been the case only over the past twenty years.   Until the
seizure of Dutch enterprises and the expulsion of Dutch nationals
in December 1957, interisland shipping was dominated by the foreign
shipping corporation known as the KPM.   This company used its
monopoly power so vigorously that by the middle of 1939 there was
only one ship larger than 100 tons in direct competition with the
KPM in the entire archipelago (Dick, 1977, p. 14).   In addition,
there were a large number of prahus because the KPM could not hold
freight rates so low as to suppress them.   After Independence the
company was unable to engage in predatory competitive tactics and
had to face increasing competition from small motor vessels as well
as prahus.   Since 1957 the large state shipping corporation Pelni
has been too inefficient to provide effective competition to small
private interisland firms (none of whom in 1974 owned more than ten
ships) or to *lokal* shipping firms and prahus (Dick, 1977).   The
industry has, therefore, become quite fragmented and it now makes
little sense to talk of monopoly capital in the formal sector.

    Given that the competition faced by prahu shipping comes
mainly from the development of firms in the small-scale motorship
sector, it is an important question whether prahu owners are able
to switch to motor vessels and share in the same upward mobility.
The evidence is that very few prahu owners have done so.   The main
reason would seem to be the great discontinuity in technology
between a prahu and even an auxiliary motor vessel, requiring
completely new expertise and involving substantial modifications to
organisation.   Lack of capital is an associated but less important
problem.   Many owners of larger prahus either singly   or in
syndicates have sufficient funds to invest in at least wooden-hulled
motor vessels, even though these are about two to three times the
cost of a prahu of the same capacity.   The fact is that they would
prefer to build two or three new prahus than one motor vessel, if
not to invest their funds instead in trade or village land as
security for their old age.   Larger prahus engaged in the booming
timber trade remain highly profitable.   Smaller prahus, which have
been hardest hit by the competition from small-scale motor vessels,
are less profitable but their owners are thereby less able to
finance investment in motor vessels.   Only a few more daring prahu
owners have had both the capital and the desire to make the transition from sail to motor vessels.   Even should their number be

increased by government subsidies for motorisation, however, the plight of the remaining small prahu owners would be worsened because the competition from motorised shipping would thereby intensify. Motorisation may help the fortunes of some prahu owners but it cannot help the whole industry.

Despite the increasing competitive pressure upon some sections of prahu shipping, it will remain a viable technology until such time as real wages begin to rise in Indonesia. As in the case of the timber trade, economic growth is in fact likely to increase the demand for some prahu cargoes. Moreover, insofar as oil prices in Indonesia follow rising world trends, sail shipping may even improve its competitiveness *vis-a-vis* motor shipping. The government would, therefore, be advised to concentrate not upon promoting motorisation but upon eliminating as far as possible the sources of discrimination against prahu shipping. These include the neglect of infrastructure in the prahu ports and the difficulties which prahu owners face in gaining access to institutional sources of finance. In addition, government cargoes are virtually denied to prahu shipping. Private interisland shipping firms and the state interisland shipping corporation are obliged to carry government cargoes such as rice, sugar, salt, cement and fertiliser at official rates below opportunity cost, even though much lower than official rates would still be greater than the opportunity cost if the cargoes were in part carried by prahu. Ideally, the government would not merely provide prahu owners with better access to institutional sources of finance but raise interest rates generally to better reflect the relative shadow prices of labour and capital and thereby redress the balance in favour of more labour-intensive technologies. This would run counter, however, to the strong vested interests in a cheap capital policy.

The failure of the government to revise their policies in this way may stem in large part from well-intentioned ignorance. Dick (1973b, p. 103) quoted the case of one senior port official who accompanied a foreign adviser on an inspection of the prahu port which, although it lay within easy walking distance of his office, he admitted to never before having visited. Similarly, officers of the Department of Agriculture seldom visit factories unless to attend an official opening of a new project. Speaking with prahu owners or captains, farmers or businessmen simply to gain a better understanding of their problems would constitute an admission that officials were not already well-informed of their problems and thereby undermine their self-importance. If those in the prahu industry wish to draw a particular problem to the attention of the government they must do so through their association Pepelra (*Persatuan Pengusaha Pelayaran Rakyat*: Prahu Shipowners Association), which the government regards as the proper channel for communication of industry views. Government policy is, therefore, based upon bureaucratic prejudice as much as upon the facts of the situation.

Official ignorance of the role and organisation of prahu shipping may reflect not only intellectual laziness and bureaucratic arrogance, however, but also some fundamental attitudes towards the modernisation process. The government appears to interpret its role as promoting the development of the modern sector, implying both modern technology and modern forms of organisation· Long-term credit at very low or negative real

interest rates and taxation concessions upon capital-intensive new
investments both serve this purpose.   Modernisation would not be
promoted by allowing informal sector firms the same access to these
types of subsidies.   'Protection all round' would defeat their
purpose which is none other than to discriminate in favour of the
modern or formal sector.   A cheap interest policy cannot be aban-
doned because it is the basis of the government's modernisation
strategy.   This interpretation is consistent with the emphasis
devoted to the motorisation of sailing prahus as the government's
only substantive policy towards prahu shipping (see Dick, 1975b,
pp. 94-9)for a full discussion of motorisation policy).   By
motorisation prahus would take their place on at least the fringe
of the modern sector.   Another embarrassing sign of backwardness
would thereby be eliminated.   The same motivation probably lies
behind the banishment of smaller prahus, which are less of a tourist
attraction, from ports near main city centres to more remote locations where, invariably, the promised improved facilities have not
been completed.   The intention does not seem to have been to
deliberately penalise the prahus, which officials appear happy to
tolerate — neither directly encouraging nor directly discouraging
them — provided they are out of sight.   Once out of sight, however, they tend to be forgotten.

     The Indonesian government would therefore appear to support
what Emmerij (1974, p. 202) has called the 'inherent disadvantage'
argument on the development of the informal sector.   This argument,
he suggests, runs as follows:

>   ...with marginal adaptations, it is the industrial
>   technology of the West that must be the basis of economic
>   growth...This technology implies a scale of operation, a
>   degree of expertise and an institutional organisation
>   beyond the capabilities of small entrepreneurs...The two
>   types of enterprise compete neither for consumers nor for
>   resources, or, to the extent that they do the industrial
>   technology is almost invariably the more efficient.
>   Hence a policy of confining foreign exchange, finance
>   capital and state favours to the formal sector is techno-
>   logically and economically realistic and does not in any
>   way hinder the small-scale sector, which, in any case,
>   could not take advantage of these benefits.

At the same time, however,

>   ...legal restrictions on the informal sector should be
>   eliminated and...assistance should be given to particularly
>   promising small-scale enterprises which - against the odds
>   - do seem capable of "making the jump".

The conclusion to which this line of argument leads is that

>   ...the fostering of industrial technology does not in any
>   important way harm the small-scale or informal sector, and
>   that any harm that does result is the inevitable conse-
>   quence of the struggle between the efficient and inefficient.
>   While...(this) may have somewhat unfortunate consequences such
>   as a slow rate of employment growth, excessive foreign

involvement in strategic industries, and income
inequality...these problems must be solved by means
other than the encouragement of an informal sector
which either is inefficient or, if efficient, has no
growth potential.

The contrary view is what Emmerij (1974, pp. 202-3) has called the
'structural disadvantage' argument:

...the fact that most indigenous enterprises are small
is the consequence of the structure of an economy in
which a number of policy measures favour the informal
sector.   Legal harassment of small enterprises and the
imposition of health and safety regulations are only the
most obvious.   Equally, or even more, important is the
competitive advantage enjoyed by large enterprise,
especially as a result of state measures reducing the
cost of capital (duty-free import of capital goods, low
interest rates) and restricting competition (high tariffs,
quotas, and building, health and safety regulations)...
(The) economic success (of large-scale firms) is...a
consequence of the privileges they enjoy, not of inherent
technical or economic efficiency.

Both lines of argument, which Emmerij seems to have summarised most
fairly, have two serious deficiencies.   First, they neglect the
importance of intermediate technologies and intermediate forms of
organisation.   Second, they overlook the considerable opportunities so well exploited in Japanese and Chinese industralisation of
integrating different technologies and forms of organisation at
differing stages of production in the same industry.   The formal/
informal sector dichotomy suffers from the same deficiencies.
Overcoming them is the challenge for future research and policy in
this field.

4.   CONCLUSION

When an attempt is made to define rigorously the formal and informal
sectors, it becomes clear that the dichotomy is an empty one.
Presumably it is meant to encompass more than technology as recognised in the old modern/traditional dichotomy.   This at least had
the merit of simplicity because the distinction between mechanical
and non-mechanical power was easily quantifiable.   Yet if
organisation is also taken into account, the neat dichotomy dis-
appears and is replaced by a continuum which overrides differences
in technology.   While there is a clear dichotomy between large
corporations and petty traders, for example, as more highly
organised activities, prahu and junk shipping falls somewhere in
between.   Accordingly, it seems useful to distinguish between
three main forms of organisation: corporate (or 'rational bureaucratic'), non-corporate, and unincorporated.   The non-corporate
form is characterised by fragmentation of individual capital, exercise of direct personal management and consequently small size, the
importance of intermediaries, and reliance upon personal relationships and profit-sharing to maintain organisational loyalty.   These

characteristics may be found in small-scale motor shipping as well
as in prahu and junk shipping and even nominally formal sector
shipping firms display some of them.   Their utility in the economic
and social environment suggests the inappropriateness of development efforts based upon the 'rational bureaucratic' form of
organisation.

        Government policy discriminates against prahu shipping in its
neglect of port infrastructure and in the provision of long-term
capital at low or even negative real rates of interest to formal
sector firms through state banks to which prahu owners have no
access.   This discrimination is substantially weakened, however,
by the freedom of prahu shipping from the regulation imposed by the
government upon the formal sector.   The main competition faced by
prahu shipping comes not in fact from the formal sector but from
small-scale motor shipping.   Although the operators of such
shipping receive somewhat better port facilities than prahu shipping
and have access to institutional capital, their competitiveness
does not seem to reflect primarily any discrimination in their
favour.   Rather, it seems to arise from the upward mobility of
successful traditional-commercial trading firms, at least on the
fringe of the informal sector, able to adopt more modern technology
and accumulate capital.   The failure of prahu shipping firms to
display similar upward mobility seems to stem from their reluctance
to concentrate capital in the unfamiliar modern technology of
motorships.   Hence, in economists' jargon, there is factor
immobility.   This may be partially overcome by subsidies to prahu
owners investing in motorisation.   Nevertheless, while this may
benefit an enterprising few, it will merely worsen the competition
from motor vessels faced by the remaining owners of sailing prahus.
Until such time as rising real wages and perhaps a falling opportunity cost of capital renders pure sail shipping uneconomic, the
government would be advised to adopt positive policies to make
better use of a technology which economises on scarce capital and
utilises abundant labour to produce the cheapest possible sea
transport services.   Even if existing forms of discrimination are
not eliminated, some offsetting assistance could be provided as a
second-best measure.   This seems unlikely, however, because
support of a traditional technology would run counter to the
government's apparent modernisation strategy.   Perhaps the best
the prahu shipping firms can hope for is a continuing absence of
direct regulation which will permit them to survive because, unlike
some other unmechanised technologies, sailing prahus remain
commercially viable at existing distorted relative factor prices.

REFERENCES

Dick, H.W. (1975a),   'Prahu Shipping in Eastern Indonesia',
                           Bulletin of Indonesian Economic Studies,
                           11(2), pp. 69-107.

Dick, H.W. (1975b),   'Prahu Shipping in Eastern Indonesia',
                           Bulletin of Indonesian Economic Studies,
                           11(3), pp. 81-103.

Dick, H.W. (1977),   The Indonesian interisland shipping
                           industry: a case study in competition
                           and regulation, unpublished Ph.D.
                           thesis in Economics, RSPacS, Australian
                           National University, Canberra.

Emmerij, L. (1974),   'A New Look at Some Strategies for
                           Increasing Productive Employment in
                           Africa', *International Labour Review*,
                           110, pp. 199-219.

Feuerwerker, A. (1958),   *China's Early Industrialization: Sheng
                           Hsuan-huai and Mandarin Enterprise*,
                           Cambridge, Mass.

Hayashi, T. (1972),   'The Shipping Brokers and Transport
                           Companies of Soochow' in A. Watson
                           (trans), *Transport in Transition*,
                           Michigan Abstracts of Chinese and
                           Japanese Works on Chinese History,
                           No. 3, Michigan University, Ann Arbor,
                           pp. 35-52.

Hou, C.M. (1965),   *Foreign Investment and Economic Devel-
                           opment in China, 1840-1937*, Cambridge,
                           Mass.

International Labour   *Employment, Incomes and Equality: A
Office (1972),   Strategy for Increasing Productive
                           Employment in Kenya*, International
                           Labour Office, Geneva.

Kosaka, T. and   'Junk Ownership and Operation in North
Nakamura, Y. (1972),   China' in A. Watson (trans), *Transport
                           in Transition*, Michigan Abstracts of
                           Chinese and Japanese Works on Chinese
                           History, No. 3, Michigan University,
                           Ann Arbor, pp. 53-6.

Koizumi, T. (1972),   'The Operation of Chinese Junks' in
                           A. Watson (trans), *Transport in Transi-
                           tion*, Michigan Abstracts of Chinese and
                           Japanese Works on Chinese History,
                           No. 3, Michigan University, Ann Arbor,
                           pp. 1-12.

Long Term Fleet
  Development Team (1973),   Study on the long term development
                                 planning of the Indonesian interisland
                                 fleet, Interim Report, Indonesian
                                 National Shipowners Association,
                                 Jakarta.

McGee, T.G. (1973),   'Peasants in the Cities: A Paradox, A
                                 Paradox, A Most Ingenious Paradox',
                                 Human Organization, 32(2), pp. 135-42.

Nagasaka, H. (1972),   'Junk Ownership in Soochow' in A.
                                 Watson (trans), *Transport in Transition*,
                                 Michigan Abstracts of Chinese and
                                 Japanese Works on Chinese History,
                                 No. 3, Michigan University, Ann Arbor,
                                 pp. 71-7.

Nakamura, Y. (1972),   'Shipping Brokers in North China' in
                                 A. Watson (trans), *Transport in Transi-
                                 tion*, Michigan Abstracts of Chinese and
                                 Japanese Works on Chinese History,
                                 No. 3, Michigan University, Ann Arbor,
                                 pp. 15-34.

Rimmer, P.J. (1976),   'A Framework for Considering the Trans-
                                 port Needs of Urban Areas and Non-urban
                                 Areas in Southeast Asia' in *Journal of
                                 the Society of Automotive Engineers*, 36
                                 pp. 30-9.

Sethuraman, S.V. (1976),   'The Urban Informal Sector: Concept,
                                 Measurement and Policy', *International
                                 Labour Review*, 114(1), pp. 69-81.

Teshima, M. and Arai, Y.   'Junk Crews in Soochow' in A. Watson
  (1972),   (trans), *Transport in Transition*,
                                 Michigan Abstracts of Chinese and
                                 Japanese Works on Chinese History,
                                 No. 3, Michigan University, Ann Arbor,
                                 pp. 57-70.

CHAPTER 11

THE ENVIRONMENT OF INFORMALITY:

A COMPARISON BETWEEN CARIBBEAN AND PACIFIC[*]

HAROLD BROOKFIELD[**]

1. INTRODUCTION

One of the more striking features of the contemporary human
geography of the eastern islands of Fiji, identified by the United
Nations Educational, Scientific and Cultural Organisation (UNESCO)/
United Nations Fund for Population Activity (UNFPA) Project
(1977)[***], was the difficulty encountered by islanders seeking to
diversify production for the market from under the massive 'coconut
overlay' that has spread a one-crop economy across an ecologically
varied region of rich natural potential. The enterprise of individual farmers in growing crops for the urban market in Suva was
'helped' by the formation of a National Marketing Authority in
1971, but in practice this organisation has interpreted its role
more in relation to holding down prices for the urban consumer, so
that farmers have been poorly served both by low prices and a poor
collection record. It is useful to compare this situation with
that on ecologically similar outer islands in the Caribbean where a
large trade in vegetable produce for the more industrialised
islands has grown up and has been sustained through many years.
The comparison will lead us to some thoughts on the role of the
informal sector in transport and rural development.

2. FREIGHT FORWARDING AND THE ECONOMY OF ST VINCENT[****]

St Vincent in the Windward Islands was a 'late developing' island
by Caribbean standards. Although there was early settlement from

---

[*]   The substantive material in this paper is extracted from a
paper prepared by the writer for the United Nations Educational,
Scientific and Cultural Organisation (UNESCO) for a United Nations
Conference on Trade and Development meeting on the transport
problems of outer islands. It must, therefore, be stated that all
opinions expressed are those of the writer and do not necessarily
reflect the views of UNESCO.

[**]   Professor H.C. Brookfield is Professor, Department of
Geography, University of Melbourne, Melbourne, Victoria.

[***]   Professor Brookfield was Chief Technical Adviser of the
UNESCO/UNFPA (United Nations Fund for Population Activity) Project.

[****] Work in St Vincent was carried out in 1971 and 1972.   The
present tense refers to those years.

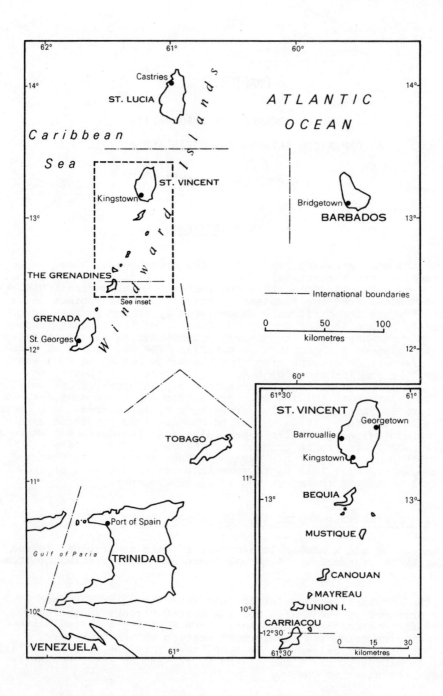

Fig. 11.1: Caribbean; inset showing St Vincent and The Grenadines.

Barbados, and some sugar plantations were established, most of the
northern part of the island was taken from the Caribs only at the
end of the eighteenth century.   A varied plantation economy was
set up, growing sugar, coconuts, and arrowroot in particular, but
by 1970 sugar was no longer exported, the arrowroot industry had
declined seriously, and the principal export staple had since 1953
become bananas, grown by between 7000 and 8000 registered growers,
graded at packing stations and again at the wharf, and shipped on a
regular weekly schedule by Geest Line ships to the United Kingdom.
Some 80 per cent of farmers in the island participated in the
business which, however, offered only very minimal returns; if
farmer's labour and family labour were costed at the going agricultural wage, production was taking place at a loss in 1972.

       Members of the Arrowroot Association, by contrast, comprised
only 210 growers of whom seventeen, classed as 'large growers',
provided 67 per cent of production both by weight and value.   Two
private factories survived; two others were maintained by the
Arrowroot Board.   This industry, however, was in severe difficulties because of its labour intensity; while some small growers provided co-operative help to each other, large growers were having
difficulty in obtaining labour at $EC2.40 - 4.00 per day*.   One of
the few remaining large estates closed down and was subdivided in
1968.   Export was by occasional foreign-going vessels, at an
average interval of a month, which often picked up nothing else at
St Vincent, and some arrowroot went to Barbados for trans-shipment.

       Apart from small quantities of nutmegs, mace, coffee and lime
juice, and the supply of West Indian vegetable crops and whole
coconuts to the immigrant market in Britain and North America, to
be discussed below, this represented virtually the whole of the
surviving staple export production of the St Vincent economy for
metropolitan markets.   With the tourist industry operating
virtually as an enclave industry on certain of the Grenadines, and
represented only by a few small hotels on the main island, this was
by itself a very inadequate base for a population of 80,000 including some 10,000 farmers.   St Vincent is a mountainous volcanic
island, its central and northern part still largely in forest and
dominated by the periodically active Soufriere, which has mantled
much of the island with volcanic ash in the recent past.   The
eastern windward side of the island has some extensive areas of
open rolling country, but the north and west are deeply dissected
so that the leeward valleys are too close to the mountains to be
dry.   In the northwest is an area accessible only by boat, and some
northern communities are also periodically cut off by land in wet
weather when the road is often blocked.   Less than half the island
is cultivable.   There is only one town, Kingstown, on a sheltered
bay in the southwest, but three smaller townships survive from a
former period when the island had no comprehensive road system.
Kingstown was provided with a large-ships wharf by overseas aid
toward the end of the colonial period, and there is a small-ships
jetty.   An airfield, immediately east of Kingstown, received
regular Leeward Islands Air Transport (LIAT) services up and down
the Windward/Leeward chain and to and from Barbados, and now handles

---

* In 1972 the United States dollar was worth two East Caribbean
dollars. The Reserve Bank does not quote the value of the East
Caribbean dollar against the Australian dollar.

almost all the passenger traffic outside the country; there is also
a small airfield on a tourist island in the southern Grenadines,
and two of these islands also have jetties with safe anchorages for
small ships.   The two largest, Bequia and Union, have miniature
towns.   The Grenadines, by contrast with St Vincent itself, on the
other hand, produces a wide range of root crops and vegetables,
dominated by sweet potatoes, the taros (eddoes, dasheen *Colocasia*
sp. and tannia, *Xanthosoma* sp.) and yams.

        Supply of vegetables and copra to Barbados, with its special-
ised sugar-growing economy, has probably been an element in the St
Vincent economy since the nineteenth century, and in the nineteenth
and early twentieth centuries vessels carried St Vincent vegetable
produce also to Trinidad and even Guyana, bringing back rice from
the latter.   This interisland trade was never an important activity
of the Europe-based vessels, which cruised down the chain dropping
imports and picking up exports, and handling the better-paying
passenger traffic.   It is even less so today when frequent and
regular overseas cargo/passenger service is confined to the specialised and expensive Geest Line ships, other foreign-going vessels
are infrequent and most imports are trans-shipped at Barbados and
Trinidad and brought to St Vincent on a variety of vessels.   This
service is dominated by 'Federal' ships which had been intended to
form the core of a national shipping line for the abortive West
Indian Federation and still ply regular cargo/passenger services
through the islands (see Keirstead and Levitt, 1963).   These ships
carry little agricultural produce which both originates and terminates within the West Indies.

        The island agricultural trade has therefore remained almost
wholly the business of the auxiliary schooners, vessels of from
thirty to sixty tons which still voyage mainly under sail up and
down the islands.   Still smaller vessels, based mainly within the
Grenadines, trade between St Vincent and its own outer islands,
and also down to Carriacou, where produce is trans-shipped to and
from Grenada, sometimes being trans-shipped both at Union and
Carriacou on the way (Fig. 11.1).   The rapid urban/industrial
growth experienced in Trinidad and Barbados, and the tourist development that has also taken place on Barbados, Antigua and other
Leeward islands since the Second World War, has created a considerable growth in demand for the agricultural produce of the Windward
Islands, and during the 1950s and early 1960s it seems that there
was quite intense competition for this traffic, accompanied by
alternating shortages and gluts on the urban markets which played
havoc with the prices received by farmers, traffickers* and shipowners alike.   St Vincent, therefore, set up an Agricultural
Marketing Board to buy produce in accordance with demand at regulated prices, and thus stimulate the growth of vegetable production
on the island as a substitute for the ailing export staples.

---

* Traffickers, or 'speculators', are traders in agricultural
produce who buy from farmers or in the Kingstown market and consign
at their own expense to agents in the markets at Bridgetown
(Barbados), Port-of-Spain (Trinidad) and other places. Their continuing role is discussed in detail below.

Today, by their own estimate, they handle between 70 and 75 per cent of the whole business, but as we shall see below, this gross figure is rather illusory.   Their regulated prices, and their insistence that all produce sold to them be bought only in Kingstown, delivered there by the farmers or their agents, are causes of discontent; the cost to farmers of getting produce to Kingstown varies from around $EC0.20 to as much as $EC2.50.

The fruit and vegetable business has, however, now been taken up by almost all farmers in St Vincent, large and small.   It is very difficult to quantify this business. The Agricultural Marketing Board buys almost $EC1,000,000-worth a year, dominated in weight terms by sweet potatoes and taro for the Trinidad market, but including also a very much wider range of higher-value produce, much of which is grown by only a small number of farmers.   The outlets for farmers include: the Agricultural Marketing Board, the Kingstown market and lesser markets in Georgetown and Barroualie, hawking, and most significantly traffickers, who buy directly from the farmers, sometimes at their houses, sometimes on the farm, sometimes even in the field.   With regard to the Agricultural Marketing Board, data were extracted from sample daily records covering twelve days during which goods valued at approximately $EC24,000 were delivered.   Sixty-three per cent came from the windward areas of the island; 36 per cent was drawn from within eight kilometres of the centre of Kingstown, but almost 30 per cent came from areas twelve to sixteen kilometres distant, while the sparsely peopled settlements on the northern tip of St Vincent contributed 4 per cent, in addition to supplying charcoal carried by boat to Kingstown and hawked around the town.   Examination of these data shows that the dominance of root crops is sustained in almost every part of the island and that there is only a very weak tendency for remoter communities to specialise in goods with a higher-value/weight ratio (Table 11.1). This form of specialisation varies more with size of farm, and type of operator, than with distance.

Kingstown market is a second major outlet, and one in which middlemen/women as well as producer-sellers operate extensively. The weekly Kingstown market, operating on Friday and Saturday, is a mixture of producer-sellers and middlemen.   The result of a survey, details of which are unfortunately still in the limbo where lost postal articles find a haven, showed that only 19 per cent of sellers, mainly from near Kingstown, produce their own goods, while 23 per cent bought their produce in the country area, 17 per cent off buses arriving in the town, 27 per cent from the farmers and 14 per cent from middlemen.   More than a third of the vendors had no other occupation, and more than half became market-sellers in their teens, sell in the market regularly and trade only on their own behalf. There is a good deal of within-market trading and it is the main centre of supply for the Grenadines and even Carriacou. The ship that goes down the Grenadines on a Saturday is heavily laden with market produce, some of which is immediately trans-shipped at the terminus, Union, onto schooners sailing on to Carriacou in Grenada; a few very vocal trafficking women handle this business*.

---

* The market survey was conducted on two Saturdays in 1972 by an enthusiastic team of girls from Kingstown High School. Apologies, but largely on behalf of Canada Post, are due to these helpers for the loss of all but the preliminary analysis of their data.

TABLE 11.1:   ST VINCENT CROP DELIVERIES TO THE
AGRICULTURAL MARKETING BOARD ON A SAMPLE OF 12
DAYS IN 1972

Distance band from Kingstown km	Fruit %	Vegetables %	Root crops %	Other %	Total tonnes	Value of deliveries EC$/kg
0 - 2	4.5	11.6	83.9	–	5.26	0.18
2 - 4	1.3	20.1	78.6	–	6.95	0.20
4 - 6	0.7	13.9	85.4	–	24.67	0.19
6 - 8	3.9	11.4	83.9	0.8	22.77	0.19
8 - 10	18.6	16.3	65.1	–	4.87	0.29
10 - 12	–	18.3	81.2	0.5	7.55	0.23
12 - 14	0.9	18.2	80.8	–	17.43	0.29
14 - 16	1.1	4.9	93.7	0.3	9.11	0.22
16 - 18	–	2.6	97.4	–	1.82	0.16
18 - 20	–	10.3	78.8	10.9	2.76	0.32
20 - 22	–	35.5	64.3	–	0.04	0.34
22 - 24	–	100.0	–	–	0.00	0.55
24 - 26	–	2.7	97.3	–	5.49	0.16

Source: St Vincent Agricultural Marketing Board.

The exports of the Agricultural Marketing Board are analysed in Table 11.2; the Agricultural Marketing Board does put some produce on sale in Kingstown, but this is mostly rejected produce (like the bananas put on sale by the Banana Board), and their main concern is with export.   It is clear from Table 11.2 that the Agricultural Marketing Board has conceived its major function in terms of creating a new 'staple export' for St Vincent in its vegetable produce, so that they have searched widely for outlets and no less than 39 per cent of their exports in 1972 went to 'temperate' countries with West Indian populations, outstandingly Britain.   The produce, which is consigned by the Geest Line ships, goes mainly to a Vincentian company established in the United Kingdom and specialising in the retailing of West Indian produce through shops and market-stallholders in those British towns with a large immigrant population from the West Indies.   Supplies to Canada and New York go mainly by air.   Though the base of the Agricultural Marketing Board traffic is the supply of sweet potatoes and, to a lesser extent, taro to Trinidad, their energies are obviously directed to the search for a wider market.   Within the island trade, their most important role is to control the supply and price of sweet potatoes sent to Trinidad; beyond this large but basic trade, it could be that as much as 50 per cent still remains in the hands of the traffickers.

TABLE 11.2:   EXPORTS OF ST VINCENT VEGETABLES, FRUIT AND
COCONUTS BY THE AGRICULTURAL MARKETING BOARD BETWEEN
JANUARY AND NOVEMBER 1972

Destination	Value		Months in which supplies sent
	$EC	Per cent	Number
Trinidad	379,343	45.7	11
United Kingdom	286,252	34.5	11
Barbados	57,804	7.0	11
Guyana	51,084	6.2	7
United States of America	19,766	2.4	1
Canada	11,036	1.3	4
Bermuda	6,012	0.7	4
St Lucia	5,983	0.7	5
St Maarten/St Thomas/St Croix	5,089	0.6	3
Belgium	3,874	0.5	2
Antigua/Montserrat	2,046	0.3	3
Dominica	1,315	0.2	3
Grenada	658	0.1	2

Source: St Vincent Agricultural Marketing Board.

Including all 'peripheral' part-time dealers, there may be as many as sixty traffickers in St Vincent, but the core group numbers only about twenty.   They are people in very varied circumstances and of very varied origins.   One, an emigrant to Britain in 1951, left his job as a telephone operator to join his Bajan (Barbados) brother-in-law in the business of importing West Indian produce into Britain.   He tried to deal through the Agricultural Marketing Board but found that they gave preference to the established company, so

returned to St Vincent himself to handle the exporting end of the
business.   Like other successful traffickers, he buys root crops
carefully, wraps them individually, and relies on his personal contacts to get crops out of the ground at exactly the right stage.
The business continues unsatisfactorily, however, and he is now
shifting to importing fish from Britain, split peas from Europe,
and flour for sale on the local market.

This man is exceptional.   The range also includes another
man, operating in a big way, whose wife spends much of her time in
Trinidad telephoning home every second day or so on the state of
the market there; he uses agents only when his wife is at home in
St Vincent.   In Trinidad, she sells to agents who in turn sell to
traders on the Port-of-Spain market, and she keeps in constant
touch with the state of demand — she telephoned her husband during
our interview — so that he can adjust his buying most accurately
to what is required.   His business prospers, even if his marriage
is slightly unusual.   A little lower down the scale is a man who
consigns to contacts in Trinidad only about once a month.   He is
also a farmer, and went into trafficking to widen his profit opportunities.   Unlike the bigger operators, who regard the Agricultural
Marketing Board as a valuable stabilising influence in the market,
he considers that the government organisation squeezes the small man
out of the more profitable lines.   He buys all over the island,
but has no telephone with which to keep informed, so his business
is always a gamble.

At the bottom of the range in one sense, but not in others,
are two women in partnership, both of whom went into trafficking at
an early age to help support their families.   When interviewed
they were packing produce to take to Barbados on the 'Federal Palm'
as personal cargo.   They go both to Barbados and Trinidad, and
rarely consign; they sell to middlemen, or more rarely directly to
market vendors.   More than once, they have chartered a vessel at
$EC1000 to go up to the Dutch island of St Maarten, more than 500
kilometres distant.   There is good business there for St Vincent
produce, but no return cargo except salt from Antigua, and they have
to run the risk of customs, for this trade is illegal.   They have
no advantage of telephone, and depend entirely on their personal
networks for information.   They protested strongly at the intrusion
into the business of an American, who was operating a motorised
vessel with ventilated hold, and had contracts with Barbados hotels
who preferred to deal with a regular supplier — and perhaps preferred to deal with a European.   He had operated from St Lucia and
Dominica, but because supplies there were short was now entering
the St Vincent trade, buying regularly and reaching Barbados ahead
of the regular traffickers, so that there was no market when the
latter arrived.   The two ladies had tried to organise a protest
against him, because he was taking money from local people, but it
came to nothing.

Traffickers depend entirely on the schooners, which operate
frequently but irregularly.   Outside harbour, they generally use
only sails to save money; their crews are relatively large but they
handle most of their own stevedoring, and the ships need repair two
of even three times a year.   Rates charged were in 1972 $EC18/ton
to Trinidad and $EC12/ton to Barbados.   However, as an agent
pointed out:

There are many weaknesses in the system.   Goods are
almost always understated so that a stated 600 lb of
eddoes [taro] could be 6000 lb.   Crates are underestimated though these are always measured; cubic
measure is found to be the best way to make charges.
The content also may not be stated; eddoes could become
potatoes and so on.   Large quantities of liquor are
also carried.   One schooner is from Bequia, two are
from Union, owned and crewed.   [Ship A] has paid
$10,000 of fines in Trinidad, but the owner always
claims ignorance.   It is not worthwhile to check;
there are too many ways of cheating...Sacks are charged
$1.20 whatever the size, so some traffickers sew two
sacks together.   Vessels are never fully laden going
south; the profit is northbound, carrying general cargo
and usually fully loaded.   The crews are not really
large, though they are also stevedores, unlike on the
iron boats.   But though wages are low, they make up
for it on the pilfering and smuggling.   Delays add to
costs; boats have to wait up to 14 days for a berth in
Port-of-Spain instead of staying only two or three days
(Interview, Kingstown, August 1972).

There are also leakages in the system.   Most ships are crewed
in the Grenadines, and call there on both outward and homeward
journeys.   Thus, the 'supermarket' in Clifton, Union Island, is
stocked only with goods from Trinidad; contraband unloaded in the
Grenadines can later enter Kingstown at the small-ships wharf without further check; even vessels entering Kingstown directly from
Trinidad and Guyana have often found means of concealing the most
valuable part of their cargoes against the most stringent checks.
In volume and value as recorded, the outward traffic from the
islands amounts to only a third of the inward traffic of imported
goods and the products of manufacture in Port-of-Spain or Bridgetown.   It is these imports, including trans-shipped imports, from
Port-of-Spain and Bridgetown that fill the ships and keep them in
profit; the export traffic of yams, taro, cassava flour (Farine),
tomatoes, chillies, carrots, ginger and so on, really provide no
more than partial back-loadings to fill the vessels.

Not too much reliance can be placed on the outward ships'
manifests held in the Port Office in Kingstown.   Not only do they
omit the substantial leakage through the Grenadines, but they may
also be inaccurate in their own right, as the statement quoted above
demonstrates.   For what they are worth, however, estimates based on
ships' manifests held in the Customs Office in Kingstown show the
approximate amount of tonnes of fruit, vegetables and livestock,
together with coconut products, exported in the months of January
1971 and March and April 1972, data for the last month being
probably incomplete (Table 11.3).

Much of these 'quantities' are made up of estimated cubic
tonnage, 'weight' conversions of livestock, and so on.   The ships
also carry empty bottles, boxes and gas cylinders going back down
to Trinidad, but these are not shown here.   All that can perhaps
be said is that in a good month 300 to 400 tonnes of Vincentian
produce is shipped out by the schooners, representing a significant
proportion of total island production.   But with so much of the

TABLE 11.3: FRUIT, VEGETABLE, LIVESTOCK AND
COCONUT EXPORTS FOR SELECTED MONTHS

Destination	January 1971 tonnes	March 1972 tonnes	April 1972[a] tonnes
Barbados	137	56	70
Trinidad	284	220	80
Antigua	8	-	-

a Possibly incomplete.

Source: Customs Office, Kingstown.

business passing through informal channels and poorly recorded, it
is perhaps better to limit generalisation from this information and
from Table 11.3, to say that the total island traffic, excluding
the exports outside the region, is probably worth about $EC1,000,000
a year on 1972 values.

The persistence of a form of local shipping capable of handling cargo in small quantities over sea distances of several hundred
kilometres, using sail power at sea for economy, and employing
comparatively small crews because of the availability of stevedoring help ashore, has undoubtedly facilitated diversification of the
agricultural economy of this island. Although the regional market
is not productive of large profits, it is more rewarding and more
stable than the overseas export market to the farmer, and offers
opportunity for entrepreneurship at several levels. The so-called
'informal sector' embraces a very large part of this business,
including the sea transport itself, and shows its characteristic
ability to spread the benefits of market participation thinly, but
widely. However, the sea transport itself is the most vulnerable
link in the chain. Most of the schooners are more than thirty
years old and some are more than fifty years old. New schooners
continue to be built, especially on Bequia which has long specialised in this craft, but at a rate insufficient to replace losses.
'Iron boats' are quite widely replacing the schooners in the
Caribbean island trade, demanding greater regularity and a more
formal manner of operation. There are fewer schooners in operation each year and lack of transport is a very definite constraint
to further expansion of agricultural enterprise on St Vincent. As
of 1972 the need for new initiatives in this area has already become
pressing.

3.   DETERIORATION OF SHIPPING SERVICES IN THE EASTERN
ISLANDS OF FIJI

The problem of a one-crop outer island region

The eastern islands of Fiji, like most island areas to the east and
north, the New Hebrides and Solomons, and the outer islands of Papua

New Guinea, grow precisely the same range of crops as the islands of eastern Caribbean. However, the historical evolution of these economies has been very different. Colonial entry into these regions in the later nineteenth century did not destroy the previously-existing indigenous systems, as it had in the Caribbean, but subordinated them wholly to its aims. Large areas of land were alienated, mostly to small-scale capitalists whose immediate origins and financial backing lay in the young economies of Australia, New Zealand and New Caledonia. With such limited backing the attempts of most of the settlers to undertake the labour-intensive cultivation of high-value crops failed, because labour was scarce and its importation, though possible, was beyond their means. Only the more highly-capitalised sugar venture in Fiji succeeded, using Indian indentured labour, and this only on the two main islands. There was never even a short period of planter wealth and influence comparable to that experienced in the West Indies, and a high proportion of planters soon fell into debt to trading companies, which quickly developed vertical integration including control over line-haul and feeder shipping, production, processing and marketing. The crop which succeeded was copra, being in this period in rising demand in Europe thanks to the popularisation of soap among an increasingly affluent working class, and being also a crop with relatively small labour needs, capable of storage for long periods, and readily transportable with minimal technological aids. In the outer islands copra became virtually a means of exchange, and as such was imposed also on the indigenous population from whom taxes and church payments were accepted in copra. A 'coconut overlay' descended over the whole outer island region of the South Pacific between 1880 and 1910, absorbing the best coastal land in almost all areas, and replacing a formerly diversified resource use system, which had supported extensive indigenous trade with the monotony of a one-crop economy. To a great degree, this still remains true of a large part of the outer-island areas of the South Pacific to this day (Fig. 11.2).

The copra industry of the South Pacific did not, however, serve a local or regional demand, but was directed almost entirely to remote markets, mainly in Europe. As modern shipping services evolved they were geared to the collection of copra from estates and agents, and the distribution of supplies, including foodstuffs for the workers that were often imported rather than locally grown. The situation quickly became as it was described by Couper (1967, p. 263):

> The copra trade reaches out to every inhabited island in the three archipelagoes [Fiji, Tonga, Gilbert and Ellice Islands] and it determines to an overwhelming extent the pattern of shipping services. In the GEIC there is little inward movement of any other commodity to the port towns. This results directly from the poor agricultural environment of these islands, from their remoteness from markets for handicrafts, and their inability to market sea resources either internally or externally through inadequate curing and transportation arrangements.

> In Tonga, local self-sufficiency in foodstuffs normally exists and trade in fresh produce is usually a personal one, or for the New Zealand and American Samoa export

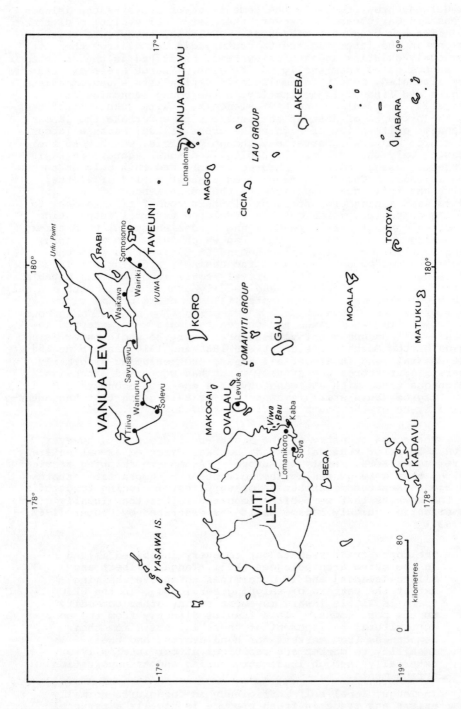

Fig. 11.2: Fiji.

markets.   The situation in Fiji is different.
Here a potential exists for the flow of many commodities in addition to copra, for there are fertile
islands capable of producing these and there is a
constant demand for them in the port towns.   The
limitation to this trade is definitely one of transportation.

As the island trade developed, however, its configuration was determined entirely by the export crop, and although passengers with
personal cargo have always been carried on interisland sections,
there has been negligible interest until recent years in the
carriage of consignment cargo other than copra, timber and other
bulky commodities.   In the later nineteenth century there was
still a considerable number of island-owned vessels, but as these
perished they were rarely replaced, so that by the modern period
since 1945 almost all transport has been controlled from the port
towns of each island group.

The deterioration of service

In eastern Fiji it has never been the practice to operate
vessels around the outer islands; at least since the 1870s these
islands have been served by local vessels operating from Levuka and
later Suva.   Ring-routes and loop-routes (in which a vessel
doubles back to one earlier point before returning to its home port)
have often been followed, and subsidies for certain principal services were introduced as early as 1912.   Nonetheless, there has —
as in other parts of the Pacific — been a gradual pattern of with-
drawal of service from the most outlying places, and this accelerated in recent years.

The operating costs of vessels in the Pacific trade have
always been rather different from those in the Caribbean.   Power
replaced sail much earlier and more completely than in the Caribbean, and almost no commercial vessels have voyaged under sail
alone in the Pacific for more than a quarter of a century.   Perhaps
this is partly because of generally longer sailing distance, but
more important was the concentration of control into company hands;
as Couper (1967) demonstrates, there is still extensive informal
use made of commercial voyages, but the informal sector at sea has
itself almost perished.   There are other differences also.   Larger
crews are generally carried in order to make ships quite independent
of the shore for stevedoring at all outports; the absence of
wharves, necessitating use of workboats, has encouraged this practice.   The largest element in operating costs has therefore consistently been the wages and victualling of the crew, amounting to one-
third the voyage costs of a 'representative steel-hulled vessel' on
the Fiji internal service in 1969-71 (Baker, 1974, p. 169).   The
advanced age of most ships has also ensured that engine repairs and
vessel maintenance costs have been a major cost heading.   The
difficult navigational conditions — perhaps best recounted by
Hilder (1961) — often imposed severe delays so that undue periods
of time were frequently spent in handling only small quantities of
cargo.   The whole business has become increasingly vulnerable to
higher costs, and pressures for steep increases in freight rates
began to mount toward the end of the 1960s and have become increasingly severe in the 1970s.   However, freight rate increases have

generally been restrained, whether by the government regulation, by
a sense of social responsibility, or simply by assessment of the
capacity of consumers to pay.   As a result the cost increases have,
at least in part,had to be compensated in other ways, and this has
been achieved principally by further contraction of services.   More
islands and more outports have lost service altogether; ships spend
less time on voyage, call less frequently, and thus carry more cargo
per voyage.   In eastern Fiji, the average copra load per vessel
entering Suva from the eastern islands increased from 11.58 tonnes
in 1969 to 16.58 tonnes in 1974, an increase of 43 per cent.   This
was accomplished through a decline of only 5.5 per cent in the total
number of voyages between the two years, but by a reduction of 31.0
per cent in the number of islands visited per voyage.

        Where whole islands lose service, the cost can be much more
severe.   In the absence of locally-owned seagoing vessels, it
becomes necessary to charter ships to carry copra to the nearest
pick-up point, and to buy supplies for local consumption on the
island.   At the remote island of Cikobia, north of Vanua Levu, for
example, there has been intermittent direct shipping service until
the last two years.   A government-sponsored copra grading station
was then established on the Vanua Levu mainland, and ships began to
call only at this point, and to cease calls at other places in its
region.   For the Cikobia people, this meant that each tonne of
copra sold earned them $F40 less than it did before.   People from
other remote islands pay a comparable 'hinterland penalty' reducing
their effective income from 15 per cent to 30 per cent, at present
prices.   This penalty is likely to increase sharply in consequence
of rising costs of fuel.

Island initiative and government support

        As indicated Couper (1967) observed that these islands could
supply commodities other than copra.   As late as the 1950s the
Lomaiviti islands were still supplying vegetables to Levuka in
canoes of indigenous design (O'Loughlin, 1956), while farmers in
the south of the large and fertile island of Taveuni — as large as
Barbados — were,on their own initiative,taking or consigning taro
and especially yaqona (a locally-grown stimulant) to the Suva
market.   At some time around this period Indo-Fijians began
business in the 'trafficking' of yaqona from Taveuni and the
Lomaiviti islands, and this has now become a major business.   It
employs about a dozen middlemen on Taveuni; it earned a few hundred
growers an estimated $F150,000 in 1975 and the crop in the ground
was probably worth about $F1,000,000 at 1976 prices, more valuable
than a year's production of copra from the island's groves*.

        Yaqona is a durable crop, capable of storage over long periods
without deterioration.   The vegetable crops on the other hand are
all perishable in the medium to short term.   Taro, which should be
relatively durable, suffers especially in Taveuni from a corm rot
which develops rapidly once the crop is out of the ground.
Nonetheless, Taveuni obtains very high yields of taro (varying
between nine and twenty-six tonnes/ha in our yield measurements).

---

* The rate of exchange was $A1 = $F1.1 on 21 November 1977.

Small groups of Taveuni farmers made a number of attempts to market
their taro in Suva and elsewhere in the 1960s, and the Department
of Fijian Affairs gave them assistance by engaging vessel space and
assisting with collection.   In 1971 Government set up a National
Marketing Authority among whose objectives were:

(a) to provide a guaranteed market for specified primary produce at a
     pre-determined price for different production zones;

(b) to maintain a steady flow of reasonably priced, high quality
     market produce;

(c) to assist in Government's drive to combat inflation by dampen-
     ing upward spirals in produce prices.

In their first few months of activity the National Marketing
Authority bought most of their taro on Taveuni, but at a price
regarded by farmers as derisory.   Subsequently the National Marketing Authority seem to have given priority to the aim of holding
down the cost of market produce for the urban consumer and most of
their buying has been close to Suva.   Their performance on all the
islands has been poor and on Taveuni lamentable; in 1975 and the
first ten months of 1976 they bought respectively only 30.6 per
cent and 48.4 per cent of their pre-determined quota, and at such
irregular intervals that much of the farmers' crop was lost.   The
National Marketing Authority have concerned themselves only with
vegetables and fish from the outer islands; the yaqona trade has
been left almost entirely to the middlemen, some of whom also handle
taro.

     The quality and quantity of shipping services has been a major
factor in the poor performance of the National Marketing Authority
in the outer islands.   Irregular shipping with pace and itinerary
determined by a relatively non-perishable crop — copra — is not
at all well suited to handle trade in perishable vegetables.   The
inner islands of Lomaiviti, together with Kadavu to the south of
Suva, have good and frequent connection by small vessels.   Lau is
too remote, and too infrequently served to participate significantly
in the supply of the capital.   Taveuni occupies an intermediate
position; most of its shipping is now in the 200-400 ton category,
but calls are irregular — two or three vessels may arrive almost
simultaneously followed by no ship in more than two weeks.   Vessels
voyage the coast of Taveuni, nearby Vanua Levu and small islands,
for copra; perishable cargoes have to be fitted in where possible,
and not always at the end of the island voyage.   Coupled with a
buying policy which treats Taveuni taro as only a reserve source of
supply, the effect has caused great dissatisfaction and threatens
to destroy a genuine farmers' initiative.

4.   CONCLUSION: FORMAL OR INFORMAL?

A beleaguered set of small traders, operating by methods which range
from something very close to 'formal' company operation to the most
'informal' together with the persistence of a transport mode which
suits their style of business, have facilitated the widespread
diversification of the whole agricultural economy of St Vincent.
Is this, then, a method of operation suited also to Fiji, and if

so what steps are required to facilitate its development?   Both
regions have marketing boards, the one rather more flexible in its
operation than the other, but both boards have found their decision-
making and style of operation more strongly influenced by the
market than by the needs of the suppliers.   The boards have offered
growers the incentive to produce regularly, except that in Fiji the
actual buying performance has been notably inferior to the promise.

Eastern Fiji also has its middlemen, but principally in the
yaqona trade; they too range in scale from men who operate out of
formerly-established premises, operating utilities which advertise
their business, down to traders of very small scale.   Some of these
Fiji 'traffickers' also buy and consign vegetable produce, as well
as such goods as empty bottles, but their role in the island trade
is much more marginal than that of the Vincentian traffickers.
Moreover, and this is part of the wider Fijian problem, almost all
are Indo-Fijians, though some Melanesian-Fijians are involved in
the Yaqona business from certain islands.   Is it, then, the plural-
istic structure of the Fijian economy and society, rather than lack
of opportunity, that has constrained the development of traffickers
in response to a felt need in eastern Fiji?

If this be so, however, it would seem to call for greater
rather than the lesser support of individual enterprise alongside
the National Marketing Authority, to provide a service which this
organisation is either unable or unwilling to perform.   It can be
argued that what both the regions under study here really need is
an 'intermediate' sector of trade, capable of entry by men and
women with little capital, but enjoying access to credit, good
information on the state of the market, and facilities for storing
and packaging of produce.   The role of the marketing boards should
be in the regulation of prices by means of being the largest buyer
and seller, not by acquiring a quasi-monopoly and using it in
accordance with decision-making concentrated at the centre.

In this connection, however, there is also need for a bias in
pricing in favour of the producing areas and their resident traders.
So far as Fiji is concerned, it is not difficult to agree with
Lipton's (1977) argument that the rural population is exploited in
the interests of the urban buyers of their produce, whether these
buyers are of coconut products in Europe or of taro in Suva.   Only
in the yaqona trade, which is still producing for an unsatisfied
market, do the growers feel that they receive an adequate price.

Bayliss-Smith (1977, p. 65) puts it in this way:

If a Koro villager sells taro to the NMA [National
Marketing Authority] he receives 13.2 cents per kg
(6¢/lb).   It can be assumed that he or his family
will supply most of the labour needed to produce the
crops and that labour will therefore have to be with-
drawn from the subsistence sector, necessitating at
least a partial dependence on purchased foods.   However, the $132 per tonne return from taro only allows
the purchase of 600,000 kcal in average store prices,
or 884,200 if the diet were to be rice and flour in
equal proportion.   If on the other hand the producer

consumed the tonne of taro himself he would gain instead up to 1,322,100 kcal in direct food energy ...it is not surprising that most producers on Koro regard selling the crop as being a waste of energy, because in the most literal sense this is precisely what it is.

The margin for traders is depressed by this level of pricing, the object of which is to put taro on the Suva market at 10-11¢/lb, after meeting all costs.   In other words both farmers' incomes and the scope for rural enterprise are restricted in consequence of this application of a national low-wage/cheap-food policy designed to encourage investment in the country, principally in industry and tourism.   The creation of an environment for small-scale enterprise, that is for 'informality' in rural areas requires a more equitable share of the gains from trade between town and country.

ACKNOWLEDGEMENTS

In material from the UNESCO/UNFPA Project in Fiji, the work of John Campbell and Richard Bedford has been used as well as the writer's own.   Work in St Vincent was supported by McGill University, and was shared with Stanley Iton, who collected some of the data; preliminary analysis was by Christian Girault, and later analysis in Melbourne by Pauline and Alan McLean.   The paper was typed, and in large measure edited, by Tyna Charles.   In the field, the assistance of Daryll Tarte and Captain 'Kai-lau' in Fiji, and in St Vincent of George Leigertwood and Messrs Sprott and Sealey of the St Vincent Agricultural Marketing Board, is also gratefully acknowledged.

REFERENCES

Baker, J.R. (1974),   Transfer costs in the overseas and
                               internal shipping services of Fiji and
                               Tonga, unpublished Ph.D. thesis in
                               Human Geography, Australian National
                               University, Canberra.

Bayliss-Smith, T. (1977),   'Koro in the 1970's: Prosperity Through
                               Diversity', UNESCO/UNFPA Population and
                               Environment Project in the Eastern
                               Islands of Fiji, *Island Report No. 2*,
                               Development Studies Centre (ANU) for
                               UNESCO, Canberra.

Couper, A.D. (1965),   *Report on the Inter-insular Shipping
                               and Trade of Fiji*, Australian National
                               University, Canberra.

Couper, A.D. (1967),   The island trade: an analysis of the
                               environment and operation of seaborne
                               trade among three island groups in the
                               Pacific, unpublished Ph.D. thesis in
                               Geography, Australian National
                               University, Canberra.

Hilder, B. (1961),   *Navigator in the South Seas*, London.

Keirstead, B.S. and   *Inter-territorial Freight Rates and
 Levitt, K. (1963),   the Federal Shipping Service*, Institute
                               of Social and Economic Research, Univer-
                               sity of the West Indies, Kingston.

Lipton, M. (1977),   *Why Poor People Stay Poor: A Study of
                               Urban Bias in World Development*, London.

O'Loughlin, C. (1956),   *The Pattern of the Fiji Economy: the
                               National Income 1950-53*, Legislative
                               Council of Fiji, Council Paper No. 44
                               of 1956, Suva.

UNESCO/UNFPA (1977),   *Population, Resources and Development in
                               the Eastern Islands of Fiji: Informa-
                               tion for Decision-making*, UNESCO/UNFPA
                               Population and Environment Project in
                               the Eastern Islands of Fiji, Development
                               Studies Centre (ANU) for UNESCO,
                               Canberra.

AFTERWORD

AFTER THE 'BALL' IS OVER...

R. GERARD WARD[*]

After the day and a half during which the papers of this seminar
were presented and discussed the main impression which emerged was
that of the complexity of the topic.   That impression remains in
the revised papers presented here and it marks the growing maturity
of studies of the informal sector.   With greater insight into this
complexity we must beware of over-rigid categorization and simplification which, though useful for prescriptive purposes, may limit
our understanding.   One of the strong implicit, and often explicit,
themes which runs through all the papers is that the formal-informal
classification breaks down when we are forced (perhaps reluctantly)
to examine the real world.   McGee (Chapter 1) and J.C. Jackson
(Chapter 2) both express some unease about this breakdown.   They
show very clearly how sector blinkers, or academic categorizations,
have hindered our appraisal of the reality of the 'informal sector'
and how the supposed contrasts between the two poles of the model
simply do not exist when examined in detail.   Drakakis-Smith notes
(p. 103) that his own bi-polar model of housing is simply an aid to
understanding.   Surely we should not be too concerned when such a
preliminary categorization is overrun by the complexity revealed by
better empirical information.   We must expect the exceptions and
the variants — only by finding these can we hope to reach a better
understanding.   The formal/informal categorization will have served
its purpose when we move to a better one.   So, I do not share what
appears to be a slight case of depression in the face of complexity.
Perhaps it arose when the enthusiastic pursuit of a new idea began
to lose its thrust — or the idea proved not to be such a sharp
tool as it seemed at first.

We must acknowledge that each attempt to categorize puts a
screen between us and our real subject; and by our very use of words
we often lose rather than gain clarity.   The concept of efficiency
is touched on in discussions of fish marketing and vegetable
marketing (Chapter 2), but we have not sufficiently pursued the
question of efficiency for whom, and by what criteria it should be
measured.   In discussion the point was made that cost, taste, and
time might all be used in measuring 'efficiency' and certainly we
should not assume 'efficiency' has only one meaning.   Perhaps the
implications of Buddhist economic assumptions, as described by
Schumacher (1974), need to be borne in mind a little more often.

* Professor R.G. Ward is Head of the Department of Human Geography,
Research School of Pacific Studies, The Australian National
University, Canberra.

During the seminar several speakers expressed doubts about
whether there could be any policy prescriptions for the informal
sector — let us not tie ourselves up with the thought that any
policy automatically makes something formal and therefore is not to
be countenanced.   The papers in this volume show, not that there
should be no policies, but that the policies must be carefully
tailored to fit the particular conditions.   Undoubtedly some
improvements might be made on the basis of a number of criteria,
even in the 'efficient' system J.C. Jackson describes in Chapter 2,
but they would certainly be very different from the changes in
marketing which might benefit the Guadalcanal vegetable producers
and vendors described in Chapter 3.   Although we are all aware of
the danger of generalized prescriptions, we should not be too
surprised when politicians and administrators assume homogeneity or
adopt foreign images of the city or the economic system.   This is
what academics do when we construct bi-polar models and become constrained in our thought patterns by these models.   It may be
necessary in some situations to devise policies which can be
supportive of the informal by being deliberately restrictive of the
formal.   The Third World provides innumerable examples of policies
which deliberately foster the formal sector and restrict the
informal but the converse is rarely tried and deserves consideration in certain circumstances.

Let me make two other comments in similar vein.   One is that
just as our models take us away from reality, so do the use of terms
which carry strong associations which may or may not be relevant.
Undoubtedly the international capitalist system is deeply involved
as a causative factor in all the problems we have been talking
about.   But I get uneasy when, for example, we are told that 'squatting is considered illegal because it violates laws of property — one
of the inalienable institutions of capitalist economies' (p. 115).
Surely this needs to read 'capitalist and socialist economies';
State-owned property tends to be just as sacrosanct as private
property.   This is an omission which Franklin (1965) also makes in
the paragraph McGee quotes in his paper (p. 10).   Franklin notes
that in *both* capitalist and socialist systems labour becomes a
commodity to be hired, and dismissed by the enterprise, but then
appears to imply that *only* in the capitalist system of production
does this fact become disruptive of traditional societies.   This
is patently not the case as Franklin makes clear elsewhere in his
paper (1965:159-60).   In seeing some of the political or ideological links more clearly than we have done in the past, we must not
simplify others out of existence.   Let us look at exactly where
the power and political influence lies, and the consequence of
possession of that power, regardless of tags.

I would like to re-emphasize that other example of oversim-
plification pointed out by R. Jackson (Chapter 7), and made explicit
by Bathgate (Chapter 3) and Jellinek (Chapter 5).   The predominantly
urban problems discussed in this volume cannot be considered
separately from the rural context in which the towns are imbedded —
again a bi-polar model is tending to mislead us.   To extend Johnstone's point in Chapter 4, I wonder whether we might find (if we
cared to look and compare) that not only is housing in small towns
often as poor as, or worse than, housing in large cities, but that
in some situations it may be worse still in rural villages.   Let
us not let the Anglo-Saxon belief that 'God made the country, and

man made the town' (Cowper, 1785) mislead us and prevent us from looking at rural poverty as well as urban.

When looking at the Third World those of us from the developed world tend to forget the parallels in our own societies. I do not want to imply that development is unilinear but, for example, we tend to think of circular migration and associated informal economic activities as African, Asian, or Pacific phenomena. However, an examination of *Akenfield* (Blythe, 1969) or Thistlethwaite's (1964) work on nineteenth century trans-Atlantic migration, makes it clear that circular migration on both international and intra-national scales is an old European phenomenon as well, and it is also highly developed in Western Europe today. Similarly one might find close parallels to the *pondok* in nineteenth century New York or Chicago as well as in twentieth century Indonesia. Examination of these parallels might be instructive — as much to indicate what policies should *not* be pursued as for any use of them as a model for the less developed world. Furthermore greater awareness of the detail of change in the less developed world may help to illuminate aspects of the historical geography and economic history of the developed world.

The interest aroused in this seminar far exceeded expectations. We have been surprised and gratified at the range of disciplines represented at the meeting in Canberra in July 1977. For those present it was a most stimulating meeting. For me, it was an encouraging contrast to a major international conference I attended the previous week on the theme of Appropriate Technology for Development, held in that most inappropriate of locales — the Bali Beach Hotel. At the Canberra meeting there seemed to be more concern for real people suffering real poverty in real places than I found in that other supposedly high level meeting of experts. We must be concerned with the question of the ethics of involvement which McGee (Chapter 1) raised at the outset. Personally I was far less worried about this at the end of this seminar than I was after several days in Bali, filled with suggestions for solutions involving more international conferences, more supra-national bodies to co-ordinate work in appropriate technology (a supra national organization to design a better spade?), computer banks of data and the like. In this volume I think we are somewhat closer to reality, which is where we should be.

REFERENCES

Blythe, R. (1969),   *Akenfield, Portrait of an English Village*, New York.

Cowper, W. (1785),   'The Sofa', *The Task*, London, line 749.

Franklin, H. (1965),   'Systems of Production: Systems of Appropriation', *Pacific Viewpoint*, 6(2), pp. 145-66.

Schumacher, E.F. (1974),   *Small is Beautiful, a Study of Economics as if People Mattered*, London.

Thistlethwaite, F. (1964),   'Migration from Europe Overseas in the Nineteenth and Twentieth Centuries', in H. Moller (ed.), *Population Movements in Modern European History*, New York, pp. 73-92.

21